Wargaming
The Peninsular War
1808–1814

Wargame Scenarios: The Peninsular War 1808–1814

Jon Sutherland
and Diane Canwell

Pen & Sword
MILITARY

First published in Great Britain in 2014 by
Pen & Sword Military
An imprint of
Pen & Sword Books Ltd
47 Church Street
Barnsley
South Yorkshire
S70 2AS

Copyright © Jon Sutherland and Diane Canwell, 2014

ISBN 978 1 84415 947 5

The right of Jon Sutherland and Diane Canwell to be identified as Authors of this Work has been asserted by them in accordance with the Copyright, Designs and Patents Act 1988.

A CIP catalogue record for this book is available from the British Library.

All rights reserved. No part of this book may be reproduced or transmitted in any form or by any means, electronic or mechanical including photocopying, recording or by any information storage and retrieval system, without permission from the Publisher in writing.

Typeset in Palatino Light by Chic Graphics

Printed and bound in England by
CPI Group (UK) Ltd, Croydon, CR0 4YY

Pen & Sword Books Ltd incorporates the Imprints of Aviation, Atlas, Family History, Fiction, Maritime, Military, Discovery, Politics, History, Archaeology, Select, Wharncliffe Local History, Wharncliffe True Crime, Military Classics, Wharncliffe Transport, Leo Cooper, The Praetorian Press, Remember When, Seaforth Publishing and Frontline Publishing.

For a complete list of Pen & Sword titles please contact
PEN & SWORD BOOKS LIMITED
47 Church Street, Barnsley, South Yorkshire, S70 2AS, England
E-mail: enquiries@pen-and-sword.co.uk
Website: www.pen-and-sword.co.uk

Contents

Introduction vii
Map of Peninsular War Battle................................. ix
Using the Scenarios x

Chapter 1   The Coming of the Peninsular War 1

Chapter 2   Opening Moves................................... 4
              Battle of Valls, 25 February 1809................. 6
              Battle of Vimiero, 21 August 1808 13
              Battle of Corunna, 16 January 1809............. 21

Chapter 3   Portugal, Retreat and Counter Invasion 29
              Battle of Talavera, 28 July 1809................ 33
              Battle of Almonacid, 11 August 1809............ 41
              Battle of Tamames, 18 October 1809 45
              Battle of Ocaña, 19 November 1809 48
              Battle of the River Coa, 24 July 1810 52
              Battle of Bussaco, 27 September 1810 56
              Battle of Sabugal, 3 April, 1811................. 60
              Battle of Barrosa, 5 March 1811 64
              Battle of Albuera, 16 May 1811................. 68
              Battle of Fuentes de Oñoro, 3-5 May 1811 75
              Battle of Saguntum, 25 October 1811 88

Chapter 4   Wellington Takes the Offensive 96
              Battle of Salamanca........................... 101

Chapter 5	Collapse and Defeat 119
	Battle of Vitoria, 21 June 1813. 122
	Battle of Castalla, 13 April 1813 131
	Battle of Sorauren, 28 July 1813 139
	Battle of Orthez, 27 February 1814 148
	Battle of Tarbes, 20 March 1814 154
Chapter 6	Armies of the Peninsular War. 163
Chapter 7	The War in the Peninsula 193
Chronology	 216
Further Reading 222

Introduction

In 2008 the Spanish and the Portuguese celebrated the bicentenary of the beginning of the Peninsular War. The war was a six-year struggle to overthrow a French regime imposed on Spain. The war would cost the protagonists over a million lives.

For wargamers the Peninsular War offers the very best of Napoleonic wargaming. There are set-piece battles, innumerable skirmishes, the use of deception tactics and sieges.

Throughout the war many of the most famous British and French regiments saw action in the peninsula. Battle honours, such as Salamanca, Corunna and Vitoria still adorn the regimental flags of British regiments. Whether the wargamer is an Anglophile or a Francophile, the Peninsular War represents a microcosm of the Napoleonic conflict. It was a sprawling world war and the peninsula became a battle ground where great generals, such as Wellington and Soult, would lead their men in the great struggle between the two implacable enemies: Britain and France.

Many wargamers will have been attracted to the Peninsular War as a theatre to play Napoleonic wargames by the Sharpe novels and television series. Many of the Sharpe novels are based loosely on the historical events that took place between 1808 and 1814. In fact the Peninsular War has far more to offer than set-piece battles and it can be played in any scale and at any level, from skirmish to mass pitched-engagements.

This book aims to offer the wargamer a brief but comprehensive history of the Peninsular War. The narrative of the war is punctuated with twenty examples of battles that can be refought using the *Grand Battery* Napoleonic wargame rules published by Pen & Sword. Each of the battles is first described for historical detail, and then orders of battle, along with a description of the abilities of the troops, are given. Each key objective is outlined and victory conditions suggested. In order to aid the setting up of a particular battle, each of the engagements has a basic map, which assumes an 8 x 5 foot playing surface. All key terrain features are included, as well as the opening positions of each of the divisions or brigades.

Wargamers will find the background information on each of the battles and each of the twenty scenarios invaluable in helping them prepare to replay the engagement. In choosing twenty likely battles over a six-year

WARGAME SCENARIOS

period it is inevitable that we may well have missed out your favourite engagement. We have concentrated on trying to offer battles that give wargamers the opportunity to use the same formations as often as possible and to build up typical armies, which could fight in the widest variety of different engagements. You will discover that we have chosen battles that range from engagements that are little more than skirmishes to huge pitched battles that could require several hundred figures. We have largely avoided focusing on sieges, although it is important to remember that siege warfare played a big role in the Peninsular War. Often, a force moving to relieve a besieged position brought about a field engagement when the besiegers sought to prevent the raising of a siege.

The battles are broadly broken down into four sections. The first section covers the opening engagements through to the battle of Corunna. The second section covers a wider period, from the spring of 1809 through to 1811; in other words, from Talavera through to Saguntum in October 1811. The third section just features one battle, albeit a significant one: Salamanca in July 1812. The final batch of battles runs from Vitoria in June 1813 through to Tarbes in March 1814.

Obviously many wargamers will want to fight the Peninsular War as a campaign, with casualties, replacements and reinforcements all being applied to armies from battle to battle. With a theatre as large as the peninsula it is not always possible to necessarily achieve this, as the size and nature of the armies fluctuated enormously over the six years and, in some cases, battles were fought either by the British, the Portuguese or the Spanish without any allied support. We have included a chapter *War in the Peninsula*, which offers a generic set of army lists and background in order to begin fighting a Peninsular War campaign.

Pen & Sword will have online resources and new scenarios, as well as rule clarifications, at www.penandswordbooks.co.uk. You will also find downloadable cards, templates and ready reference sheets. Have fun and good wargaming.

Jon Sutherland and Diane Canwell

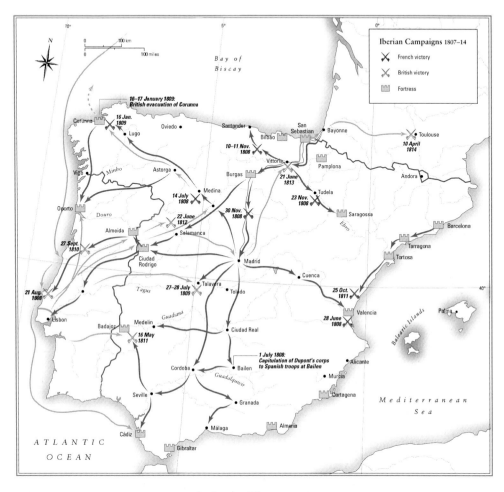

Peninsular War 1807-14

Using the Scenarios

The orders of battle for each of the engagements are designed so that wargamers can choose to refight the battle on a grand scale, representing all of the key units. It is not always practical to assemble such large forces, particularly for some of the bigger engagements. For small-scale, but still representative, battles, each of the army lists shows in italics the necessary units to refight the cut-down version of the battle. Effectively, this is to enable a battle to be fought with fewer units and with the prospect of being able to complete the game in an evening. Players may wish to represent divisions or brigades with other units drawn from the full order of battle.

Chapter 1

The Coming of the Peninsular War

In July 1807 Napoleon's France dominated Europe. He had led his troops to stunning victories against Austria, Prussia and Russia. With a secure eastern front and peace with Russia, along with dominance in central Europe, Napoleon's eyes fell on Spain and Portugal.

To nullify Britain, Napoleon had instituted the Continental System. It aimed to boycott British goods and deny them markets in Europe. Spain and Portugal at this time were major holes in this strategy. Napoleon had failed to sustain a significant challenge to Britain's naval supremacy. The Danish fleet had been destroyed at Copenhagen in 1801 and the French had been humiliated at Trafalgar in 1805. Napoleon was therefore forced to attempt a different strategy to compel Britain to come to terms. Trade barriers closed Austrian and Russian ports to British shipping. The British responded by setting up a counter-blockade, aiming to prevent neutral merchant shipping from trading with any part of the French Empire.

A British monopoly on goods such as sugar, spices and coffee meant that these were in short supply in continental Europe, added to which British cloth and metal supplies had dried up. Rather than adversely affecting Britain, it was Europe that suffered, stoking up anti-French feeling. The French Continental System was not without success, but ultimately it was never widespread enough or consistent enough to bring Britain to its knees. Sweden continued to be a valuable entry point into Europe (until 1810) and Russian ports reopened to the British in 1812.

In the end, it would be Napoleon's decisions to try to impose the Continental System on Portugal and Spain in 1808 and on Russia in 1812 that would lead to his ultimate defeat. So convinced was Napoleon that economic pressure, coupled with selective military action, would bring Britain to the negotiating table that he had outlined grandiose plans. He intended to invade Spain with French and Russian troops and take

WARGAME SCENARIOS

Gibraltar. He would then seize Constantinople, drive into Africa and reclaim France's lost possessions in India.

In the period running up to the Peninsular War, Spain was an uncertain ally for the French. Spain was making diplomatic noises that alarmed Napoleon. Napoleon feared the prospect of Spanish attacks through the Pyrenees whilst his armies were engaged in operations against Prussia. Technically Spain was a compliant ally, even providing troops to garrison the Baltic; nonetheless Napoleon reinforced his troops in the Pyrenees as a precautionary measure.

Portugal was in an altogether different and difficult position. On the one hand it faced the prospect of French and Spanish invasion if it did not toe the Continental System line, whilst on the other it was certain in its fears that Britain would seize its colonies if Portugal complied with the French.

By the summer of 1807 it was clear that Portugal's attempt to balance the two impossible alternatives was not working. They had brought in limited anti-British measures, but had not gone as far as France or Spain demanded. War was becoming inevitable.

In the Treaty of Fontainebleau the French and Spanish agreed to partition Portugal. In the complex political climate, the Spanish First Minister of King Charles IV, Godoy, was promised a sizeable chunk of land for himself in Portugal. Godoy was intriguing against the Spanish heir, Prince Ferdinand and saw himself as Charles's natural successor. Undoubtedly Napoleon played on this ambition.

On 18 October 1807 General Junot began moving a 25,000-man Corps across Spain with the intention of compelling Portugal to submit to the Continental System. Junot's men marched across the difficult terrain and entered Lisbon on 30 November. The Portuguese had given up without a fight. Some 25,000 Spanish troops were also moving to cross into Portugal. The Portuguese monarch, Prince John, had even tried to stave off invasion by declaring war on Britain, but it had failed. Prince John abandoned his capital hours before the French entered Lisbon. The Royal Navy conveyed him into exile in Brazil.

Riots broke out in Lisbon on 13 December, the citizens seemingly less compliant and unwilling to accept occupation despite the position of the authorities. Nonetheless it had been a cheap victory for the French and now Napoleon, to some extent justified, believed that Spain would fall as easily. It would be the last piece in the Continental System jigsaw and would close Europe to Britain. Not only that, it would give him the vast Spanish wealth and a valuable pool of new troops.

THE COMING OF THE PENINSULAR WAR

Undoubtedly the Spanish had never recovered their naval strength after Trafalgar and their army was poor. Unknown to Napoleon, Spain was broke and the value of Spain's colonial possessions questionable, given the dominance of the Royal Navy. Abruptly, Napoleon cast aside the Treaty of Fontainebleau, sending 70,000 extra men into Spain under Monce, Dupont and Duhesme. Meanwhile he built up extra reserves in the Pyrenees.

Godoy tried to salvage what he could from the increasingly desperate situation. He suggested that Prince Ferdinand marry into the Imperial French family. This would have given Napoleon a puppet Spanish ruler, but Napoleon rejected the proposal.

With growing concern the Spanish saw French influence pour into their country. On 16 February 1808 the French seized Barcelona and the Spanish-held frontier posts and more French troops crossed the border into Spain.

Prince Ferdinand dismissed Godoy, and there were riots and disorder until Charles IV abdicated in favour of his son. Murat, now the Commander-in-Chief of French forces in Spain, marched into Madrid at the head of 20,000 men. He refused to recognize Ferdinand as monarch and instead Ferdinand was invited to meet with Napoleon in Bayonne to discuss the situation.

Napoleon decided that Ferdinand must abdicate. Napoleon used Charles IV and Godoy to attest that Ferdinand had seized the throne in an unlawful way. Ferdinand did abdicate and Charles surrendered his own rights to Napoleon. The throne was then handed over to Napoleon's brother, Joseph. It was to be a dreadful mistake. The Spanish had never been very happy with either Charles or Ferdinand, but now Napoleon had imposed a foreign dictator as a monarch.

On 2 May 1808, Madrid citizens, seeing the last of their royal family disappearing into exile, rose up against the French garrison under Murat. Murat responded with extreme violence. The Dos de Mayo Rising, as it became known, was the beginning of a popular revolt against the French. The Asturias, calling up 18,000 men, declared war on France on 25 May, to be quickly followed by other Spanish provinces. The Peninsular War was now underway.

Chapter 2

Opening Moves

Spain was in widespread revolt by the middle of May 1808. However, the main Spanish military strength was concentrated in the north-west and south-west. The French, on the other hand, had troops in Portugal, Madrid, along tenuous lines of communication stretching back to Bayonne, and forces in Catalonia. None of the smaller French detachments was safe, the supply lines were under constant threat and communications in peril everywhere.

Murat, however, viewed the situation with optimism. He believed that opposition to the French occupation could easily be handled with flying columns. Consequently, in cooperation with Napoleon, Murat instituted a plan to handle the situation:

- A large French reserve would be retained in Madrid.
- Dupont would take a force to Cordova and Seville.
- Moncey and Duhesme would deal with Valencia and Cartagena.
- Bessières would hold open communication and supply lines in the north.
- Detached forces would be sent to put down the revolts in Santander and Saragossa.

The first move saw Dupont (13,000 men) arrive in Andujar on 5 June. Dupont then pushed onto Cordova, where Don Pedro de Echavarri had amassed around 13,400 men and eight guns. The vast bulk of this Spanish force consisted of raw recruits and when they formed up against Dupont at the Alcolia Bridge the Spaniards were routed in minutes and Cordova was looted. This set the tone for the war, as the Spanish retaliated by butchering French stragglers.

Dupont was deep in rebel territory and uncertain of his lines of communication so he pulled back towards Anduja. Moving towards him was General Castaños at the head of some 34,000 men.

Murat had sent Dupont reinforcements and on 27 June 6,000 infantry and 600 cavalry under Vedel arrived at La Carolina. Despite this Dupont did not take the offensive and instead he held back. Further troops arrived under Gobert (primarily to ensure that the routes to Madrid were kept open). But still Dupont did not attack. He now had over 20,000 men at his disposal.

Castaños took the offensive, splitting his forces into three columns. He led 12,000 men against Anduja, Coupigny (8,000 men) marched on Villa Neuva and Reding (10,000 men) headed for Mengibar. The plan was for Castaños to demonstrate in front of Anduja whilst the other two forces swung around the French flank.

The attack came on 14 July. The two opposing forces jockeyed for position, but on 16 July Reding's men had driven the French out of Mengibar and crossed the River Guadalquivir. Gobert had rushed reinforcements to stem the Spanish advance, but in the fighting he had been mortally wounded and his men were flooding back towards Baylen.

Vedel was sent to help stem the tide but found that Gobert's successor, Dufour, had ordered a retreat back to La Carolina. The French believed that the Spanish were threatening the supply route back to Madrid. They were, but the Spanish there were not part of Reding's force but levies. Reding himself and his troops were still at Mengibar.

With Vedel and Dufour to the north, Dupont was virtually isolated. Reding and Coupigny advanced on Dupont at around noon on 17 July, believing that the bulk of the French were still near Andujar. Reding marched unopposed into Baylen that evening and was ordered to attack Dupont's rear at first light.

Vedel was approaching with 11,000 men, although Dupont could not have known this. Dupont had begun to retreat from Andujar and in the early hours of the morning of 19 July his lead troops collided with advanced units of Reding's force. Reding quickly organized his 14,000 men and twenty guns on dominating hills to the west of Baylen. In order to prevent himself from being outflanked, he sent a small force to cover the road from La Carolina.

The French were still uncertain as to what they had blundered into and they threw forward just 3,000 men, which were easily dealt with by the Spaniards. Dupont now realized that there were more Spanish ahead of him than he had expected and that he needed to move fast, because he feared that Castaños might only be a short distance behind him. Foolishly Dupont made a series of uncoordinated attacks, with regiments being thrown into the attack the moment they arrived on the battlefield.

By 1230 Dupont had made no serious headway and Castaños was indeed approaching. Dupont made a last ditch attempt to break through.

WARGAME SCENARIOS

The Spanish began to waver but the French lacked sufficient men to deliver the final blow and fell back once again. At this point Castaños attacked Dupont's rearguard. Dupont's Swiss troops deserted him and he was forced to seek surrender terms.

The battle had been an absolute disaster. Vedel had been held up by one of Reding's brigades and had contributed virtually nothing. In all, 20,000 French troops became prisoners of war. Dupont and the senior officers were shipped home, but not the rank and file.

Meanwhile, Moncey was marching to deal with the rebels in Valencia. He arrived on 26 June and found the rebels had thrown up fortifications and earthworks, and that some of the surrounding fields had been flooded. His 9,000 men faced around 20,000 rebels, mainly peasants. He demanded that the city surrender but this was rejected, so he began his attack on 28 June, easily pushing back the outer defences of the city. Once his men reached the city walls they came under intense fire and in the first two attacks Moncey lost 1,000 men. It was clear to him that he lacked the resources to storm the city. Duhesme, with a supporting column, had failed to arrive, so Moncey decided to pull back and hope to lure the Spanish out as he fell back on Madrid.

Cervellon, the Spanish commander, had placed troops barring the route that the French had taken. Instead the French moved off in another direction. Moncey still hoped to draw the Spaniards to him. But it was a wasted effort and he eventually marched back into Madrid.

Background to the Battle of Valls
So far the two French plans had failed, but there now remained the situation in Catalonia. General Duhesme had been given 5,500 Italians and 7,000 French to hold Barcelona and then deal with rebel forces in both Lerida and Manresa. He was also expected to provide Moncey with assistance. Duhesme had despatched 3,000 men to help Moncey and a further 3,000 to deal with the two centres of insurrection. As General Schwartz made for Lerida and Manresa he came up against determined resistance in the shape of Spanish militia. He immediately called for reinforcements. The only thing Duhesme could do was to recall General Chabran with his 3,000 men that were en route to Moncey. Everywhere Duhesme turned there were Spanish militia units, or levies, known as Somatenes.

Duhesme was making for Gerona but behind him his lines of communication were severed. Arriving outside of Gerona he was heavily held and just like Moncey he realized that there was no way that the city could be taken. Reluctantly he slunk back to Barcelona.

OPENING MOVES

More troops were obviously needed. By 5 July just a small proportion of a new force, which was supposed to be 8,000 men under General Reille, had assembled in southern France. With less than 2,000 men Reille headed for Catalonia.

By mid-July Reille was joined by the rest of his division and he tried his luck against Rosas. Once again it was too strong and instead Reille turned south and headed for Gerona. This seemed to galvanize Duhesme, who marched out to join him, running into innumerable Somatenes on the way. The two French commanders combined on 24 July near Gerona. They now had sufficient artillery to start a siege.

Whilst the French were settling down around Gerona, General Del Palacio and 5,000 regular Spanish troops, supported by Somatenes, were surrounding Barcelona. To begin with Duhesme ignored the calls for help, believing that Gerona would fall any day. Unbeknown to Duhesme another force of Spanish regulars was on its way towards Gerona.

By mid-August the Spanish regulars were in place and launched an attack, supported by an assault from Gerona itself. The attack was beaten off but this convinced the French to abandon their siege and on 16 August they destroyed their siege equipment and Duhesme headed back towards Barcelona and Reille to Figueras.

Duhesme's key priority was to relieve Barcelona. He was under continual attack from the Somatenes and even his supply columns and troops on the coastal road were under fire from the Royal Navy. By the time he broke through to Barcelona on 20 August he had had to abandon all of his guns, much of his ammunition and the bulk of his baggage.

So far the French attempts to deal with Catalonia had ended in failure, but Napoleon was determined to bring the region under his control. In late October he sent General St-Cyr to join up with Reille. The new French commander began his campaign by beginning the siege of Rosas. The campaign began on 7 November and it would take the French until 26 November to achieve a breach and a foothold in the town. The Spanish garrison of some 3,000 men held on for as long as they could with Royal Navy support, but eventually French pressure paid off and the stronghold was taken.

This effectively removed the threat to the French rear, leaving the bulk of the French forces free to move toward Barcelona. St-Cyr left Reille to hold the road open to France and marched with 17,000 men in mid-December, heading first for Gerona. St-Cyr was in a dilemma; it would take time to seize Gerona and by then it might be too late to help Duhesme. Secretly St-Cyr sent back his guns and baggage to Reille and

WARGAME SCENARIOS

bypassed Gerona, making straight for Barcelona. The Spanish surrounding the city, under General Vives, amounted to some 24,000 men. The Spanish had no idea that the French had bypassed Gerona and did not learn that St-Cyr was on his way until 11 December. As it was, Vives did not move the bulk of his force to deal with the French threat and marched just 8,500 infantry and 600 cavalry to Cardadeu, where they were attacked by St-Cyr on 16 December.

St-Cyr left a small rearguard to prevent attacks from the garrison at Gerona and formed up 13,000 men to literally plough their way through Vives' small force. The first attack failed when the leading French columns deployed too broadly. St-Cyr took personal command and formed his men up into a narrow column for the second attack. It was entirely successful. The raw Spanish recruits suffered 2,500 casualties and lost most of their guns. In all, the engagement cost the French 600 casualties.

St-Cyr marched on towards Barcelona and entered the city on 17 December. He did not settle for this and instead reorganized his forces. He set off to bring Reding and Caldagues to battle. The French outnumbered the available Spanish forces. They had 18,000 men to the Spanish 15,000. St-Cyr found the Spanish on 21 December. He launched a diversionary attack on the bridge at Molins de Rey whilst the bulk of his troops swung around the Spanish right. Reding, outmanoeuvred, began to retreat. Most of the Spanish managed to get away, but General Caldagues was captured along with 1,200 men and twenty-five guns.

The next few weeks saw rest, recuperation and reorganization for both protagonists. Reding took over from Vives and received 6,000 reinforcements. By February 1809 he was ready to begin operations once again.

Reding sent a division, under Castro, to Igualada. St-Cyr immediately responded by marching the bulk of his army to deal with Castro, whilst Souham and a small force kept an eye on Reding, who by then was in the Gaya Valley. The French engaged Castro on 17 February. After a desperate struggle and in fear of being outflanked, Castro retreated, but the French continued to pursue and the bulk of Castro's force was destroyed.

Meanwhile, Reding marched towards Valls, arriving there in the early hours of 25 February. Souham's small force was pushed aside and the Spanish began crossing the River Francoli. St-Cyr was desperate for a major engagement and Reding gave him the opportunity by deploying, rather than retiring. The Spanish even gave St-Cyr sufficient time to bring up fresh troops. In all, St-Cyr managed to march over 13,000 men to the battlefield to deal with Reding's 11,000 men and eight artillery pieces. At around 1700 the French began crossing the River Francoli. They came

OPENING MOVES

under heavy fire but the enormous French columns terrified the Spanish and, before the French closed with them, the bulk of the Spanish army was running. Reding tried everything he could to stem the tide and at the head of a charge he was mortally wounded. Reding's men fled towards Tarragona. Several Spanish senior officers were killed, wounded or captured, 1,500 men had been taken prisoner and the same number killed or wounded. All of the Spanish baggage and guns were lost. St-Cyr had achieved victory for the loss of 900 killed and wounded.

St-Cyr could not deal with Tarragona as he did not have any siege equipment. But the city could be as effectively dealt with by blockade, as there was an epidemic in the city and it was effectively a prison for the beaten Spanish army.

Gaming the Battle of Valls, 25 February 1809

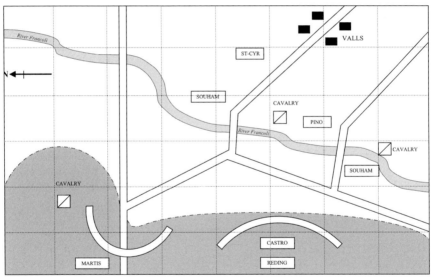

Valls Wargame Set Up

This was a crushing defeat for the Spanish, yet there is a chance that the Spanish army can at least hold the French for a time and not disintegrate. The key to the battle is not necessarily territory or physical objectives, although control of the ridge is very important. This is a battle that revolves around the Spanish army standing and holding off the French for as long as possible and inflicting casualties on them. For the French, they must attempt to destroy the Spanish army at the earliest opportunity.

WARGAME SCENARIOS

The river is fordable at all points, but obviously disorganizes the unit crossing. All French units begin the game with 'advance' orders. The Spanish all have 'hold' orders.

Reding's Army

The key objective is to hold the ridge and inflict as many casualties as possible on the French. At Game Turn 12 the Spanish have the option of withdrawing from the battlefield. If they do this then they win the game by managing to exit five or more regiments that are not routing or have been forced to leave the battlefield.

C in C: Reding	*Able*
Castro	*Cautious*
Swiss Regiment	*Green Cautious*
Granada Regiment	*Green Cautious*
Sante Fé Regiment	*Green Cautious*
Antequera Regiment	Green Cautious
Martis	*Cautious*
Walloon Guards	Veteran Confident
Castile Regiment	Green Cautious
Baza Regiment	Green Cautious
Soria Regiment	Green Cautious
2nd Savoia Regiment	Green Cautious
Palma Militia	Green Cautious
1st Hussar Regiment	Experienced Steady
2nd Hussar Regiment	Experienced Steady
Foot Artillery Battery – 3 medium guns	Green Cautious

St-Cyr's Army

The French will win a decisive victory if they have cleared the ridge line of intact Spanish units by Game Turn 10. They can also win a decisive victory if the Spanish army has less than six intact units on the battlefield by Game Turn 8. They will draw if the Spanish have managed to extract at least 4 intact regiments by Game Turn 14.

C in C: St-Cyr	*Gifted*
Souham	*Able*
1st Léger	*Experienced Steady*
42nd Line	*Experienced Steady*

OPENING MOVES

Pino	*Able*
1st Léger	Experienced Steady
2nd Léger	Experienced Steady
4th Line	Experienced Steady
6th Line	Experienced Steady
7th Line	Green Steady
Napoleon Dragoons	Experienced Steady
Italian Chasseurs	Experienced Steady
24th Dragoons	Experienced Steady
Field Artillery Battery – 3 medium guns, 1 medium Howitzer	Experienced Steady

The War in the North
In the north, Bessières had 25,000 men to deal with the troubles in the northern provinces. He overran Logrono on 2 June 1808. Other detachments overcame Santander and Reynosa. Attention now turned to the more difficult problem of Valladolid. Centred round Valladolid was Cuesta's Army of Castile, at that time around 5,000 men. The troops were predominantly inexperienced volunteers and Cuesta had just 300 experienced horsemen and four guns. Undaunted, Cuesta decided to take the offensive rather than wait for Bessières to deal with him. Promptly he cut the road between Burgos and Madrid. Cuesta and his men, eager for battle, would not have long to wait.

On 12 June, Lasalle, at the head of some 9,000 men, closed with the Spanish at the Bridge of Cabezon over the River Pisuerga. It was over in a matter of minutes. The inexperienced Spaniards were slaughtered and what remained of the force fled back to Valladolid. Lasalle lost just fifty men. He followed up, overrunning the city and in a blink northern Spain was virtually secure. Santander fell on 23 June.

There was still fighting to be done and at Saragossa the Spanish commander, Palafox, had managed to scrape up 7,500 men, a handful of guns and a small cavalry force. General Lefebvre-Desnouettes had been sent to deal with Palafox by Bessières. The French engaged Palafox at Tudela on 8 June. The Spanish, under Lazan, mustered 2,000 levies and 3,000 armed peasants against 5,000 French infantry and 1,000 cavalry. The result was a foregone conclusion and in fact Lazan was routed twice. Palafox moved 6,000 men to Alagon, stiffened by 500 regulars, four cannons and 150 cavalry. It was not enough and they were swept aside and what remained of the force fled towards Saragossa.

The French arrived outside the city on 15 June. Inside were around

WARGAME SCENARIOS

11,000 defenders. Lefebvre believed that a determined assault would break the spirit of the Spanish recruits and consequently he launched an attack against the west side of the city, whilst his Poles tried to take the Santa Engracia Gate. French artillery would keep the defenders' heads down. The Polish cavalry managed to break through all the way into the city but they suffered heavy casualties. The French infantry had managed to get into the western quarter, but determined resistance forced them to retire. Ultimately, with no support the Poles too had to pull out.

The French tried again. They broke through the western gate, but once again could make very little headway. Reluctantly they pulled back for a second time. Lefebvre waited for reinforcements. An infantry regiment arrived on 21 June, with news that more troops were on their way. Lefebvre was in a precarious position; he had already lost 700 men and his spies told him that 4,000 more Spaniards were en route to the city.

Leaving just half of his troops screening the city, he marched with 3,000 men to attack the Spanish reinforcements. He managed to rout them and only a handful of the Spaniards managed to make it to the city.

Meanwhile, General Verdier arrived at the head of 3,500 men. He had brought with him vital siege cannons. Verdier took over and his first job was to clear Monte Torrero, which had 500 Spanish troops on top of it. It was an ideal position for the French siege guns, as it dominated the city. By 30 June forty-six French guns opened up on the city from the hill and after twelve hours of continuous bombardment Verdier launched his first infantry attack. He met with no greater success, losing 500 men. He now determined to settle down for a long siege. The problem was that he had not managed to cut off the city entirely, as it lay on the banks of the Ebro River. Daily, fresh Spanish troops and supplies were coming in, whilst he was stuck in hostile territory with just 1,300 men. Every day the French trenches inched forward, with the artillery batteries getting closer and closer to the walls.

On 4 August Verdier ordered that section-by-section the walls would be cleared of Spanish artillery and then bombarded to make breaches. As soon as the breaches were made he threw in an assault, but it was thrown back. Verdier persisted and overran part of the city. The Spanish launched furious counterattacks, trying to push the French out. By the following day the French position in the city was tenuous and between the two protagonists around 2,000 men had been killed. Unable to make any serious headway, Verdier abandoned the siege on 13 August. Everything he could not take with him was destroyed. The French had lost 3,500 men, the Spanish at least that and perhaps more, added to which hundreds of civilians had been killed or wounded.

After his defeat Cuesta tried to reorganize at Benavente. He demanded fresh levies of troops and, above all, regulars. He received very little support until Galicia sent General Blake to assist him at the head of 25,000 men. Cuesta thought himself to be Blake's superior and he assumed command. Consequently, on 12 July Cuesta, at the head of a far larger force than he had had just days before, set out to retake Valladolid.

Bessières quickly learned that the Spanish were en route. He had with him around 1,400 men; less than ten percent of this force was cavalry. He was confident that he could deal with the Spanish. The two armies met close to Medina de Rio Seco on July 14. Between them Cuesta and Blake had 21,000 infantry, 600 cavalry and twenty guns. The Spanish dispositions on the battlefield were less than impressive, with a gaping hole in the front line commanded by Blake and troops under Cuesta too far back in reserve. Bessières noticed the deficiency immediately and aimed to break through the gap in Blake's line. Blake tried his best to hold the French off but he was being constantly outmanoeuvred and the French were working round his flank. Cuesta had not moved up.

Suddenly the French unleashed their cavalry through the gap between the Spanish lines, and the French infantry made their frontal assaults. In moments Blake's troops broke, chased by jubilant Frenchmen. Bessières now turned his attention to Cuesta. He formed up a line that would have given Cuesta time enough to retreat across the River Sequillo to safety. Instead the old general stood his ground. In fact Cuesta launched his own attack against Bessières' right and centre. But he was now outnumbered. The loss of Blake had cost the Spanish 3,000 men and all of their artillery pieces. As more French troops moved up, Cuesta's men became trapped and they promptly broke. The French, however, were exhausted and failed to chase and catch the bulk of the Spanish force.

Background to the Battle of Vimiero
General Junot had been charged with the difficult job of occupying Portugal. With 26,000 men he had less than one man for each of the 30,000 square miles in the country. At any time the country could rise up in full revolt and in fact it did, centred on Oporto, where a militia was formed and regular units flocked to the new army.

At the same time Britain was reluctant to become involved on the mainland of Europe against the French alone. They had been content for a time to merely contain and sting the French with the Royal Navy. The prospects of hurting the French even more in the Peninsula were good, with the certain support of both the Portuguese and the Spanish.

The first move was to snatch General La Romana's Spanish troops from under the noses of the French at Gothenburg. The Royal Navy managed to get out 15,000 Spanish garrison troops. Elsewhere money was being sent to rebel and guerrilla units in the Peninsula.

Junot was acutely aware of the fact that the British could land in Portugal at any time. He began to concentrate his troops, primarily in fortresses and in Lisbon. As the French withdrew from the countryside the rebellion spread.

By now Junot had 26,000 men in and around Lisbon. He sent a detachment of 7,000 to deal with an insurrection near the Guadiana River. These troops routed a rebel force of 3,000 on 29 July. Despite the victory there was shattering news; Sir Arthur Wellesley had landed at Mondego Bay with a British Expeditionary Force.

With reforms to the British army, the British government had worked out that they could afford to send 40,000 men to the Peninsula. They would lack cavalry and there would certainly be supply difficulties. As it was, Wellesley landed at the head of 18,000 infantry and 400 cavalry. Sufficient horses were available for five artillery batteries and just half of the cavalry, but undaunted Wellesley had decided to move immediately onto the offensive. On 9 August, at the head of six British brigades and a Portuguese brigade, he began his march along the coast towards Lisbon. Ahead of him was General Delaborde's division, slowly withdrawing ahead of the allies towards Lisbon. He was eventually brought to battle at Roliça on 17 August.

Delaborde had mustered 6,000 men and five guns at around the time that Wellesley had landed but was now reduced to about 4,000 men. Set against him were 13,000 British, 2,000 Portuguese and eighteen guns.

Wellesley formed up in an arc in the hope that he could perform a pincer movement and envelop the French. In the nick of time Delaborde pulled out of the trap, falling back a mile. Wellesley tried again and this time on a ridge the French stood. As the British began to threaten the flanks it was time for Delaborde to pull out. He fell back in relatively good order, having inflicted 500 casualties on the allies.

Wellesley did not choose to pursue but instead marched on Vimiero, where another 4,000 British troops had just landed.

Shortly before dark on 15 August Junot marched his troops towards Villafranca. Here he learned that Delaborde had fallen back to Montechiqu and that Wellesley was close to Vimiero. Pulling together as many troops as he possibly could, Junot had 14,000 men and twenty-three guns. By

OPENING MOVES

dawn on 21 August Junot had arrived at Vimiero: Wellesley had taken up defensive positions along a chain of hills running south-west to north-east. Vimiero was at the centre.

Wellesley had believed that Junot would attack his right wing and had reinforced it, but in fact Junot instantly rejected this option and aimed for Vimiero itself and Wellesley's left flank. He sent 3,000 infantry and 600 cavalry to the north, under Brennier, to outflank Wellesley. Wellesley was not about to fall for the trick and immediately moved men from his right to his left and centre. Junot responded, sending another brigade, under Solignac, to support Brennier. This now left him with around 8,000 men to attack Vimiero.

Junot launched the assault in three deep lines, colliding first with the British brigades of Fane and Anstruther, holding a mound in front of the village. The French made little progress but the British were under enormous pressure. In fact the French attack on Fane broke down into chaos as they came under flank fire and they fell back in disorder. Charlot's brigade was met with crushing volleys from Anstruther's men and they too broke and fell back.

Junot now threw in his Grenadiers; two battalions of them. They were hopelessly outnumbered by three British battalions and twelve guns and were shot to pieces. Junot now had two Grenadier battalions left and sent them in. They got as far as the village but sheer weight of numbers told against them. As they fell back, 500 allied cavalry, led by Colonel Taylor, charged them but Taylor in turn was charged by French cavalry.

Meanwhile, General Brennier had moved north trying to find a way around the British-held ridge. They found a gap at Ventosa and with Solignac's men in the lead they advanced into a trap held by seven British battalions, under Bowes, Ferguson and Nightingale. The French were shot to pieces and Solignac was badly wounded. Brennier's force now appeared and managed to scatter two British regiments and recapture three guns that had been abandoned by Solignac. The engagement was already lost, however, and Brennier retreated back into the ravine. Here he too was wounded and taken prisoner.

After two-and-a-half hours the whole of the French army was in retreat, but Wellesley had not followed up, largely because Sir Harry Burrard had just arrived to take over command of the expeditionary force. Although he had allowed Wellesley to fight the battle, Burrard was reluctant to risk pursuit in fear that Junot might spring a trap. The battle cost the French 2,000 casualties and thirteen guns. The allies lost 720 men. As a result of the defeat the Convention of Cintra was signed. It handed Portugal back to the Allies and Junot's men would be conveyed back to

WARGAME SCENARIOS

France by the Royal Navy. The evacuation began on 13 September and took seven weeks.

The French had entered Portugal with over 30,000 men. Between 2,000 and 3,000 had been killed, a similar number had deserted and 25,747 were repatriated.

Gaming the Battle of Vimiero, 21 August 1808

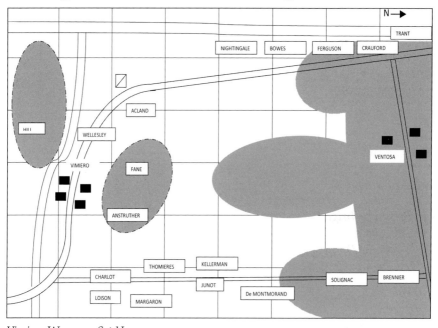

Vimiero Wargame Set Up

The orders of battle are somewhat confused for the French, but we have attempted to provide a complete listing of units. This has the potential to be a large battle due to the number of regiments per brigade or division. If you wish to reduce the number of units involved then simply reduce the three- and four- regiment brigades to two, and the two-regiment brigades to one etc.

Wellesley's Army
The Allies should remain on the defensive until at least Game Turn 6. After that, they may launch a counteroffensive against the French with the objectives of destroying or capturing at least one of the French Divisions. If this has already been achieved, then a decisive victory is achieved by

OPENING MOVES

forcing either a second French infantry division to retreat or forcing the French Grenadiers to retreat.

C-in-C: Lieut Gen Sir Arthur Wellesley	*Gifted*
1st Brigade – Major General Rowland Hill	*Able*
1st Battalion, 5th (1/5th) Foot Regiment (944)	*Experienced Steady*
1/9th Foot (761)	*Experienced Steady*
1/38th Foot (953)	Veteran Confident
2nd Brigade – Major General Ronald Craufurd Ferguson	*Able*
1/36th Foot (591)	*Veteran Confident*
1/40th Foot (923)	*Veteran Confident*
1/71st Foot (935)	Veteran Confident
3rd Brigade – Brigadier General Miles Nightingale	*Able*
1/29th Foot (616)	*Veteran Confident*
1/82nd Foot (904)	*Veteran Confident*
4th Brigade – Brigadier General Barnard Foord Bowes	*Able*
1/6th Foot (943)	*Veteran Confident*
1/32nd Foot (870)	*Veteran Confident*
5th Brigade – Brigadier General Catlin Craufurd	*Able*
1/45th Foot (915)	*Veteran Confident*
91st Foot (917)	*Veteran Confident*
6th Brigade – Brigadier General Henry Fane	*Able*
1/50th Foot (945)	*Veteran Confident*
1/60th Rifle Foot (604)	*Elite Confident*
2/95th Rifle Foot (4 companies) (456)	Elite Confident
7th Brigade – Brigadier General Robert Anstruther	*Able*
2/9th Foot (633)	*Veteran Confident*
2/43rd (Monmouthshire) Foot (721)	*Veteran Confident*
2/52nd (Oxfordshire) Foot (654)	Veteran Confident
2/97th Rifle Foot (695)	Veteran Confident

WARGAME SCENARIOS

8th Brigade – Brigadier General Wroth Palmer Acland	Able
2nd Foot (731)	Veteran Confident
20th Foot (7½ companies) (401)	Veteran Confident
1/95th Rifle Foot (2 companies) (200)	Elite Confident
Lieutenant Colonel William Robe (RA), two-and-a-half companies (226 men, 16 guns)	Veteran Confident
Lieutenant Colonel C. D. Taylor's 20th Light Dragoons (240), 6th Portuguese Cavalry Regiment (104), 11th Portuguese Cavalry Regiment (50), 12th Portuguese Cavalry Regiment (104), Lisbon Police Cavalry (41)	Green Steady Note this is counted as one regiment of cavalry
Lieutenant Colonel Nicholas Trant (Portuguese detachment)	Able
12th Infantry (605)	Green Steady
21st Infantry (605)	Green Steady
24th Infantry (304)	Green Steady
Porto Caçadores (562)	Experienced Steady
4th Portuguese Artillery (2 guns, 210 men)	Green Steady

Junot's Army

The French will win a decisive victory if they manage to break or capture four of the British brigades and capture Vimiero. If they have failed to take Vimiero by Game Turn 12, they may force a draw if they manage to withdraw two French Divisions, or one division and the Grenadiers voluntarily from the battlefield. Alternatively, if the French can overwhelm the combined brigades of Nightingale, Ferguson and Bowes and have intact units within two moves of Vimiero by Game Turn 12, then they will have won a victory. Note that the totals for men in each regiment include the Grenadiers (of which there were around 2,000), hence the Grenadier battalions do not have totals of men.

Commander-in-chief: General de Division Jean-Andoche Junot, Duke of Abrantes	Able
Division Delaborde – General de Division Henri François Delaborde	Able

OPENING MOVES

1st Brigade – General de Brigade Antoine François Brennier de Montmorand
3/2nd Light Infantry (1,075)
3/4th Light Infantry (1,098)
1 and 2/70th Line (2,358)

Able

Green Steady
Green Steady
Experienced Steady

2nd Brigade – General Jean Guillaume Thomières
1 and 2/86th Line (1,945)
4th Swiss Infantry Regiment (2 companies) (246)

Able

Experienced Steady
Experienced Steady

Division Loison – General de Division Louis Henri Loison
1st Brigade – General Jean Baptiste Solignac
3/12th Light Infantry (1,253)
3/15th Light Infantry (1,305)
3/58th Light Infantry (1,428)

Able

Able
Experienced Steady
Green Steady
Green Steady

2nd Brigade – General de Brigade Hugues Charlot
3/32nd Line (1,034)
3/82nd Line (963)

Able

Green Steady
Green Steady

Cavalry Division – General de Brigade Pierre Margaron
1st Provisional (ex-26th) Chasseur a Cheval (263)
3rd Provisional Dragoon (640)
4th Provisional Dragoon (589)
5th Provisional Dragoon (659)
Squadron of Volunteer Cavalry (100)

Able

Experienced Steady

Green Steady
Green Steady
Green Steady
Green Steady

Reserve – General François Étienne de Kellermann
1 and 2/1st Regiment Reserve Grenadiers
1 and 2/2nd Regiment Reserve Grenadiers

Gifted

Experienced Steady
Experienced Steady

Artillery, engineers and train: (700); Four batteries (23 guns)

Experienced Steady

WARGAME SCENARIOS

Napoleon was clearly alarmed at not only the lack of progress, but also the serious reverses that his troops had suffered in the Peninsula. He scraped up 130,000 men from Germany and earmarked them for operations in Spain. By 3 November they had begun to assemble at Bayonne.

Meanwhile, the situation still remained difficult for the French in the Peninsula. As far as most of the Spanish were concerned the French had been beaten and it would only be a matter of time before they evacuated the country. They could not have been more wrong. The Spanish could not even agree on an overall commander-in-chief and this would be a continual problem, until finally in 1812 Wellington became Commander-in-Chief of allied forces in the Peninsula. In the false belief that the war had effectively been won, the Spanish failed to exert any real pressure on the French.

Blake, however, had gathered 32,000 men together and on 10 September he began moving on Bilbao. On 20 September he captured the city but by now the French were stirring and troops were crossing into Spain. Ney led 10,000 men against Bilbao, easily taking the town, but then he left just 3,000 men as a garrison and fell back to the Ebro. He took up a position at Logrono, facing 10,000 Spanish troops under Pignatelli.

There was another Spanish force of 15,000 at Lodosa and Calahorra and yet more, some 7,000, at Tudela. This was the Spanish Army of the Centre, which had been created by Castaños.

Although the Spanish outnumbered the French they failed to take advantage of the fact. As they began to stir it was Ney that attacked Pignatelli, whilst more French troops attacked Lodosa. Both engagements were a disaster for the Spanish. Pignatelli's recruits were routed and Lodosa was captured along with its important bridge.

Meanwhile Blake had decided to reopen his offensive and moved once again on Bilbao. The French were forced to evacuate in the face of enormous pressure on 11 October. Blake held 11,000 men in reserve and then waited until late October before he got underway once again. By now the French had been reinforced. There was confused fighting and manoeuvring until Blake decided to halt at Espinosa on 10 November. Blake had around 23,000 men and ten guns. Marshal Victor's corps made the first probing attacks but was held off. Another attempt was made in the afternoon. On the following day the French worked around Blake's left and then launched a frontal assault. The Spanish broke and fled back towards Reynosa. By this time Blake had lost all of his artillery and was down to 12,000 men.

The enormous French reserves brought in from Germany began to move under Marshal Soult on 10 November. The main central force made

OPENING MOVES

for Burgos with an ultimate destination of Madrid. French troops spread out to the left and the right, some to deal with Blake and others to deal with Castaños.

Soult ran into a Spanish force led by Belvedere at Gamonal on 10 November. Soult's troops were primarily cavalry; some 5,000 of them supported by a pair of infantry brigades. Belvedere's men were swiftly overrun. The French lost a handful of men and Belvedere's force was destroyed, with 2,500 dead and wounded and 1,000 prisoners. This effectively secured Burgos.

Ney was sent off to encircle the Spanish Army of the Centre and Reynosa to cut off Blake's retreat. The French were now ready to move directly on Madrid. Napoleon concentrated 20,000 troops. On every front the Spanish were now under serious pressure.

Castaños had retreated to Tudela. On 21 November Castaños discovered that the French were behind him. He had 26,000 men with him; insufficient to break out of a trap and consequently he withdrew. It was too late. On 23 November Marshal Lannes closed on Castaños and in the ensuing battle the Spanish lost 4,000 men and twenty-six guns.

Meanwhile, on 22 November, Napoleon, now with 45,000 men, resumed his march on Madrid. He ran into 9,000 Spaniards, led by General San Juan, defending the Somosierra Pass. The Spanish had sixteen guns. An initial cavalry charge by just eighty-seven Polish horsemen was beaten off by the Spaniards, but as the French infantry advanced the Spanish began to break. Napoleon launched 1,000 cavalry at the pass and the Spanish fled.

Napoleon marched into Madrid on 1 December, easily overwhelming hastily-improvised defence works. The Spanish Junta quickly surrendered and many of the Spanish units that still remained began to melt away.

By the middle of December there were 40,000 French troops in Madrid. Even Junot's men that had been repatriated were marching back into Spain. Other French marshals and their commands were stamping out resistance across Spain. It seemed that Spain was now firmly in French hands, but Napoleon was wrong. The British had not been idle. They had been organizing a large force at Lisbon and were now ready to strike.

Background to the Battle of Corunna
The new commander of the British forces in the Peninsula was Lieutenant-General Sir John Moore. He took up his position on 6 October 1808. His instructions were to advance into Leon with 20,000 troops. Meanwhile another 12,000 troops under General Sir David Baird landed at Corunna

and were due to meet up with Moore near Valladolid. Moore left 10,000 men to protect Portugal and began moving towards Salamanca. Baird landed at Corunna on 26 October. Both he and Moore found the roads and local organization chaotic. Both columns made extremely slow progress.

Intelligence was also flawed. For some time Moore was unaware that Madrid had fallen to the French and he also believed that the French in the Peninsula barely numbered 80,000. In fact there were nearly 250,000.

Some good news was that Blake had pulled together around 23,000 men. This news convinced Moore that he should move against Soult and force the French to bring troops out of Madrid to deal with the situation. By 20 December Moore had linked up with Baird. There was a cavalry action at Sahagun on 21 December. What Moore could not know, however, was that Napoleon was rushing troops north to reinforce Soult, as he already knew that Moore's troops had passed through Salamanca.

Ney's VI Corps was moving at the head of 80,000 French troops and had forced the Guadarrama Pass and was approaching Villacastin. By 24 December it was abundantly clear that Moore was in danger of falling into a trap. In order to avoid the disaster he began to retreat towards Corunna.

Cavalry units clashed at Benavente on 26 December, when Lefebvre's guard cavalry fell foul of the 10th Hussars. Lefebvre was captured. There was another engagement on 30 December when General La Romana lost 3,000 men at Mansilla. By the end of the year the British troops had reached Astorga.

As far as the French were concerned the British threat had receded, and Napoleon returned to Madrid with the bulk of the troops, leaving Soult to finish them off. Soult, now with 25,000 infantry and 6,000 cavalry, continued to press the British retreat. A rearguard and deserters were overrun at Bembibre and Villafranca. La Romana meanwhile had been heading for Orense after his disastrous battle. French troops under Franceschi intercepted the Spaniards at the Foncebadon Pass and virtually eliminated La Romana's force.

By 11 January Moore had reached Corunna. His troops were in poor condition having marched and counter-marched in poor weather and with few supplies. As far as Soult was concerned the destruction of 4,000 barrels of gunpowder by the British seemed to signal the fact that Moore was ready to evacuate the Peninsula.

Sure enough the Royal Navy was there to ensure Moore's escape, but he was not yet ready to throw in the towel. The British troops formed up outside Corunna. The key point of the defensive line was Monte Moro. Soult overran British forward positions on 15 January and then set up

OPENING MOVES

artillery batteries to open fire on the main British lines. By lunchtime on 16 January the French troops were in position to launch a major attack along the length of the British line. The battle got underway at 1400.

The first blow fell on Elvina, to the centre right of the British line. A determined counterattack by the 50th and 42nd Infantry drove the French out of the village. In turn the 50th was counter-charged and routed, but Moore threw in additional troops, including a pair of foot guard battalions. The small village became the focus of both commanders' attentions. Moore was mortally wounded by artillery fire, but the British troops were gaining the upper hand.

Meanwhile, on the British right, Fraser's 3rd Division held off determined attacks by cavalry led by Franceschi and Lahoussaye. Although the French had been prevented from delivering a perhaps fatal blow to the British army, Moore had been killed and replaced by General Hope and the British did indeed evacuate 26,000 men. It had almost ended in absolute disaster for the British. They had lost 7,000 men during the campaign, but Napoleon had been forced to take his eyes off the ball and had not completed his conquest of the Peninsula. For now Portugal was safe.

Gaming the Battle of Corunna, 16 January 1809

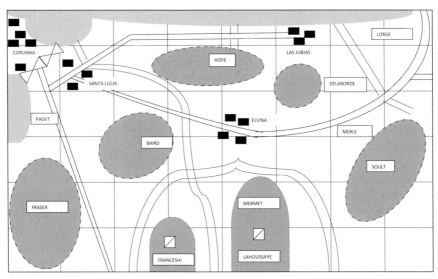

Corunna Wargame Set Up

Moore's Army

This may appear to be a considerable force, but in reality it amounted to

WARGAME SCENARIOS

just 15,000 men. It would therefore be perfectly possible to scale down the force and have a single battalion representing each of the brigades. The British objective is to prevent the French from driving them into the sea and hold the line as well as Corunna itself. The British are outnumbered. The British will win if they are still in possession of the three hills closest to Corunna on Game Turn 15. They will draw if they still hold on to two of them.

C-in-C: General Moore	*Able*
1st Division – General Baird	*Able*
Warde	*Able*
1/1st Foot Guards	*Veteran Confident*
2/1st Foot Guards	*Veteran Confident*
Manningham	**Able**
3/1st Foot	Veteran Confident
1/26th Foot	Veteran Confident
2/81st Foot	Veteran Confident
Bentinck	**Able**
1/42nd Highland	Veteran Confident
1/4th Foot	Veteran Confident
1/50th Foot	Veteran Confident
2nd Division – General Hope	*Able*
Crawford	*Able*
71st Light	*Veteran Confident*
92nd Highland	*Veteran Confident*
36th Foot	*Veteran Confident*
Leith	**Able**
1/51st Foot	Veteran Confident
2/59th Foot	Experienced Steady
2/76th Foot	Experienced Steady
Hill	**Able**
1/2nd Foot	Veteran Confident
1/5th Foot	Veteran Confident
2/14th Foot	Veteran Confident
1/32nd Foot	Veteran Confident

OPENING MOVES

Catlin — Able
1/36th Foot — Veteran Confident
1/71st Foot — Veteran Confident
1/92nd Foot — Experienced Steady

3rd Division – General Fraser — *Able*
Beresford — *Able*
1/6th Foot — *Veteran Confident*
1/9th Foot — *Veteran Confident*
2/23rd Foot — *Experienced Steady*
2/43rd Foot — Veteran Confident

Fane — Able
1/38th Foot — Veteran Confident
1/79th Foot — Veteran Confident
1/82nd Foot — Experienced Steady

4th (Reserve) Division – General Paget — *Able*
Anstruther — *Able*
1/95th Rifles — *Elite Confident*
1/52nd Light — *Veteran Confident*
1/20th Foot — *Veteran Confident*

Disney — Able
1/28th Foot — Veteran Confident
1/91st Foot — Experienced Steady

Artillery: The British mustered just 12 artillery pieces for the battle, and ideally they should be allocated fairly evenly to each of the divisions. In some accounts, the British are given 9 guns. In this case, 3 of the guns Moore gave to Paget; the remaining 6 he placed in pairs along the crest of Monte Mero. Artillery is Experienced Steady. In this case, give the British just 1 field gun.

Soult's Army
The army list may be shorter, but each of the regiments are large with up to four battalions each. If you are scaling down the British, then still retain all of the regiments in the French force to give them a degree of flexibility. There are some good units in this army, but the French do not want a Pyrrhic victory. The French win if they capture two or more of the hills

WARGAME SCENARIOS

closest to Corunna, or they manage to destroy or capture two of the British divisions.

C-in-C: Marshal Soult	*Able*
Infantry Division – General Merle	*Able*
2nd Light Regiment (3 btns.)	Elite Confident
4th Light Regiment (4 btns.)	Veteran Confident
15th Line Regiment (3 btns.)	Veteran Confident
36th Line Regiment (3 btns.)	Veteran Confident
Infantry Division – General Delaborde	*Able*
17th Light Regiment (3 btns.)	Veteran Confident
76th Line Regiment (4 btns.)	Veteran Confident
86th Line Regiment (3 btns.)	Veteran Confident
4th Swiss Regiment (1 btn.)	Elite Arrogant
Infantry Division – General Merment	*Able*
31st Light Regiment (4 btns.)	Veteran Confident
47th Line Regiment (4 btns.)	Veteran Confident
122nd Line Regiment (4 btns.)	Veteran Confident
2nd Swiss Regiment (2 btns.)	Elite Arrogant
3rd Swiss Regiment (1 btn.)	Elite Arrogant
Cavalry Division – GdD Franceschi	*Able*
Light Cavalry Regiment	*Veteran Arrogant*
Light Cavalry Regiment	*Veteran Arrogant*
Light Cavalry Regiment	Veteran Arrogant
Dragoon Regiment	Experienced Steady
Cavalry Division – GdD Lahoussaye	*Able*
Dragoon Regiment	*Experienced Steady*
Dragoon Regiment	*Experienced Steady*
Dragoon Regiment	Experienced Steady
Dragoon Regiment	Experienced Steady
Cavalry Division – GdD Lorge	*Able*
Dragoon Regiment	*Trained Impetuous*
Dragoon Regiment	*Trained Impetuous*
Dragoon Regiment	Trained Impetuous
Dragoon Regiment	Trained Impetuous

OPENING MOVES

Artillery: The French deployed some 36 guns at Corunna. Broadly, depending on your scaling down of the battle, the French should have six times the number of British guns available to them. In this case give the French 6 field guns; they should be Experienced Steady.

Three days before the battle of Corunna the vanguard of the Duke of Infantado had been brought to battle at Uclés. The Spanish army was what remained of the Army of the Centre, which had retreated to Cuenca, but on Christmas Day had begun its advance on Madrid. At that stage Madrid was held by around 9,000 French troops and Infantado had 20,000 men available. However the Spanish advanced too slowly and on 8 January another 20,000 French became available and Victor marched out to deal with the Spanish threat with 16,000 men. The leading Spanish units, comprising of 9,500 infantry, 2,000 cavalry and four guns, under Venegas, were quickly routed. The Spanish lost over 1,000 killed or wounded: all of their artillery and 6,000 men were taken prisoner. The remainder of Infantado's troops retreated into Murcia. Here he was reinforced and the Spanish moved back toward Madrid. Again the French tried to close with them, but apart from a handful of inconclusive skirmishes the Spanish proved elusive. French cavalry, however, was able to inflict enormous casualties and the Spanish strength slowly dripped away.

Meanwhile, in Estremadura, Cuesta was reorganizing his forces. Victor had been instructed by Napoleon to plan an invasion of Portugal and to deal with Cuesta. One of Victor's divisions was driven from strong positions at the Ibor Gorge. By late March Cuesta began moving on Victor's camp at Medellin. Cuesta had 20,000 infantry, 3,000 cavalry and thirty guns. Victor could muster 13,000 infantry, 4,500 cavalry and fifty guns.

Cuesta advanced on a four-mile front on 28 March. Victor deployed his troops with the bulk of his cavalry on the wings. As the long, thin Spanish line closed, French cavalry charged its flanks, only to be driven back. The French infantry became jittery and it was clear that the only option was to pull out. On the verge of breaking, French cavalry made one last determined effort and crashed into an open Spanish flank. The long, thin lines of infantry were dangerously exposed and cut to pieces by the French. In moments Cuesta's whole left wing melted away.

On the French left more cavalry was thrown forward, supported by French infantry. The Spaniards were also hit from the rear by French cavalry from the right that had swung all the way round the back of the enemy's force. Faced with the prospect of either being slaughtered on the

WARGAME SCENARIOS

spot or cut down whilst they ran, the Spanish routed, with French cavalry hard on their heels. By the time the French gave up the pursuit 8,000 Spanish were dead, 2,000 were prisoners and twenty guns had been taken. Around 1,000 French had been lost. Victor had certainly given Cuesta a rough ride, but he still lacked the resources to invade Portugal.

Chapter 3

Portugal, Retreat and Counter Invasion

With the evacuation of the British forces after the battle of Corunna it appeared that the French had a free hand to now invade Portugal once more. On paper the French strength was still strong, but in reality fewer than half of the men were fit for duty.

Soult, however, began to move towards Portugal on 30 January 1809. But it was not until 9 March that he crossed into Portugal. Opposing him were just 10,000 men under General Silveira and, after a Portuguese corps of 4,000 men was lost when their commander ignored orders and dug in to defend Chaves, Silveira was in even more desperate straights.

Soult marched on Oporto, but found his path blocked by 25,000 irregulars. They were not to prove to be any particular problem and they scattered as the French advanced. They were far better suited for guerrilla work. As Soult approached Oporto he discovered that it was garrisoned by 30,000 men and 200 guns. All he could muster against them was 13,000 infantry and 3,000 cavalry. Undeterred, Soult launched a series of probes and on 29 March launched a division against each flank of the Portuguese army. The Portuguese responded by reinforcing their flanks. This was precisely what Soult had hoped. Timed to perfection he launched a concealed division under Mermet. In a matter of minutes the defence-works had been overrun and Oporto lay at Soult's feet. The Portuguese army tried to get away as best it could, but with its back to the River Douro thousands of soldiers and civilians were killed; perhaps as many as 20,000. The French also captured all of the artillery. With Oporto captured Soult still found himself deep in hostile territory. He was losing men to the guerrillas every day.

Ney had been left to deal with the rebellion in Galicia with just 17,000 men against an estimated 30,000 guerrillas. Ney tried everything to suppress opposition but he also had to contend with Spanish regulars and the presence of the Royal Navy. It was May before any help was sent to Ney and even then it was only 7,000 men. When Kellermann's men arrived it was not to reinforce Ney but to prompt him to take part in a new offensive. Together they were to tackle Asturias. No sooner had the French marshals got underway than there were problems rapidly developing with the return of the British.

Wellesley resumed command of the British on 22 April and had 23,000 men. The force was still building and by the beginning of May he could call on 30,000 British troops and 16,000 Portuguese. Wellesley's plan was to advance on Oporto with 18,500 men and twenty-four guns. Beresford would march with 6,000 men towards Lamego and a further 12,000 men would be put in positions around Abrants.

By the early hours of 10 May Wellesley's troops were approaching Oporto. Soult had not taken sufficient precautions and he had insufficient men to hold the city. Soult was in danger of being completely surrounded and as a consequence he retreated before it was too late. Wellesley could now turn south and seek a decisive engagement.

Meanwhile, the war continued in Aragon. The French had achieved great progress. At large were just 4,000 Spanish troops under Lazan and some guerrillas. Junot was responsible for the south of the province and Mortier the northern part. However the struggle for Aragon was not over and worse still Junot was being stripped of troops. Some were escorting prisoners into France and other had been lent to Kellermann. In fact by April Junot was down to just 15,000 men.

At the beginning of May Spanish militia overran the French garrison at Monzon. The French immediately tried to retake it but found themselves surrounded by guerrillas and most of the force had to surrender.

Blake was also active in Aragon. He had taken command of the Army of the Right. He was brought to battle by Suchet on both 23 May and 15 June, first at Alcaniz and then at Maria.

Suchet had joined his command on May 19 and immediately set out to deal with Blake. The French marched to Hijar, reaching there on 23 May. Suchet had fourteen battalions of infantry, five squadrons of cavalry and eighteen guns. Sitting astride three hills to the east of Alcaniz was Blake's 9,000 troops. Blake also had nineteen artillery pieces.

The French attempts to break the line ended in defeat, but Blake did not pursue and instead he incorporated men from Valencia into his army. So he now had 25,000 effectives. He decided to move against Saragossa.

Suchet was desperate for extra troops but so far nothing had arrived. By 13 June Blake was just 20 miles from his target and by this time his force had been reduced to 20,000 men in three divisions, under Lazan, Roca and Areizaga. Lazan and Roca remained on the left bank of the River Huerba, heading for Maria. Suchet was determined to deal with the enemy and on 14 June his lead troops collided with the Spanish. Suchet left 2,000 men to guard against a flanking move from Areizaga, drawing up his remaining 9,000 men to face Blake. Suchet decided to hold on, as he had received news that 3,000 reinforcements were on their way, but on 15 June Blake launched an attack on the French right. The attackers were cut to pieces and fell back in confusion.

Suchet was now sure that the reinforcements would arrive by 1400. All he had to do was to continue to apply pressure. There was then a hailstorm and shortly after this had cleared the French reinforcements, under Roberts, arrived. Suchet could now advance. He hit Blake's right and in a short time Blake's flank was turned and his army was cut off from any prospect of linking up with Areizaga. Ultimately Blake chose to pull back rather than risk losing his whole army.

But Suchet was on his tail and on 16 June he headed for Blake's camp. Blake retired again but he was losing men to desertion. Blake and Suchet faced one another once again at Belchite on 18 June. Blake had 12,000 men and seven guns whilst Suchet had 13,000 men.

An unfortunate accident was to seal the Spanish defeat when a shell hit Blake's ammunition stores. The Spanish thought they were being attacked from the rear and routed. By now Blake had just 9,000 men left.

The British army left Abrantes on 28 June with the purpose of linking up with Cuesta. Wellesley's men consisted of four divisions and thirty artillery pieces; some 20,000 men. There were an additional 8,000 men either in Lisbon or marching to join the main field army. 1,500 Portuguese were with them but most of the Portuguese army was left to secure the frontier. Wellesley was marching to join Cuesta, who was heading for Almaraz with 34,000 infantry, 7,000 cavalry and thirty guns. The French had absolutely no idea what was happening.

The French had fallen back to Talavera by 26 June. Cuesta was close and Wellesley some days march behind. The allies believed that Victor would have around 22,000 men with him at Talavera, with the possibility that King Joseph could reinforce him with 12,000 more. There was also the distinct possibility that Sebastiani, who was then at Madridejos, could also march to reinforce Victor. The allies believed he had 10,000 men but in fact he had double that amount. There was also the possibility that further French troops could be drawn into the engagement.

Wellesley and Cuesta were confident that with their combined 56,000

WARGAME SCENARIOS

men they could handle the possibility of 34,000 French at Talavera. As a precautionary measure moves were made to try and draw possible French reserves away by threatening Madrid.

By 18 July Wellesley had reached the River Alberche. He now moved towards Oropesa in order to fully link up with Cuesta. There was an initial clash between the lead Spanish cavalry units, British cavalry and some French at around noon on 22 July.

Wellesley was desperate to come to grips with the French, but Cuesta was not so hasty. In fact the Spanish did not advance again until 24 July. The next move by Cuesta nearly ended in disaster. He arrived close to Toledo on 25 July only to find 50,000 French barring his way. What the allies did not know was that Soult had been given overall command and he was marching his army to try and get behind the allies. Cuesta instantly retreated. The French saw their opportunity: now they could prevent a junction between Cuesta and the British. However French cavalry were not sufficient to stop Cuesta working round and reaching the River Alberche.

Meanwhile, Wellesley had thrown some of his troops over the Tagus and immediately ran into lead French units. As Cuesta's men began to arrive the allies formed a 3-mile line, running from Talavera northwards. The British would hold the northern end of the line, whilst the Spaniards would hold Talavera. It was a good position and they mustered some 52,000 men who would face 46,000 under the command of King Joseph.

There was initial vicious fighting on 27 July, which saw two battalions of the King's German Legion routed. There was near disaster but luckily Hill threw Stewart's brigade in and broke the French attack.

By the morning of 28 July the bulk of the French army was fully deployed, its primary strength facing the British-held sector. At 0500 the French artillery began to open fire. On the extreme left of the allied positions they could see Ruffin's division advancing towards them. Hill, occupying higher ground, poured flanking fire into them as they approached. He was reinforced by a battalion of Sherbrooke's and together they broke Ruffin's division, killing or wounding 1,300.

There was a long lull before the next French attack when eighty guns opened fire on Hill's positions at 1400. Half an hour later the entire left wing and centre of the French army began to advance. The French took enormous casualties.

Sherbrooke's men targeted Sebastiani and Lapisse, but came under tremendous artillery and skirmisher fire. Sherbrooke's eight battalions waited patiently until the French were within 50 yards. Simultaneously 4,000 British muskets opened fire. Then the British charged. The leading

PORTUGAL, RETREAT AND COUNTER INVASION

French battalions disintegrated. As the French routed they broke up successive lines of columns moving up behind them.

Sherbrooke's division pressed too hard and the French rallied and shattered the whole division. The French then recommenced their advance. There were precious few British reserves left.

Wellesley scraped together a battalion and six guns, which was sufficient to give his shattered units time to rally. To the south Campbell was under pressure, but once again the French were held off. The French now tried to turn the British left but British cavalry and a whole Spanish infantry division, supported by Albuquerque's cavalry, was ready. The French came on but seeing the enormous numbers of allied cavalry they formed a square. The allied cavalry took huge casualties in the difficult terrain but both sides were now nearly spent.

Joseph had a 5,000 man reserve but the bulk of Cuesta's Spanish army had not yet been committed and he could not risk using up his last troops. The battle was over.

Talavera was a Pyrrhic allied victory. The British lost 5,500 and Cuesta, including the retreat from Toledo, had lost 1,200. French losses were higher at over 7,000, including Lapisse and many field officers.

Gaming the Battle of Talavera: 28 July 1809

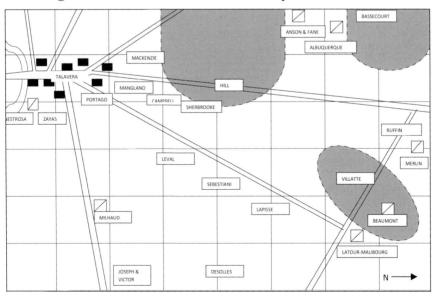

Talavera Wargame Set Up

WARGAME SCENARIOS

Though a costly victory for the Allies, this was the first of a handful of battles that made a major difference to the fortunes of the French in the peninsula. The Battle of Talavera was a victory for a combined British and Spanish army, followed by Fuentes D' Onoro in 1811 and Salamanca in 1812. The French never really recovered from these blows.

Wellesley and Cuesta's Army

This is a large force with a significant Spanish contingent that will need careful deployment and handling. The Spanish in particular are somewhat unreliable and should not be relied upon for any major work. The Allies will win if they can retain a cohesive front line which includes Talavera and the high ground to the north until Game Turn 15. If the Spanish are reduced to fifty percent on the battlefield (including dead, captured and routed) then this is an automatic loss. The Allies can also win by eliminating one of the French corps.

C-inC: Wellesley — *Gifted*
Cavalry Division: Lieutenant-General William Payne — *Able*

Fane's Brigade: Sir Henry Fane — *Able*
3rd Dragoon Guards — *Experienced Steady*
4th Dragoons — *Experienced Steady*

Cotton's Brigade: Sir Stapleton Cotton — Able
14th Light Dragoons — Experienced Steady
16th Light Dragoons — Experienced Steady

Anson's Brigade: George Anson — *Able*
23rd Light Dragoons — *Experienced Steady*
1st Light Dragoons, King's German Legion Experienced Steady

First (Sherbrooke's) Division: Sir John Coape Sherbrooke — *Able*
H Campbell's Brigade Brigadier General Henry Campbell — Able
1st Battalion, Coldstream Guards — Veteran Confident
1st Battalion, 3rd Guards — Veteran Confident
One company 5/60th Foot — Elite Confident

PORTUGAL, RETREAT AND COUNTER INVASION

Cameron's Brigade: Sir Alan Cameron of Erracht Able
1/61st Foot Veteran Confident
2/83rd Foot Veteran Confident
One company 5/60th Foot Elite Confident

Langwerth's Brigade: Brigadier General Ernst (Baron Langwerth) Able
1st Line Battalion, King's German Legion Veteran Confident
2nd Line Battalion, King's German Legion Veteran Confident
Light Companies, King's German Legion Veteran Confident

Low's Brigade: Brigadier General Sigismund (Baron Löw) Able
5th Line Battalion, King's German Legion Veteran Confident
7th Line Battalion, King's German Legion Veteran Confident

Second (Hill's) Division: Sir Rowland Hill Able

Tilson's Brigade: Brigadier General Christopher Tilson Able
1/3rd Foot Veteran Confident
2/48th Foot Veteran Confident
2/66th Foot Veteran Confident
One company 5/60th Foot Elite Confident

R Stewart's Brigade: Richard Stewart Able
29th Foot Veteran Confident
1/48th Foot Veteran Confident

Third (Mackenzie's) Division: Sir Alexander Mackenzie – Mackenzie's Brigade *Able*
2/24th Foot *Veteran Confident*
2/31st Foot *Veteran Confident*
1/45th Foot Veteran Confident

Donkin's Brigade: Sir Rufane Shaw Donkin Able
2/87th Foot Veteran Confident
1/88th Foot Veteran Confident
Five companies 5/60th Foot Elite Confident

WARGAME SCENARIOS

Fourth (Campbell's) Division: Sir Alexander Campbell – A Campbell's Brigade: Sir Alexander Campbell   *Able*
2/7th Foot   *Veteran Confident*
2/53rd Foot   *Veteran Confident*
One company 5/60th Foot   *Elite Confident*

Kemmis's Brigade: Colonel James Kemmis   Able
1/40th Foot   Veteran Confident
97th Foot   Veteran Confident
One company 5/60th Foot   Elite Confident
Lawson's Battery   *Experienced Steady*
Sillery's Battery   *Experienced Steady*
Elliot's Battery   Experienced Steady
Rettberg's Battery   Experienced Steady
Heyse's Battery   Experienced Steady

Spanish Army of Estremadura

General in Chief: Lieutenant General Gregorio de la Cuesta   *Able*

Major General of Infantry: Major General J. M. de Alos   Cautious
Vanguard: Brigadier General José Zayas   *Cautious*
2nd Voluntarios de Catalonia   *Green Cautious*
Cazadores de Barbastro (2nd battalion)   *Green Cautious*
Cazadores de Campo-Mayor   Green Cautious
Cazadores de Valencia y Albuquerque   Green Cautious
Cazadores Voluntarios de Valencia (2nd battalion)   Green Cautious

1st Division: Major-General Marques de Zayas   Cautious
Cantabria (three battalions)
Granaderos Provinciales   Green Cautious
Canarias   Green Cautious
Tiradores de Merida   Green Cautious
Provincial de Truxillo   Green Cautious

PORTUGAL, RETREAT AND COUNTER INVASION

2nd Division: Major General Vincente Iglesias — Cautious
2nd Majorca — Green Cautious
Velez-Malaga (3 btns) — Green Cautious
Osuna (3 btns) — Green Cautious
Voluntarios Estrangeros — Green Cautious
Provincial de Burgos — Green Cautious

3rd Division: Major-General Marques de Portago — *Cautious*
Badajoz (2 btns) — *Green Cautious*
2nd Antequera — *Green Cautious*
Imperial de Toledo — Green Cautious
Provincial de Badajoz — Green Cautious
Provincial de Guadix — Green Cautious

4th Division: Major-General R. Manglano — *Cautious*
Irlanda (2 btns) — *Veteran Confident*
Jaen (2 btns) — Veteran Confident
3rd Seville — *Green Cautious*
Leales de Fernando VII (1st battalion) — Green Cautious
2nd Voluntarios de Madrid — Green Cautious
Voluntearios de la Corona — Green Cautious

5th Division: Major-General L. A. Bassecourt — *Cautious*
Real Marina, 1st Regiment (2 btns) — *Green Cautious*
Africa (3rd battalion) — *Green Cautious*
Murcia (2 btns) — Green Cautious
Reyna (1st battalion) — Green Cautious
Provincial de Sigüenza — Green Cautious

Major General of Cavalry: Major General R. de Villalba, Marquis de Malapina — Cautious
1st Division: Lieutenant General J. de Henestrosa — *Cautious*
Calatrava — *Green Cautious*
Voluntaris de España — *Green Cautious*
Imperial de Toledo — *Green Cautious*
Cazadores de Sevilla — Green Cautious

WARGAME SCENARIOS

Rey	Green Cautious
Reyna	Green Cautious
Villaviciosa	Green Cautious
Cazadores de Madrid	Green Cautious
2nd Division: Lieutenant-General Duque de Albuquerque	Cautious
Carabineros Reales (one squadron)	Green Cautious
Infante	*Green Cautious*
Alcantara	*Green Cautious*
Pavia	Green Cautious
Almanza	Green Cautious
1st and 2nd Hussars de Estremadura	Green Cautious

Notes: In all the Spaniards deployed 7,000 cavalry in the battle. The Spanish artillery was 30 guns in the engagement; they should be spread across the army. They should be given 3 Green Cautious batteries.

Joseph's Army

This is a powerful force that must be deployed and used quickly, otherwise the Allies will dig in and hold their positions: do not expect them to take the offensive. The French win if they manage to reduce the Spanish forces to fifty-percent effectiveness on the battlefield, or eliminate two British divisions (no units that are able to be given a hold order as a minimum). The French can draw if they can destroy twenty-five percent of the Spanish and break one British division without losing one of their corps.

C-in-C: Joseph – King of Spain	Cautious
1st Corps: Marshal Victor	Gifted
1st Division: General François Amable Ruffin	Able
9th Léger (3 btns)	*Veteran Confident*
24th Line (3 btns)	Veteran Confident
96th Line (3 btns)	Veteran Confident
2nd Division: General Pierre Bellon Lapisse	Able
16th Léger (3 btns)	*Experienced Steady*
8th Line (3 battalions)	Experienced Steady

PORTUGAL, RETREAT AND COUNTER INVASION

45th Line (3 battalions)	Experienced Steady
54th Line (3 battalions)	Experienced Steady
3rd Division: General Eugène-Casimir Villatte	*Able*
27th Léger (3 battalions)	*Veteran Confident*
63rd Line (3 battalions)	Veteran Confident
94th Line (3 battalions)	Veteran Confident
95th Line (3 battalions)	Veteran Confident
Corps-Cavalry: (General) Beaumont	*Able*
5th Chasseurs	*Trained Impetuous*
2nd Hussars	*Trained Impetuous*
4th Corps: General Sebastiani	*Able*
1st Division: Sebastiani	
28th Line (3 battalions)	*Experienced Steady*
32nd Line (3 battalions)	Experienced Steady
58th Line (3 battalions)	Experienced Steady
75th Line (3 battalions)	Experienced Steady
2nd Division: General Cyrus Valence	**Able**
4th Polish Regiment (2 battalions)	Experienced Steady
3rd Division: General Jean François Leval	**Able**
Nassau (2 battalions)	Experienced Steady
Baden (2 battalions)	Experienced Steady
Hesse-Darmstadt (2 battalions)	Experienced Steady
Holland (2 battalions)	Experienced Steady
Frankfort (1 battalion)	Experienced Steady
(General) Merlin's Light Cavalry	*Able*
10th Chasseurs	*Trained Impetuous*
26th Chasseurs	*Trained Impetuous*
Polish Lancers	Trained Impetuous
Westphalian Chevaux-Légers	Experienced Steady
1st Dragoon Division: General Marie Fay Latour-Marbourg	*Able*
1st Dragoons	*Trained Impetuous*

WARGAME SCENARIOS

2nd Dragoons	*Trained Impetuous*
4th Dragoons	Trained Impetuous
9th Dragoons	Trained Impetuous
14th Dragoons	Trained Impetuous
26th Dragoons	Trained Impetuous

2nd Dragoon Division: General Edouard Jean Bapiste Milhaud — Able

5th Dragoons	Experienced Steady
12th Dragoons	Experienced Steady
16th Dragoons	Trained Impetuous
20th Dragoons	Trained Impetuous
21st Dragoons	Trained Impetuous
3rd Dutch Hussars	Experienced Steady

Troops from Madrid (place under Joseph's personal command)

12th Léger (3 battalions)	Experienced Steady
51st Line (3 battalions)	Experienced Steady
King's Guard Infantry	*Trained Impetuous*
King's Guard Cavalry	*Trained Impetuous*
27th Chasseurs (2 squadrons)	Experienced Steady

Artillery: It is unclear just how many guns were available to the French in this battle. You should allocate them in proportion to the army lists in the *Grand Battery* rules. They should be given around 6 batteries in total.

Background to the Battle of Almonacid

For the allies the strategic situation was actually quite dangerous. Wellesley and Cuesta believed that Soult had around 15,000 men, whereas in fact he had 50,000. Soult moved through the Tagus Valley, almost with impunity. When Wellesley discovered that Soult was approaching the mountain passes he managed to persuade Cuesta to send additional troops to guard them, under Bassecourt. But Soult had already reached Plasencia, cutting off Wellesley's communication lines. Still under the misapprehension that Soult's force was smaller, Wellesley marched with 18,000 men and arrived at Oropesa on 3 August.

Ney's VI Corps had already swept the Spanish away from the passes and in fact across the Tagus at Almaraz. Bassecourt was also falling back on Oropesa. On the night of 3 August Mortier's V Corps had reached the bridge at Arzobispo and skirmished with Wellesley's cavalry.

PORTUGAL, RETREAT AND COUNTER INVASION

Both sides managed to capture despatches. The first allowed Wellesley to know the true strength of Soult's forces. The second, that Soult now had in his hands, disclosed Wellesley's position, strength and plans. Wellesley wanted to retreat immediately, but Cuesta wanted another crack at the French.

Cuesta finally conceded and began his retreat along with Wellesley. Soult was hard on the heels of Cuesta's rearguard and launched a surprise attack on them on 8 August. The Spanish were caught unprepared and the rearguard was scattered. Despite desperate allied action the French pressed on, crossing the Tagus at Almaraz. The French, however, did not pursue into the mountains. Ney had been ordered to return to Leon and Soult had been told not to march any further west. King Joseph feared that the allies would swing around and take Madrid.

The new French operations would be against Venegas. King Joseph concentrated troops between Toledo and Madrid but Venegas, unsure of how many troops the French had, resolved to go on the offensive. By dawn on 11 August Venegas's army took up positions on the hills on either side of the town of Almonacid. His troops were drawn up in a long line. He had 24,000 infantry and around 2,800 cavalry. Against him Sebastiani could deploy 14,000 men. Sebastiani attacked Venegas's centre and right with his own division, supported by Milhaud's cavalry. The other two divisions struck against the enemy left. Giron's brigades were pushed back and with pressure to their front and flank Zerain and Lacy could not hold. The Spanish army fell back, attempting to maintain order, but King Joseph's reserves were now moving up and the Spanish army collapsed. Vigodet's division was all that stood in the way of complete destruction. Nonetheless 3,500 Spaniards were killed or wounded and 2,000 were captured at a cost of 2,400 French.

Gaming the Battle of Almonacid: 11 August 1809

In this battle, the French could muster some 14,000 troops in total against a Spanish force of some 24,000 infantry, 2,800 cavalry and forty guns. The main point of the battle is for the French to dislodge the Spanish from the line of hills and to inflict as high casualties as possible on the enemy. For the Spanish, the primary objective is to hold as long as possible whilst not jeopardising the army's ability to extract itself as intact as possible. We have provided the strengths of each of the divisions by battalion allowing you to choose the scale to suit your available figures.

WARGAME SCENARIOS

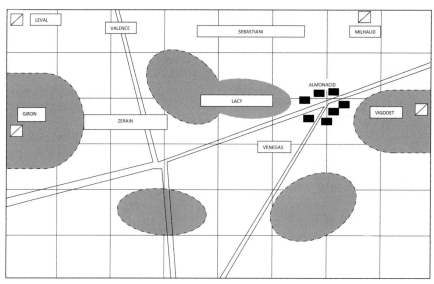

Almonacid Wargame Set Up

Sebastiani's Corps

You are outnumbered and you are attacking a force that holds the high ground. In the battle, the Spanish centre was held by Sebastiani and the Spanish left was overwhelmed by local superiority. Do not expect the Spanish to mount an attack; you have the initiative. To achieve a decisive victory you must break or destroy three of the four Spanish divisions. To win a minor victory, you must break or destroy two of the four Spanish divisions. Any other result will be a draw.

1st Division – Sebastiani: (C-in-C)   *Able*
– 12 battalions *(4 battalions)*   *Experienced Steady*

2nd Division – Leval: *Able*
– 9 battalions *(3 battalions)*   *Experienced Steady*

3rd Division – Valence: *Able*
– 6 battalions *(2 battalions)*   *Experienced Steady*

PORTUGAL, RETREAT AND COUNTER INVASION

Corps cavalry – Sebastiani: *Able*
– 1 dragoon regiment and 2 light cavalry *Experienced Steady*
regiments *(1 dragoon and 1 light cavalry
regiment)*

Milhaud's cavalry: *Able*
– 4 dragoon regiments *(2 regiments)* *Experienced Steady*

Artillery: On paper, the corps would have *Experienced Steady*
*had the equivalent of around 28 guns. Give
the French 3 batteries in total.*

Venegas' Army of La Mancha
You have the numerical advantage and the opportunity to inflict high casualties on the French. Above all, you must not allow your divisions to be attacked in isolation as you will be gradually rolled up and defeated. You cannot order a retreat from the battlefield before Game Turn 10. At that point, you will win a decisive victory if you have managed to extract all of your four divisions. The units are considered saved if they are not routing from the battlefield when they make their exit. If they are forced to retreat off the battlefield, then this is acceptable. A minor victory is won if you manage to extract three of your divisions from the battlefield. Any other result is a draw. Alternatively, if you have managed to maintain your positions and hold two of the three hills on the battlefield by Game Turn 15, then you have won a crushing victory.

C-in-C: Venegas *Cautious*
Vigodet's 2nd Division: *Cautious*
– 9 battalions *(3 battalions)* *Green Cautious*

Lacy's 1st Division: *Cautious*
– 9 battalions *(3 battalions)* *Green Cautious*

Zerain's 5th Division: *Cautious*
– 7 battalions *(2 battalions)* *Green Cautious*

Giron's 3rd Division: *Cautious*
– 8 battalions *(3 battalions)* *Green Cautious*

WARGAME SCENARIOS

Bernuy's 1st Cavalry:
– 5 regiments *(2 regiments. Deploy on left)*

Cautious
Green Cautious

Rivas' 2nd Cavalry:
– 4 regiments *(2 regiments. Deploy on right)*

Cautious
Green Cautious

Artillery: On paper, this part of the army would have mustered around 40 guns. Give the Spanish 4 batteries in total.

Green Cautious

Background to the Battle of Tamames

With Wellesley and Cuesta in retreat and Bassecourt and Venegas defeated, this was a low point for the allies. There was more bad news: the Austrians had been soundly beaten. Vienna had fallen on 13 May and they had been broken at the battle of Wagram on 6 July. Within a week they had sued for peace. This meant that Wellesley could expect enormous numbers of French troops to be released from central Europe. Around this time Wellesley had become Viscount Wellington, but his elevation did not make him any more optimistic about fortunes in the Peninsula.

The Spanish were in no better a position. By the summer of 1809 General Del Parque had taken over from La Romana. He was building up his army and by late September had around 30,000 men at Ciudad Rodrigo and another 20,000 men on their way. General Areizaga had taken over Cuesta's command and had integrated Venegas's men. This created a force of around 50,000 troops, including 6,000 cavalry. There were also around 10,000 men under the Duke of Albuquerque. These were the rump of Cuesta's army.

Del Parque's army got underway towards the end of September, advancing on Ney's headquarters at Salamanca. Ney was actually away on leave and his VI Corps was under the command of Marchand. By 18 October Del Parque had taken up a position near the village of Tamames. He had 20,000 infantry, 1,500 cavalry and eighteen guns. Marchand could muster 14,000 men and fourteen guns but it was he that decided to be the more aggressive. Marchand sent a brigade to turn the Spanish left and a second column to storm the centre. Initially the action went well for the French, as Del Parque's left wing caved in. The French in the centre, under Marcognet, some six battalions, were launched against the Spanish centre. They had to approach by climbing steep slopes and immediately came under heavy artillery and musketry fire. Precisely timed, Del Parque ordered his men to charge the rapidly disintegrating French columns. The French fled.

Gaming to the Battle of Tamames: 18 October 1809

Tamames Wargame Set Up

This battle gave the French a bloody nose: in reality they were somewhat over confident and outnumbered. We have listed the whole of French VI Corps here to balance up the game, otherwise the French would have little chance in dislodging the Spanish.

Del Parque's Army of the Left

This is a golden opportunity to inflict a major defeat on the French. To win a decisive victory, break one of the French divisions and hold the ridge line with no enemy on it. A minor victory is achieved if one of these goals is attained. A draw is achieved by taking Tamames itself.

C-in-C: Duke Del Parque	*Gifted*
Maj-Gen Martin de la Carrera's Vanguard:	*Able*
– 14 battalions *(4 battalions)*	*Green Steady*
Maj-Gen Francisco Xavier Losada's 1st Division:	*Able*
– 14 battalions *(4 battalions)*	*Green Steady*

WARGAME SCENARIOS

Maj-Gen Conde de Belvedere's 2nd Division: *Able*
– 14 battalions *(4 battalions)*   *Green Steady*

Maj-Gen Francisco Ballasteros's 3rd Division: *Able*
– 15 battalions *(4 battalions)*   *Green Steady*

Maj-Gen Marques de Castrofuerte's 5th Division: *Able*
– 7 battalions *(2 battalions)*   *Green Steady*

Prince of Anglona's Cavalry Division: *Able*
– 6 regiments *(2 regiments dragoons)*   *Green Steady*

Marchand's VI Corps (Ney was on leave)

If the troops can be concentrated and you focus on dealing with the Spanish piecemeal there is a chance. A draw is won if there are no Spanish units on the battlefield other than those on the ridge. A minor victory is won if you have broken two Spanish divisions and a major victory if two have been broken and you have a division on the ridge.

C-in-C: Marchand   *Able*
Brigade Maucune: *Able*
– 6th Léger (2 btns.), 69th Line (3 btns.)   *Experienced Steady*

Brigade Marcognet: *Able*
– 39th and 76th Line (3 btns.)   *Experienced Steady*

Division Mermet   *Able*
Brigade Bardet: *Able*
– 25th Léger (2 btns.), 27th Line (3 btns.)   *Experienced Steady*

Brigade Labassée: *Able*
– 50th and 59th Line (3 btns.)   *Experienced Steady*

Division Loison   *Able*
Brigade Simon: *Able*
– Légion du Midi (1 btn.), Légion Hanovrienne (2 btns.), 26th Line (3 btns.)   *Experienced Steady*

PORTUGAL, RETREAT AND COUNTER INVASION

Brigade Ferrey: *Able*
– 32th Léger (1 btn), 66th and 82th Line *Experienced Steady*
  (3 btns.)

Cavalry – Lamotte: *Able*
– 3rd Hussars, 15th Chasseurs à Cheval *Experienced Steady*

Background to the Battle of Ocaña

Soon after the battle another Spanish division joined Del Parque and he now had 30,000 men. Brimming with confidence, he marched into Salamanca on 25 October. French reinforcements were rushed to help the VI Corps. Del Parque, now facing stiffer opposition, abandoned Salamanca on 5 November.

Shortly before Del Parque was forced to pull out of Salamanca, Areizaga began his offensive. To the dismay of the French his force suddenly appeared to the south of Ocaña. Areizaga had 48,000 infantry, 6,000 cavalry and sixty guns. It was clear to the French that he was planning to move on Madrid. King Joseph reacted quickly, pulling together as many men as possible. Luckily for the French Areizaga had hesitated and had not begun marching on Madrid until 11 November. There was a series of skirmishes and it seemed to the Spaniard that French strength was growing and reluctantly he began to withdraw, heading for Ocaña.

The French were converging on the Spanish force. On 18 November there was a major cavalry engagement. King Joseph was desperate to make sure that he brought the Spaniards to battle so that they could not elude him and threaten his capital from another direction.

King Joseph had massed 34,000 men and forty guns by 19 November, but had decided not to wait for I Corps, which was en route. Facing him were 51,000 Spanish troops. The French decided to attack the Spanish left and centre and once the Spanish reserves had been committed a massed cavalry attack would fall on the Spanish right.

The French centre moved forward, forcing the Spanish battalions back. Suddenly the Spanish counterattacked and Girard's division was needed to shore up the French centre. All of a sudden Milhaud's cavalry emerged and promptly routed Freire's Spanish cavalry. The Spanish flank was now exposed and with French infantry in front of them and hostile cavalry to their flank and rear, regiment after regiment was rolled up and slaughtered. Even the Spanish second line suffered the same fate.

WARGAME SCENARIOS

The reserves, under King Joseph, now moved in for the kill. Zayas's men tried to cover the retreat and together with the divisions of Copons and Vigodet they tried to hold off the French. It was a forlorn hope and these divisions were also overwhelmed. By the time the battle ended the French had taken 14,000 prisoners and fifty guns. They had lost just 2,000 killed or wounded. As for the Spanish deaths, all that can be certain is that at least 12,000 fell.

Gaming the Battle of Ocaña: 19 November 1809

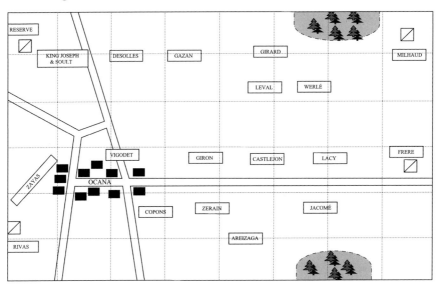

Ocana Wargame Set Up

The Spanish mustered over 50,000 men in this battle against a French force of some 34,000. The battle field is good cavalry country, as the Spanish would discover. The Spanish are brittle and need continual support to hold and inflict casualties on the French to make the battle too costly for them.

Areizaga's Army
A draw is achieved if the Spanish can extract at least four intact divisions from the battlefield by retiring after Game Turn 10. No voluntary retrograde movement is allowed until this game turn. A minor victory is achieved if there are still four intact divisions on the battlefield on Game

PORTUGAL, RETREAT AND COUNTER INVASION

Turn 15. A decisive victory is achieved if the start line is still being held on Game Turn 15 by at least four divisions.

C-in-C: Areizaga — *Cautious*

Zaya's Vanguard Division: — *Gifted*
– 7 battalions *(2 battalions)* — *Veteran Confident*

Lacy's 1st Division: — *Able*
– 9 battalions *(3 battalions)* — *Green Cautious*

Vigodet's 2nd Division: — *Able*
– 9 battalions *(3 battalions)* — *Veteran Confident*

Giron's 3rd Division: — *Able*
– 8 battalions *(3 battalions)* — *Green Cautious*

Castlejon's 4th Division: — *Able*
– 8 battalions *(3 battalions)* — *Green Cautious*

Zerain's 5th Division: — *Able*
– 7 battalions *(2 battalions)* — *Green Cautious*

Jacome's 6th Division: — *Able*
– 9 battalions *(3 battalions)* — *Green Cautious*

Freire (Cavalry Commander): — *Able*

Bernuy's 1st Cavalry Division: — *Able*
– 5 regiments *(1 regiment)* — *Green Cautious*

Rivas' 2nd Cavalry Division: — *Able*
– 4 regiments *(1 regiment)* — *Green Cautious*

March's 3rd Cavalry Division: — *Able*
– 6 regiments *(1 regiment)* — *Green Cautious*

Osorio's 4th Cavalry Division: — *Able*
– 5 regiments *(1 regiment)* — *Green Cautious*

Artillery: 6 guns — *Green Cautious*

WARGAME SCENARIOS

King Joseph's Army
Nothing but an overwhelming victory will win this battle. A draw is obtained if there are three intact Spanish divisions still on the battlefield on Game Turn 15. A minor victory is won if the Spanish are all in flight by Game Turn 12. A decisive victory is won if the Spanish are all in flight by Game Turn 10.

C-in-C: King Joseph — *Able*
Soult — *Gifted*

Division Werle: — *Able*
– 6 battalions *(2 battalions)* — *Experienced Steady*

Division Leval: — *Able*
– 9 battalions *(3 battalions)* — *Experienced Steady*

Division Gazan: — *Able*
– 12 battalions *(4 battalions)* — *Experienced Steady*

Division Girard: — *Able*
– 12 battalions *(4 battalions)* — *Experienced Steady*

Brigade Rey: — *Able*
– 6 battalions *(2 battalions)* — *Experienced Steady*

King's Guards: — *Able*
– 8 battalions *(3 battalions)* — *Green Cautious*

Division Milhaud: — *Able*
– 5 regiments *(1 regiment)* — *Experienced Steady*

Division Paris: — *Able*
– 2 Chasseur regiments, 1 light cavalry
(1 regiment) — *Experienced Steady*

Division Beauregard: — *Able*
– 1 Hussar regiment, 1 Chasseur regiment,
2 dragoon regiments *(1 regiment)* — *Experienced Steady*

Reserve Cavalry: 1 regiment — *Experienced Steady*
Artillery: 4 batteries — *Experienced Steady*

PORTUGAL, RETREAT AND COUNTER INVASION

Background to the Battle of the River Coa
As 1810 dawned it had become abundantly clear to Napoleon that all that stood in the way of a permanent conquest of Spain and Portugal was Wellington. He had intended to lead the offensive against Lisbon himself, but personal matters delayed him and instead he gave the command of the Army of Portugal to Massena. This was by no means a popular decision; at least as far as his other senior commanders were concerned. Junot did not want Massena to do any better than he had achieved. Both Reynier and Ney disliked Massena. It was hardly a promising start.

To achieve what the others had failed to accomplish Massena was given the II, VI, VIII and ultimately the XI Corps and in addition 20,000 men under Kellermann. On paper this was 90,000 men.

Conscious of the fact that the French would try another invasion of Portugal, the allies had created rings of defences and had destroyed, or at least evacuated, everything which could be considered to be of any use to the French. All of the key fortresses had been strengthened; roads were ploughed up and militia units would be available to operate behind French lines.

The defence works would become known as the 'Lines of Torres Vedras', built between November 1809 and September 1810 along two successive ridgelines. The Lines were held by 25,000 Portuguese militia men, 8,000 Spanish troops and 2,500 British gunners and marines. This enabled Wellington to assemble a further 60,000 Anglo-Portuguese troops behind the lines to deal with any French breakthroughs.

Before the French could even consider tackling Portugal there were still major campaigns to be fought across Spain. In Andalucía Bonnet's 7,000 men took Oviedo on 31 January. But the countryside was alive with guerrillas.

The British were landing raiding parties of up to 2,000 men out of Corunna. They would strike fast in northern Spain and then be evacuated to safety. This meant that it was not only virtually impossible for the French to keep lines of communication open with France, but it also tied down vital men that would be needed by Massena.

Meanwhile General Loison and elements of the VI Corps marched on Astorga. It was a sizeable Spanish-held town and was well fortified. He waited until Junot's VIII Corps arrived and they bombarded the town. On 21 April they stormed the fortification, capturing 2,500 Spanish troops.

The next target was the castle of Cuidad Rodrigo. The garrison, under Herrasti, amounted to some 5,500 troops. The Spaniards hoped that Wellington would march to their assistance if they came under siege. Ney's troops began to surround the castle on 30 May, easily dealing with some forward British units and cutting off the fortress. On 25 June the French began to batter the fortress with forty-six heavy guns. After four days there was a large breach in the north wall. After the Spanish rejected surrender terms, Ney's men stormed into the suburbs and then into the city. By this time over a quarter of the garrison was dead. Ney led an attack on the breach on 9 July. As the French advanced the Spanish surrendered and the remainder of the garrison marched out.

The British troops that had been pushed aside by the French were elements of Craufurd's light division. They were still operating in the area. By 23 July Massena had ordered the VI Corps to take Almeida. It was the last fortress blocking the invasion route into Portugal.

Craufurd's division took up a position stretching from the River Coa to a windmill close to the Almeida fortress. It was a poor position, as there was only one possible escape route, down a lane to a single bridge. Ney's men moved forward at speed, realising that he could trap and destroy the British force. The British were hopelessly outnumbered and the French broke through them easily. More by luck than by judgement, most of the 43rd got away and the division managed to rally and prevent the French from crossing the bridge to finish them off.

Gaming the Battle of the River Coa: 24 July 1810

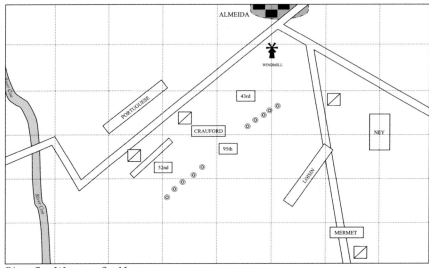

River Coa Wargame Set Up

PORTUGAL, RETREAT AND COUNTER INVASION

Craufurd seriously underestimated the force Ney was bringing up against him and the ability of the Frenchman. The Light Division could have easily been wiped out. This is a smaller-scale skirmish action, or can be fought as a regular sized battle with all the formations present. It is a holding action and then a retreat. The British need to hold long enough for the bulk of the force to get across the River Coa, the French simply have to stop them escaping.

Craufurd's Force (about 4,200 infantry, 800 cavalry, and 6 guns)
Standing and fighting is suicidal and will end in disaster. In effect, you have five regiments (including the 95th, operating as skirmishers). You receive one point for each regiment you successfully extract from the battle field. Once they are over the river, they are safe as the French did not manage to cross and chase the Light Division. If you score 3 points, this is a draw, 4 is a minor victory and 5 a decisive one.

C-in-C: Craufurd	*Able*
Beckwith's Brigade: 43rd, 95th, 3rd Caçadores	*Experienced Steady*
Barclay's Brigade: 52nd, 95th, 1st Caçadores	*Experienced Steady*

Ney's Force (20,000)
The purpose of the battle is to annihilate the Light Division. It is a golden opportunity to destroy Craufurd's isolated command. You begin with five victory points which means a decisive victory. You will lose one victory point for every enemy regiment that escapes over the River Coa, regardless of whether they are routing across it. To retain victory points, the enemy regiments must be destroyed, captured or forced to rout away and off the table away from the river. Four or more victory points is a decisive win, three is a minor win and two is a draw, any less is a loss. The French must deploy one cavalry unit on the left and the other on the right.

6th Corps Marshal Ney	*Gifted*
Division Marchand	**Able**
Brigade Maucune:	**Able**
– 6th Léger (2 btns.), 69th Line (3 btns.)	*Experienced Steady*

WARGAME SCENARIOS

Brigade Marcognet:	*Able*
– 39th and 76th Line (3 btns.)	*Experienced Steady*
Division Mermet	*Able*
Brigade Bardet:	*Able*
– 25th Léger (2 btns), 27th Line (3 btns.)	*Experienced Steady*
Brigade Labassée:	*Able*
– 50th and 59th Ligne (3 btns.)	*Experienced Steady*
Division Loison	*Able*
Brigade Simon:	*Able*
– Légion du Midi (1 btn.), Légion Hanovrienne (2 btns.), 26th Line (3 btns.)	*Experienced Steady*
Brigade Ferrey:	*Able*
– 32nd Léger (1 bat.), 66th and 82nd Line (3 btns.)	*Experienced Steady*
Cavalry Lamotte:	*Able*
– 3rd Hussars, 15th Chasseurs à Cheval	*Experienced Steady*

Almeida itself was garrisoned by 4,500 Portuguese, under Colonel Cox. They had 100 artillery pieces and the expectation was that the fortress would hold out for months. The French VI Corps surrounded Almeida, waiting for the siege train to come up with Junot. By 15 August the French had assembled fifty-three heavy guns and began to bombard the fortress. Soon they had made a breach in the southeast wall.

However it was not the French that would determine the fate of Almeida, it was misfortune. At 1900 on 26 August a leaky gunpowder barrel had been issued to one of the Portuguese batteries. The barrel had left a trail of gunpowder all the way back to the main magazine. A lucky shot from a French shell ignited the trail and detonated the main magazine, killing 700 defenders. Fire did the rest of the damage. Cox was determined to fight on, but on the following day he was forced to march out at the head of 4,000 men to become prisoners of war.

Background to the Battle of Bussaco

On 2 September the French began their advance towards Portugal. The

PORTUGAL, RETREAT AND COUNTER INVASION

French continued forward with the allies falling back and waiting to be sure of the French line of attack. The French encountered ruined roads and abandoned towns, villages and farmsteads.

On 25 September Reynier's leading troops ran into the British Light Division near Mortagoa. Wellington had chosen his intended site for battle along a nine-mile ridge, which stretched from the Sierra de Alcoba to the Mondego River. Here he deployed 52,000 men and sixty guns. There was only one major road that crossed the battlefield, leading to Coimbra. The other was simply a lane. At the northern tip of the position was the Bussaco Convent, surrounded by trees.

Massena could instantly see that infantry would have to be used to clear the slopes. As the allies were deployed on the reverse slopes he had no real idea of their strength. Consequently he believed that the allied centre was their right wing and therefore he deployed Reynier's corps to march through San Antonio and then rollup Wellington's line all the way to the convent. Once Reynier had got to the crest of the ridge two more divisions would then be unleashed.

The French came on at dawn on 27 September, preceded by skirmishers and then the divisions of Heudelet and Merle in dense, narrow columns. There was thick undergrowth and fog to add to the confusion. The French blundered into a Portuguese brigade and then came under intense fire, which brought the advance to a halt.

Meanwhile, Merle had reached the crest and suddenly found himself under intense musket and artillery fire. The lead regiment fled, carrying away the rest of Merle's division.

Reynier threw in his last men, under Foy. But by now Wellington had reinforced the position with Leith's division. They arrived just in time and the French began to retreat.

Meanwhile Ney had pushed Loison's twelve battalions forward. As they pushed aside allied skirmishers the French reached the crest, when suddenly they came under intense fire from hidden British regiments. In the first volleys 1,000 French fell.

Marchand's troops had been no more successful. They ran into thick lines of allied infantry and galling fire from well-placed batteries. Having failed on every front Ney abandoned the attack. The casualties in the battle were hugely disproportionate: the French had lost 4,500 killed and wounded, including over 250 officers. The allies had lost just 1,250 men.

WARGAME SCENARIOS

Gaming the Battle of Bussaco: 27 September 1810

Bussaco Wargame Set Up

This is a potentially large and unwieldy battle to refight. We have rolled many of the regiments together to represent composite brigades or regiments to cut down on the number of units and figures you will need to replay the battle. You may wish to unravel these combinations and fight a series of replays of the key actions along the ridge.

Allied Army
Note that the army list shows the deployment from north to south after the reserves held back by Wellington. The Allies win if they manage to break, rout, destroy or capture any French Corps and retain control over the heights. They will win a minor victory if they retain both roads through the heights by Game Turn 15.

C-in-C: Duke of Wellington — *Gifted*
RHA Battery — *Experienced Steady*
Pack's Independent Portuguese Brigade — Trained Steady
Campbell's Independent Portuguese Brigade — Trained Steady
Coleman's Independent Portuguese Brigade — Trained Steady
4th Dragoons — Experienced Steady

PORTUGAL, RETREAT AND COUNTER INVASION

Cole's 4th Division — *Able*
Campbell's Brigade — *Veteran Confident*
Kemmis's Brigade — Veteran Confident
Collin's Portuguese Brigade — Trained Steady
RA Battery — *Experienced Steady*

Craufurd's Light Division — *Able*
Beckwith's Brigade — Veteran Confident
Barclay's Brigade — Veteran Confident

Spencer's 1st Division — *Able*
Stopford's Brigade — *Veteran Confident*
Von Lowe's KGL Brigade — Veteran Confident
Packenham's Brigade — Veteran Confident
Blantyre's Brigade — Veteran Confident
RA Battery — *Experienced Steady*

Picton's 3rd Division — *Able*
Mackinnon's Brigade — *Veteran Confident*
Lightburn's Brigade — Veteran Confident
Champalimaud's Portuguese Brigade — Trained Steady
RA Battery — *Experienced Steady*

Leith's 5th Division — *Able*
Barnes's Brigade — *Veteran Confident*
Spry's Portuguese Brigade — Trained Steady
Eben's Portuguese Brigade — Trained Steady
RA Battery — *Experienced Steady*

Hill's 2nd Division — *Able*
Stewart's Brigade — *Veteran Confident*
Inglis's KGL Brigade — Veteran Confident
Craufurd's Brigade — Veteran Confident

Hamilton's Portuguese Division — *Able*
Campells' Portuguese Brigade — *Trained Steady*
Fonesca's Portuguese Brigade — Trained Steady

French Army
The French win a major victory by having captured the convent and the

WARGAME SCENARIOS

two roads passing through the heights. They win a minor victory if they control one of the roads and they have broken, destroyed, routed or captured two Allied divisions.

C-in-C: Massena   *Able*
12pdr Foot Battery   Veteran Confident
8pdr Foot Battery   *Veteran Confident*

Mountburn's Cavalry   *Able*
3rd/6th Dragoons   *Trained Impetuous*
11/15/25th Dragoons   Trained Impetuous
6pdr Horse Battery   *Veteran Confident*

Reynier's 2nd Corps   *Able*
Soult's Cavalry   *Able*
Chasseurs   *Trained Impetuous*
Dragoons   Trained Impetuous
8pdr Foot Battery   *Veteran Confident*
8pdr Foot Battery   Veteran Confident

Merle's 1st Division   *Able*
2nd Light Infantry   *Veteran Confident*
4th Light Infantry   *Veteran Confident*
36th Line   *Veteran Confident*

Heudelet's 6th Division   *Able*
17th Light Infantry   Veteran Confident
31st Light Infantry   Veteran Confident
47th Line   Veteran Confident
70th Line   Veteran Confident

Ney's VI Corps   *Gifted*
Lamotte's Hussars   *Experienced Steady*
8pdr Foot Battery   *Veteran Confident*
6th Light Infantry   *Veteran Confident*
39th/69th Line   *Veteran Confident*
76th Line   *Veteran Confident*

Mermet's 2nd Division   *Able*
25th Light Infantry   Veteran Confident

PORTUGAL, RETREAT AND COUNTER INVASION

27th Line	Veteran Confident
50/59th Line	Veteran Confident
Loisin's 3rd Division	**Able**
32nd Light Infantry	Veteran Confident
26/66/82nd Line	Veteran Confident
Hanoverian Legion	Veteran Confident
Junot's VIII Corps	*Gifted*
St Croix's Dragoons	*Trained Impetuous*
8pdr Foot Battery	*Veteran Confident*
Clausel's 1st Division	*Able*
15th Light Infantry	*Veteran Confident*
19/22/25th Line	*Veteran Confident*
28/34/46/75th Line	*Veteran Confident*
Solignac's 2nd Division	*Able*
15/65/86th Line	*Veteran Confident*
Regiment Prusse	*Experienced Steady*
Regiment Irlandaise	*Experienced Steady*

Massena was determined to find his way around the allied positions. He found it near Sardao. Here he managed to reach the road linking Aporto with Lisbon. Wellington meanwhile had retreated towards Coimbra.

Massena mercilessly pushed his men on and by 11 October they had reached Villafranca and could now see the Lines of Torres Vedras. There seemed to be no way around it; everywhere there was an unbroken chain of field fortifications and artillery. Massena pulled back to Santarem and he hoped that Wellington would attack him there, but the allied general was quite happy to sit and watch the French starve to death. Massena hung on until late-February 1811, hoping against hope that supplies would arrive or that at least he would be reinforced significantly.

Reluctantly, on 4 March Massena had begun his retreat. He now had 44,000 men against Wellington's 46,000, but that only illustrated part of the equation. The French were exhausted and hungry whilst the allies were rested and well-fed.

By 22 March the French had reached Celerico. After some deliberation Massena decided that instead of continuing his retreat he would launch

WARGAME SCENARIOS

another offensive, but his commanders told him that it would only end in disaster. By 29 March Wellington had reached Guarda. Two days earlier Junot had retired from Belmonte and the French II Corps had left Sabugal.

Background to the Battle of Sabugal
Wellington, at the head of 30,000 men, reached Sabugal on 3 April, with the intention of nipping off the French in this region before they could rejoin Massena. He sent the Light Division and a pair of cavalry brigades around the enemy's left flank. Four other divisions would make a frontal attack.

Reynier's men of the II Corps were taken by surprise. They were vastly outnumbered. He desperately tried to pull away and head north to join up with Massena. The French hung on for as long as they could, but were eventually driven from the field. Massena, with his flank turned, now had to retreat towards Ciudad Rodrigo.

By 11 April what remained of Massena's army was at Salamanca. He had lost 2,000 killed, 8,000 prisoners and at least another 1,500 due to disease, starvation and desertion. Napoleon was furious and had earmarked a replacement in the shape of Marmont. But fate would determine that there would be one more engagement between Massena and Wellington before Massena's peninsular career was over.

Gaming the Battle of Sabugal: 3 April 1811

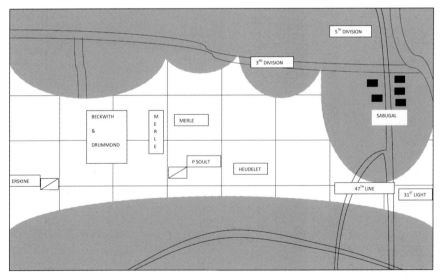

Sabugal Wargame Set Up

PORTUGAL, RETREAT AND COUNTER INVASION

The opening moves of this battle were fought in mist and fog. The French had no idea that the British were this close nor in such numbers. As such, the battle should be fought using concealed movement for as long as possible. Once the British units have been observed, the French may begin their retreat 2 turns after their observation of the British army.

Allied Army
The key objective is not territory, but the inflicting of casualties on the enemy or capturing units. The allies will win a decisive victory if three French brigades are either destroyed or captured: a minor victory if one or two are destroyed or captured.

Light Division: Major General Sir W. Erskine (C-in-C) — Able
Beckwith's 1st Brigade — Able
1/95th Rifles (4 Companies) — Elite Confident
1/43rd Light (10 Companies) — Elite Confident
3rd Caçadores (5 Companies) — Experienced Steady

Drummond's 2nd Brigade — Able
2/95th Rifles (4 Companies) — Elite Confident
1/52nd Light (10 Companies) — Elite Confident
1st Caçadores (5 Companies) — Experienced Steady
1st KGL Hussars (1 Squadron) — Experienced Steady
16th Light Dragoons (1 Troop) — Experienced Steady

3rd Division: General Picton — Able
2/5th — Veteran Confident
1/45th — Veteran Confident
5/60th — Veteran Confident
2/83rd — Veteran Confident
1/88th — Veteran Confident
2/88th — Veteran Confident
1/94th — Veteran Confident

Note that although the 5th Division is marked on the map, it did not take part in the action and marched into Sabugal without losses.

French Army
The French player must play a waiting game and cannot begin their retreat

until all British units have been observed. The purpose of the game is to save as many of your brigades as possible from destruction or capture. If you manage to exit all your infantry brigades from either of the road exit points, then you have won a decisive victory. If you manage to exit only losing one brigade, then this is a minor victory. Standing and fighting will only end in complete destruction.

2nd Corps: Reynier (C-in-C) — *Able*
Merle's 1st Division Brigade Sarrut — *Able*
2nd Léger (4 Battalions) — *Veteran Confident*
36th Line (4 Battalions) — *Veteran Confident*

Brigade Graindorge — *Able*
4th Léger (4 Battalions) — *Veteran Confident*

Heudelet's 2nd Division Brigade Foy — Able
17th Léger (3 Battalions) — Veteran Confident
70th Line (4 Battalions) — Veteran Confident

Brigade Arnaud — *Able*
31st Léger (4 Battalions) — *Veteran Confident*
47th Line (4 Battalions) — *Veteran Confident*

Cavalry Brigade: P. Soult — *Able*
1st Hussars (1 Squadron) — *Trained Impetuous*
22nd Chasseurs (1 Squadron) — *Trained Impetuous*

Divisional artillery: 2 howitzers — *Veteran Confident*

Background to the Battle of Barrosa
Meanwhile, in Andalucía, Soult had three corps, the I, IV and V, some 70,000 men. He had his own problems. There were around 12,000 Spanish, under Freire, east of Granada and some 13,000 in the northwest under La Romana. The most pressing problem, however, was Cadiz, with its garrison of 26,000 men. It was surrounded by French-held earthworks and 300 guns. But with Cadiz at the end of a five-mile peninsula, it was out of range. The island of Leon itself was separated from the mainland by 350m of water. This made it almost impossible for the French to try and storm the defences. Added to this there was nothing to stop the Anglo-Spanish fleet from going in and out at will, picking up troops, dropping them off, delivering supplies and launching amphibious operations anywhere along the coast.

PORTUGAL, RETREAT AND COUNTER INVASION

With all of this to contend with Soult had also been requested to send assistance to Massena. Rather than deplete his already over-stretched forces, Soult decided instead to deal with Badajoz on the River Guadiana.

Soult led with 13,500 infantry and 4,000 cavalry, leaving another 2,000 men to guard his supply trains. He was forced to detach another division to deal with La Romana causing him to change his plans and make for Olivenza (a minor Spanish held fortress), arriving there on 11 January 1811. After four days, Herck and his 4,000 men surrendered to Soult.

Soult now determined to try his luck at Badajoz. He began the siege on 27 January. Almost immediately he was spooked by news that a Spanish force was marching to reinforce Badajoz. It was in fact La Romana's 15,000 men, but he had just died of a heart attack and had been replaced by General Mendizabal. Soult could not stop the Spanish troops from reinforcing the garrison. Mendizabal increased the fortress defences to 7,000 and then positioned his remaining 12,000 troops on the heights of San Cristobal on the banks of the River Guadiana beside the fortress.

Gazan had rejoined Soult and on 19 February Soult detached 4,500 infantry, 2,500 cavalry and twelve guns under Mortier and sent them across the river to attack an unsuspecting Mendizabal. In a swift engagement the French cavalry saw off the Spanish horse. Immediately the Spanish infantry formed up in divisional squares. They were easy prey for the French infantry as they arrived. 1,000 Spanish were killed and 4,000 captured. The rest either fled into Badajoz or towards Portugal. This now left Soult free to deal with the fortress. By 10 March, with a 20m gap in the south wall, the Spanish surrendered. 8,000 men were taken into captivity along with masses of food and ammunition.

It was not all good news for Soult. Not only did he now discover that Massena was retreating northwards, but also that I Corps had been very roughly dealt with at Barrosa. Added to this, there was news that the army that had dealt the blow against I Corps was an Anglo-Spanish force that had landed at Algeciras and was threatening the siege of Cadiz.

Victor's I Corps had been blockading Cadiz since February 1810. The vast majority of his troops were gun-crews and sappers, and not infantry. Nonetheless he mustered 19,000 men. He was holding inside Cadiz some 20,000 Spanish and at least 4,500 British.

General Graham and Spanish General La Peña had assembled 5,000 British and 8,000 Spaniards, some from Cadiz and others from Gibraltar. They overran an outpost of I Corps on 2 March 1811. At the same time the Cadiz garrison launched a series of counterattacks.

Victor could not allow the allies to retain the initiative. He marched east

WARGAME SCENARIOS

with 10,000 men in three divisions, under Ruffin, Leval and Villatte. Villatte's command sat astride the Cadiz road near Barossa. The other two divisions headed north along the flank of the Anglo-Spanish army.

On 5 March La Peña's troops drove Villatte's men off the road and the British troops began making progress through the pine trees to the north. Victor still had two divisions with which he could deliver a flank attack. Ruffin's division suddenly appeared and Leval made for the centre of the allied army. Graham immediately responded. He sent Wheatley's brigade to deal with Leval and Dilkes's troops against Ruffin. Ahead of them raced light infantry.

The British and Portuguese skirmishers took heavy casualties, but bought enough time for Wheatley to form up his battalions and ten guns. They routed the lead French regiment, capturing its eagle and soon Leval's men were retreating.

Slightly closer to Barossa, 500 flankers under Browne held off Ruffin's division. By the time they had swept Browne aside, Dilkes had formed up and sent devastating volleys into the French columns. Ruffin's men retreated.

Victor did his best to try to rally his men, but allied cavalry arrived and the French were forced to pull back to Chiclana. In all the French had lost 2,400 against allied losses of 1,740. Controversially Graham withdrew to Leon Island, followed by the Spanish, which simply left Victor with the opportunity to surround Cadiz once again.

Gaming the battle of Barrosa: 5 March 1811

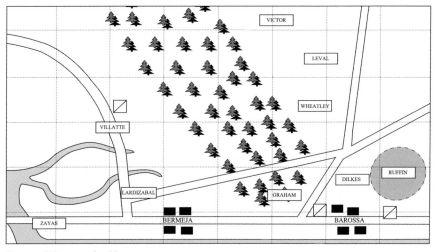

Barrosa Wargame Set Up

PORTUGAL, RETREAT AND COUNTER INVASION

This version of the battle focuses on the action involving the Anglo-Portuguese rather than the engagement between Villatte and the Spanish. You may wish to expand the engagement to incorporate this or enlarge the table to give you more space for the action around Barrosa itself.

Grahams' Army
You are spread out and on the back foot having to respond to the French threat through the woods. Wheatley and Dilkes are committed, but you must receive a message from either of these commands by courier before you can commit your reserves into the action. You win a decisive victory by breaking or destroying one of the two French commands, a minor victory if you continue to hold the road from Barrosa to Bermeja. Any other result is a draw.

C-in-C: General Graham	*Able*
1st Bde (Wheatley)	*Able*
2nd Foot Guards (2 coys)	Veteran Confident
28th Gloucester	Experienced Steady
67th Hampshire (5 coys)	Experienced Steady
87th Prince of Wales' Irish	Experienced Steady
Barnard's flank battalion (4 coys 95th, 2 coys 47th and 2 coys 20th)	Veteran Confident
2nd Bde (Dilkes)	*Able*
1st Foot Guards	Veteran Confident
3rd Foot Guards (3 coys)	Veteran Confident
67th Hampshire (5 coys)	Experienced Steady
95th Rifles (3 coys)	Veteran Confident
Brown's flank battalion (2 coys 9th, 2 coys 28th, 2 coys 82nd)	Experienced Steady
King's German Legion 2nd Hussars (2sqns)	Experienced Steady
Spanish contingent (Col. Whittingham)	*Able*
Ciudad Real Battalion	Green Steady
4th Walloon Guards	Green Steady
Spanish Horse Dragoons	Green Steady
9pdr RA (6 guns)	Experienced Steady
9pdr RA (4 guns)	Experienced Steady

WARGAME SCENARIOS

Victor's Army
With the initiative on your side, you have a chance to destroy Graham's force before he can react in time. You win a decisive victory if you have broken or destroyed Wheatley and Dilkes or if you have destroyed or broken one of them and have severed the coast road. A minor victory has been won if you have achieved one of these goals. Any other result is a draw.

C-in-C: Marshal Victor	*Able*
1st Bde (Ruffin)	*Able*
2/9th Léger	*Experienced Steady*
1/24th Line	*Green Cautious*
2/24th Line	Green Cautious
1/96th Line	*Experienced Steady*
1st Provisional Grenadiers	*Experienced Steady*
2nd Provisional Grenadiers	Experienced Steady
2nd Bde (Leval)	*Able*
1/8th Line	*Experienced Steady*
2/8th Line	Experienced Steady
45th Line	*Experienced Steady*
1/54th Line	*Green Cautious*
2/54th Line	Green Cautious
Combined Grenadiers (from 3rd battalions of 8th, 45th, 54th, 24th and 96th line, and 9th light)	Experienced Steady
1st Dragoons (3 sqns/2 sqns)	*Experienced Steady*
6 pdr foot artillery (5 guns/2 guns)	*Experienced Steady*

Background to the Battle of Albuera
Soult had left for Seville on 13 March to assist Victor. But with the danger over he was told to return to Estremadura to aid Mortier. Mortier had left a sizeable garrison in Badajoz. He had captured Campo Mayor and sent another force to tackle Albuquerque. All seemed to be going relatively well until a large allied army, under Beresford, appeared. Beresford had replaced Hill.

Beresford's army arrived at Campo Mayor on 25 March. The town was defended by a force under Latour-Maubourg, consisting of an infantry regiment and three cavalry regiments. Facing the French were 18,000 allied troops. The French did not panic, but instead began their retreat towards Badajoz. Beresford sent his cavalry, some 15,000 men, off after them.

PORTUGAL, RETREAT AND COUNTER INVASION

The British 13th Light Dragoons made first contact, routing the French 26th Dragoons and pursuing them as far as Badajoz. Mortier marched out with his reserves and routed the British cavalry and then moved to assist Latour-Maubourg.

The French were holding off the allied cavalry, with the French infantry regiment in a square. The allied cavalry under Long were massing for a charge, but Beresford arrived and stopped them, which allowed the French to withdraw. The French, facing such a large allied force, left 3,000 men to garrison Badajoz and a small force in Olivenza.

Beresford arrived at Olivenza on 9 April. Three days later he overran the fortress. He now turned his attention to Badajoz. Over the next few days Beresford was reinforced by 2,500 Spanish troops and light troops of the King's German Legion under Alten. He now had 27,000 men.

The French had not been idle and by 13 May Soult had 21,000 infantry, 4,000 cavalry and forty-eight artillery pieces en route to Badajoz.

The British had not made a great deal of progress at Badajoz and as soon as he learned that Soult was on his way, Beresford took up positions at Albuera, to confront the French. By 15 May Beresford's force had swollen to 35,000 men and fifty guns. He had been reinforced by General Blake, at the head of 8,000 Spaniards. The British were in a strong position and Beresford had chosen the ground deliberately, as he believed that the French would use the road passing through Albuera en route to Badajoz. Beresford positioned the Portuguese cavalry and Hamilton's Portuguese Division to the north of the Badajoz road. Cole and Stewart, along with Alton's brigade and 1,000 cavalry, held the centre. To the south were 12,000 Spanish infantry in four divisions, supported by allied cavalry and artillery.

The French arrived on cue, pushing back the allied skirmishers. The French massed against Beresford's centre some 10,000 infantry and three brigades of cavalry. Meanwhile, the divisions of Girard and Gazan swung around to the south against Blake's right flank. It caused enormous consternation, but Beresford drew Blake's men back at an angle and shifted his whole army to the right. The French V Corps began to advance, 8,000 men with cavalry support. In one enormous manoeuvre Soult had brought his whole army to bear on the allied right flank. Beresford hurried troops behind Blake's command to support them. By now the French were within musket range.

Stewart's second division marched up in support and raked Girard's left flank with volleys. Suddenly two French cavalry regiments ploughed into the open flank of Colborne's brigade. The men were slaughtered. Of the three leading battalions only around 400 men survived. The 31st Foot managed to form a square just in time.

WARGAME SCENARIOS

The French cavalry now swung round to attack Zayas's troops from behind. It was a dangerous situation, with Zayas's men still holding off Girard's columns. The 29th Foot arrived in the nick of time and began shooting at the French cavalry. Zayas's men held on. Girard brought up Gazan's division to support him, but by now Hoghton and Abercrombie's brigades had arrived. At this short range casualties were going to be inevitably high. In this exchange alone 2,000 French were killed or wounded and around 1,200 of Hoghton's men fell.

It was now abundantly clear that Beresford had been reinforced by Blake. As a consequence the French went onto the defensive. In desperation Beresford brought Hamilton's Portuguese brigade into the fight. But not all of the men could be spared, as Godinot's French division had launched an attack on Albuera itself.

Cole's men now moved to launch a counterattack, marching across the face of the French cavalry. It was clear to Soult that if he did not commit all of his troops then Gazan and Girard would be lost. Soult launched Latour-Maubourg against Cole's flank and moved Werlé's division to cover the V Corps' left flank. The cavalry was brought to an abrupt halt by musket fire, but the infantry closed. The French came on in narrow columns, some nine-battalions'-worth of men. Facing the 5,600 French was Myer's British brigade of 2,000. In a ferocious musketry duel lasting 20 minutes the French lost 1,800 men and the British 1,000.

This was the last straw for the French. Gazan fell back and Godinot retreated from Albuera. To cover the retreat the French cavalry reformed, supported by a handful of infantry and some artillery. The battle, however, was over. The French had lost 7,000 men; the allies had suffered 4,000 British casualties, 1,400 Spanish killed or wounded and 400 Portuguese. Beresford returned to the siege of Badajoz.

Gaming the Battle of Albuera: 16 May 1811

This was a bloody battle for both sides, and in reality as a wargame the action could quite easily focus just on the fighting on the Allied right and could ignore the action around Albuera and further north. At the very least, the actions in the south and the fight for Albuera could well be played as separate engagements.

Beresford's Army

Beresford very nearly lost this one: at the very least it was a costly draw. The Spanish troops in the front line may not be strong enough to withstand the French attack, however they did hold historically and this

PORTUGAL, RETREAT AND COUNTER INVASION

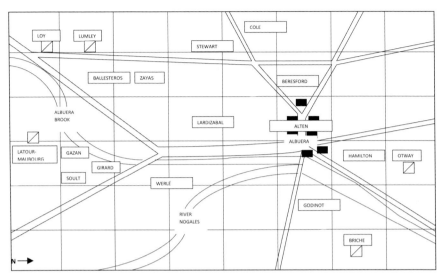

Albuera Wargame Set up

added immeasurably to the French losses. The key objective is to hold the line until at least Girard and Gazan have been broken or are no longer able to mount offensive actions. If this is achieved and Beresford has not lost a British division in doing so, then this is sufficient for a minor victory. To achieve a decisive victory, the front must be held without the loss of a division, including Albuera. At least two French divisions must have been broken or forced back beyond the Rover Nogales.

C-in-C: Marshal Beresford	*Able*
2nd Division: William Stewart	*Able*
Colborne's Brigade	*Able*
1/3rd Foot	*Veteran Confident*
2/31st Foot	*Veteran Confident*
2/48th Foot	*Veteran Confident*
2/66th Foot	*Veteran Confident*
Hoghton's Brigade	**Able**
29th Foot	Veteran Confident
1/48th Foot	Veteran Confident
1/57th Foot	Veteran Confident

WARGAME SCENARIOS

Abercrombie's Brigade	Able
2/28th Foot	Veteran Confident
2/34th Foot	Veteran Confident
2/39th Foot	Veteran Confident
Divisional Light Troops – 3 companies from 5/60th Foot	Elite Confident

4th Division: Galbraith Lowery Cole — Able
Myer's Brigade — Able
1/7th Fusiliers — *Veteran Confident*
2/7th Fusiliers — *Veteran Confident*
1/23rd R.W. Fusiliers — *Veteran Confident*

Kemmis's Brigade — Able
One company from each of the 2/27th Foot, 1/40th Foot and 97th Foot — Experienced Steady

Alten's Independent Brigade — Able
1st Light Battalion, King's German Legion — *Veteran Confident*
2nd Light Battalion, King's German Legion — *Veteran Confident*

Cavalry: Lumley — Able
De Grey's Brigade — Able
3rd Dragoon Guards — Experienced Steady
4th Dragoons — Experienced Steady

Unattached
13th Light Dragoons — Experienced Steady
British – Lefebure's Battery — *Veteran Confident*
British – Hawker's Battery — Veteran Confident
King's German Legion – Sympher's Battery — Veteran Confident
King's German Legion – Cleeves' Battery — *Veteran Confident*

Portuguese Troops under Beresford
These troops could be placed under a separate command subordinate to Beresford. Not many of these troops saw a great deal of action in the battle.

Harvey's Brigade of the 4th Division — Able
11th Regiment (2 battalions) — Green Steady
23rd Regiment (2 battalions) — Green Steady
1st Battalion, Loyal Lusitanian Legion — Green Steady

PORTUGAL, RETREAT AND COUNTER INVASION

Hamilton's Division	*Able*
2nd Line (2 battalions)	*Green Steady*
14th Line (2 battalions)	*Green Steady*
4th Line (2 battalions)	Green Steady
10th Line (2 battalions)	Green Steady
Collin's Brigade	*Able*
5th Line (2 battalions)	Green Steady
5th Caçadores (1 battalion)	Green Steady
Otway's Brigade	*Able*
Cavalry – 1st Regiment	*Experienced Steady*
Cavalry – 7th Regiment	Experienced Steady
Arriaga's Battery	Green Steady
Braun's Battery	Green Steady

Spanish Forces: General Joachim Blake

Blake's men had to withstand the full brunt of the French attacks; to begin with they lacked any real support. If played as a separate command, Blake's key objective is to hold and support the Anglo-Portuguese, but not at the cost of losing his command. If the three divisions are in danger of being overrun and there is no credible support from Beresford, then it is perfectly acceptable to withdraw towards Albuera. If this is not feasible, then a timely withdrawal from the battlefield is allowed, but not before Game Turn 10.

Blake	*Able*
Vanguard Division: Lardizabal	*Able*
Murcia (2 battalions)	Veteran Confident
Canaria (2 battalions)	Green Steady
2nd Leon	Green Steady
Campo Mayor	Green Steady
3rd Division: General Francisco Ballesteros	*Able*
1st Catalonia	*Green Steady*
Barbastro	*Green Steady*
Pravia	Green Steady
Lena	Green Steady
Castropol	Green Steady
Cangas de Tineo	Green Steady
Infiesto	Green Steady

WARGAME SCENARIOS

4th Division: Zayas — Able
2nd and 4th Spanish Guards — Veteran Confident
Irlanda — Veteran Confident
Patria — Green Steady
Toledo — Green Steady
Legion Estranjera — Veteran Confident
4th Walloon Guards — Veteran Confident
Ciudad Real — Green Steady

Cavalry: Loy — Able
Santiago — Green Steady
Husares de Castilla — Trained Impetuous
Granaderos — Trained Impetuous
Escuardron de Instruction — Trained Impetuous
Artillery: One Battery — Green Steady

Spanish Forces: General Francisco Xavier Castaños

This is a small force that should be attached to Blake.

Infantry: Carlos de España — Able
Rey — Veteran Confident
Zamora — Green Steady
Voluntarios de Navarra — Green Steady

Cavalry: Penne Villemur – one combined regiment — Trained Impetuous

Artillery: One battery — Green Steady

French Forces: Marshal Soult

Soult has a golden opportunity to defeat Beresford, but he needs to be quick. Brush aside the Spanish and deal with the British divisions as they are fed into the battle piecemeal, then roll up Beresford's army whilst pinning them with Godinot. Do not throw away the cavalry too quickly. Soult wins by having destroyed or routed the Spanish component (minor victory). A decisive victory can be obtained by destroying the Spanish and two Anglo-Portuguese divisions. A crushing victory will be achieved if the above takes place and Albuera is cleared of the enemy.

PORTUGAL, RETREAT AND COUNTER INVASION

C-in-C: Marshal Soult (5th Corps) — *Gifted*
1st Division: Girard — *Able*
2 and 3/34th Line — Experienced Steady
1 and 2/40th Line — Experienced Steady
1, 2 and 3/64th Line — Experienced Steady
2 and 3/88th Line — Experienced Steady

2nd Division: Gazan — *Able*
1, 2 and 3/21st Léger — Veteran Confident
1 and 2/100th Line — Experienced Steady
1, 2 and 3/28th Léger — Veteran Confident
1, 2 and 3/103rd Line — Experienced Steady

Werlé's Brigade — *Able*
1, 2 and 3/12th Léger — Veteran Confident
1, 2 and 3/55th Line — Experienced Steady
1, 2 and 3/58th Line — Experienced Steady

Godinot's Brigade — *Able*
1, 2 and 3/16th Léger — Veteran Confident
1, 2 and 3/51st Line — Experienced Steady

Grenediers Réunis — **Able**
45th Line — Experienced Steady
63rd Line — Experienced Steady
95th Line — Experienced Steady
4th Polish Regiment — Veteran Confident

Cavalry: Latour-Maubourg — *Gifted*
Briche's Brigade — *Able*
2nd Hussars — Veteran Impetuous
10th Hussars — Experienced Steady
21st Chasseurs — Experienced Steady

Bron's Brigade — **Able**
4th Dragoons — Experienced Steady
20th Dragoons — Experienced Steady
26th Dragoons — Experienced Steady

WARGAME SCENARIOS

Bouvier de Éclats Brigade
14th Dragoons
17th Dragoons
27th Dragoons

Able
Trained Steady
Trained Steady
Trained Steady

Unattached Cavalry:
– 1st Lancers of the Vistula/ 27th Chasseurs/   Trained Steady
  4th Spanish Chasseurs
Artillery: 3 medium guns, 1 howitzer (2 *medium guns*). Experienced Steady

Background to the Battle of Fuentes de Oñoro

Whilst Beresford focused on Badajoz and Soult, Wellington was not inactive. Wellington still faced Massena, who had not yet been replaced by Marmont. By 1 May Massena had assembled 42,000 infantry, 4,500 cavalry and thirty-eight artillery pieces. They were based at Ciudad Rodrigo. Massena aimed to relieve Almeida as his first target.

Wellington was determined to prevent this from happening and he marched to take up defensive positions at Fuentes de Oñoro. He had some 35,000 infantry, 2,000 cavalry and forty-eight guns. Over sixty percent of the force was British. Wellington deployed along a five-mile stretch of hills.

Massena's army came into view on the afternoon of 3 May 1811. Surveying the battlefield, Massena decided against attacking the northern edge of the allied line and instead decided to concentrate on storming Fuentes de Oñoro. The village itself had a considerable allied garrison. Massena intended to try to pin as much of Wellington's force as possible away from the main theatre of action by marching Reynier's men to face Erskine's 5th Division. Leading the French attack would be Ferey's division of VI Corps. They crossed the shallow Dos Casas River and into the village.

The British troops under Colonel Williams counterattacked and drove most of the French back. But the French hung on and began to slowly make progress. Wellington reinforced with three battalions belonging to the 1st Division. The British counterattacked and pushed the French out of the village. Massena responded by throwing four battalions of Marchand's division in, but with little effect.

On the following day, in response to reports from scouts, Massena discovered that Wellington's right flank was exposed. The new target would be the village of Pozo Bello. Massena earmarked 20,000 men to

PORTUGAL, RETREAT AND COUNTER INVASION

carry out this manoeuvre. As soon as the allies began to respond Ferey would try his luck again in taking the village of Fuentes de Oñoro.

Wellington was rather too canny to fall for a trick like this and had actually reshuffled during the night of 4 May. He had reinforced his right wing and had reorganised the reinforcements that had been used during the day. Nonetheless Wellington could not have anticipated the enormous numbers of French that were about to fall on his flank.

The French assault, led by Montbrun, opened at dawn on 5 May. The French cavalry saw off the allied horse around Pozo Bello. Meanwhile Marchand's division took the village. The 2nd Caçadores and the 85th Foot only managed to get away with the prompt arrival of some German Hussars. The men fell back on Houston's 7th Division.

The situation for Houston was bleak. Wellington despatched Crawford's division to help out. Allied cavalry had been making near suicidal charges against Montbrun's cavalry to hold them off. This had bought Houston valuable time and it also allowed Crawford to link up with him and slowly withdraw. With the British in squares Montbrun was reluctant to risk his men. In a short time the French had lost their initiative. They were now faced by solid and determined enemy infantry, backed up by thirty-six guns.

Meanwhile, Ferey and D'Erlon began their attack across the River Dos Casas. The French managed to drive the 71st and 79th out of Fuentes de Oñoro, but the British threw in the 2nd Battalion of the 24th Foot and began to force Ferey's men back. D'Erlon now committed three Grenadier battalions. They managed to penetrate as far as the church at the very crest of the ridge. Wellington threw in more reserves. It seemed that the French were on the verge of victory, until Mackinnon's brigade of the 3rd Division was committed. The 88th Foot drove the French out of the village and back across the river.

The French now withdrew, with Massena reluctant to commit any more men. He maintained an artillery bombardment whilst Wellington ordered his men to dig in and prepare for another assault the following day. Massena had resolved to withdraw and to order General Brennier, the garrison commander at Almeida, to destroy the fortress and retire. A message finally got through to Brennier and at around midnight on 10 May his 1,300 men broke out. Behind them Almeida exploded, as the charges detonated the gunpowder stores. Most of Brennier's men managed to make it back, but by now Massena had been replaced by Marmont.

WARGAME SCENARIOS

Gaming the Battle of Fuentes de Oñoro: 3-5 May 1811

Fuentes de Onoro Wargame Set Up

These army lists are truncated as the battle is a large one and you may wish to represent each of the divisions or corps with single regiments. The French army should outnumber the Allied one. The French mustered some 48,000 men in the engagement, the Allies only 37,606. By far the largest French corps was Losion's with 17,406 men; in other words, the equivalent of the Allied 1st, 3rd and 5th combined. Allied cavalry amounted to some 1,854, the French mustered 1,267 under Montbrun and a further 1,738 from the Army of the North.

The map focuses on the engagement that took place on 5 May rather than the manoeuvres on the two previous days. As such, not all of the forces available to the two commanders are included on the initial deployment map: you can feed in extra units as appropriate should you wish.

Wellington's Army

The battle opens with Wellington having been outmanoeuvred and desperately trying to compensate and hold the flanking move by the French. A draw is achieved by having created a continuous intact line with the available troops pivoting on the start position of the Light Division. A minor victory is won if this has been achieved and Fuentes is still held by Game Turn 12. A decisive victory is won by having achieved these goals and having broken one of the French corps.

PORTUGAL, RETREAT AND COUNTER INVASION

C-in-C: Lieutenant General Viscount Wellington	*Gifted*
Cavalry: Maj. Gen. Stapleton Cotton	*Able*
1st Brigade: Maj. Gen. Slade:	*Able*
– 1st Dragoons, 14th Light Dragoons.	*Experienced Steady*
2nd Brigade: Lieutenant Colonel von Arentschildt:	*Able*
– 16th Light Dragoons, 1st Hussars, and King's German Legion.	*Experienced Steady*
Portuguese Brigade: Brigadier General Barbacena:	*Able*
– 4th and 10th Portuguese Dragoons.	*Experienced Steady*
1st Division: commanded by Major General Nightingall	*Able*
1st Brigade: commanded by Colonel Stopford:	*Able*
– 1st/Coldstream Guards, 1/3rd Guards, 1 Coy. 5/60th Foot.	*Veteran Confident*
2nd Brigade: commanded by Lieutenant Lord Blantyre:	*Able*
– 2/24th Foot, 2/42nd Foot, 1/79th Foot, 1 Coy. 5/60th Foot.	*Veteran Confident*
3rd Brigade: commanded by Major General Howard:	*Able*
– 1/50th Foot, 1/71st Foot, 1/92nd Foot, 1 Coy. 5/60th Foot.	*Veteran Confident*
4th Brigade: commanded by Major General Sigismund, Baron Löw:	*Able*
– 1st, 2nd, 5th, 7th Line Battalions, King's German Legion, Detachments of Light Battalions, KGL.	*Veteran Confident*
3rd Division: commanded by Major General Thomas Picton.	*Gifted*
1st Brigade: commanded by Colonel Mackinnon:	*Able*

WARGAME SCENARIOS

– 1/45th Foot, 1/74th Foot, 1/88th Foot, 3 Coys. 5/60th Foot. *Veteran Confident*

2nd Brigade: commanded by Major General Colville: Able
– 2/5th Foot, 2/83rd Foot, 2/88th Foot, 94th Foot. *Veteran Confident*

Portuguese Brigade: commanded by Colonel Manley Power: Able
– 1 and 2/9th, 1 and 2/21st Portuguese Line. *Experienced Steady*

5th Division: commanded by Major General Sir William Erskine Able

1st Brigade: commanded by Colonel Hay: Able
– 3/1st Foot, 1/9th Foot, 2/38th Foot, Co. Brunswick Oels *Veteran Confident*

2nd Brigade: commanded by Major General Dunlop: Able
– 1s/4th Foot, 2/30th Foot, 2/44th Foot, Co Brunswick Oels *Veteran Confident*

Portuguese Brigade: commanded by Brigadier General Spry: Able
– 1 and 2/3rd and 1 and 2/15th Portuguese Line, 8th Caçadores *Experienced Steady*

6th Division: commanded by Major General Alexander Campbell Able

1st Brigade: commanded by Colonel Hulse: Able
– 1/11th Foot, 2/53rd Foot, 1/61st Foot, 1 Coy. 5th/60th Foot *Veteran Confident*

2nd Brigade: commanded by Colonel Robert Burne: Able
– 1/36th Foot (2nd Foot at Almeida) *Veteran Confident*

PORTUGAL, RETREAT AND COUNTER INVASION

Portuguese Brigade: commanded by Brigadier General Frederick, Baron Eben:	Able
– 1 and 2/8th Foot, 1 and 2/12th Portuguese Line	Experienced Steady
7th Division: commanded by Major General John Houston	*Able*
1st Brigade: commanded by Brigadier John Sontag:	*Able*
– 51st Foot, 85th Foot, Chasseurs Britannique, Brunswick Oels Light Infantry (8 Coys.)	*Veteran Confident*
Portuguese Brigade: commanded by Brigadier General John Doyle:	Able
– 1 and 2/7th and 1 and 2/19th Portuguese Line, 2nd Caçadores	Experienced Steady
Light Division: commanded by Brigadier General Robert Craufurd	*Able*
1st Brigade: commanded by Lieutenant Colonel Sydney Beckwith:	*Able*
– 1/43rd Foot, 1/95th Rifles (4 Coys), 2/95th Rifles (1 Coy.), 3rd Caçadores	*Veteran Confident*
2nd Brigade: commanded by Colonel George Drummond:	*Able*
– 1/52nd Foot, 2/52nd Foot, 1st/95th Rifles (4 Coys.), 1st Caçadores	*Veteran Confident*
Independent Portuguese Brigade: commanded by Colonel Ashworth:	Able
– 1 and 2/6th, 1 and 2/18th Portuguese Line Regiments	Experienced Steady
Brigadier General Howorth, 48 guns including:	Able
– Troops of Ross and Bull, Royal Horse Artillery, Batteries of Lawson and Thompson, Portuguese batteries of Von Arentschild, da Cunha and Rozierres.	Veteran Confident

WARGAME SCENARIOS

Massena's Army
The French have the upper hand with the initiative in this battle. To achieve a minor victory either one of the Allied divisions must be broken or Fuentes taken. To win a decisive victory, both of these goals must be achieved.

Army of Portugal:
Commander-in-Chief: Marshal André
  Massena, Prince of Essling, Duke of Rivoli   Able
II Corps: commanded by General Reynier   Gifted
1st division commanded by General Merle: Able
– 9 battalions: Brigade Sarrut (36th Line, 2nd   Experienced Steady
  Léger, 4th Léger)
2nd division commanded by General Heudelet: Able
– 12 battalions: Brigade Godard (70th Line,   Experienced Steady
  17th Léger); Brigade Arraud (47th Line,
  31st Léger)

Cavalry Brigade: commanded by General   Gifted
  Soult:
3 regiments (1st Hussars, 22nd Chasseurs à   Trained Impetuous
  Cheval, 8th Dragoons)

VI Corps: commanded by General Loison   Able

1st division commanded by General Marchand: Able
– 12 battalions: *Brigade Maucune (60th Line*   Experienced Steady
  (3 btns.), 6th Léger (3 btns.)); Brigade
  Chemineau (39th Line (3 bns), 76th Line
  (3 bns))

2nd division commanded by General   Able
  Mermet:
– 12 battalions: *Brigade Ménard (27th Line*   Experienced Steady
  (3 btns.), 25th Léger (3 btns.)); Brigade
  Taupin (50th Line (3 bns), 59th Line (3 btns.)

3rd division commanded by General Ferey: Gifted
– 10 battalions: 26th Line (1 btn.), Légion   Experienced Steady
  Hanovrienne, Légion du Midi, *66th Line*
  (3 bns), 82nd Line (3 btns.)

PORTUGAL, RETREAT AND COUNTER INVASION

Cavalry Brigade: commanded by General Lamotte:	Able
– 2 regiments: 3rd Hussars, 15th Chasseurs à Cheval	Trained Impetuous
VIII Corps: commanded by General Junot, Duke of Abrantes	Gifted
2nd division commanded by General Solignac:	Able
– 10 battalions: 15th Line (3 btns.), 86th Line (3 btns.), 65th Line (2 btns.), Régiment Irlandais (2 btns.)	Experienced Steady
IX Corps: commanded by General Count d'Erlon	Able
1st division commanded by General Claparéde:	Able
– 9 battalions: 1st Brigade (1/54th Line, 1/21st Léger, 1/28th Léger); 2nd Brigade (1/40th Line, 1/63rd Line, 1/88th Line); 3rd Brigade (1/64th Line, 1/100th Line, 1/103rd Line)	Experienced Steady
2nd division commanded by General Conroux:	Able
– 9 battalions: 1st Brigade, 1 Bat. 9e rgt. d'inf. Légère, 1 Bat. 16e rgt. d'inf. Légère, 1 Bat. 27e rgt. d'inf. Légère. 2nd Brigade, 1 Bat. 8e rgt. d'inf. de ligne, 1 Bat. 24e rgt. d'inf. de ligne, 1 Bat. 45e rgt. d'inf. de ligne. 3rd Brigade, 1 Bat. 94e rgt. d'inf. de ligne, 1 Bat. 95e rgt. d'inf. de ligne, 1 Bat. 96e rgt. d'inf. de ligne	Experienced Steady
Cavalry Brigade commanded by General Fournier:	Able
– 3 regiments: 7th, 13th and 20th Chasseurs à Cheval	Trained Impetuous

WARGAME SCENARIOS

Reserve of Cavalry commanded by General Montbrun:	Able
– 6 dragoon regiments: Brigade Cavrois (3rd Dragoons, 10th Dragoons, 15th Dragoons); Brigade d'Ornano (6th Dragoons, 11th Dragoons, 25th Dragoons)	Trained Impetuous
Artillery commanded by General Eblé:	Able
– 40 guns (roughly eight per corps)	Experienced Steady
Army of the North: Commander-in-Chief: Marshal Bessiéres, Duke of Istria	Able
Light Cavalry of the Imperial Guard commanded by General Lepic:	Able
– 4 regiments: 1st Lancers of the Guard, Chasseurs à Cheval of the Guard, Mameluks, Grenadiers à Cheval	Elite Steady
Light Cavalry Brigade commanded by General Wathier:	Able
– 4 regiments: 5th Hussars, 11th, 12th and 24th Chasseurs à Cheval	Trained Impetuous
Artillery: 6 guns.	*Experienced Steady*

After hearing of the huge losses at the battle of Albuera, Wellington replaced Beresford with Hill, who had just returned from England. He gave Hill the 2nd and 4th Divisions, Spanish troops and a large number of cavalry. He left the 3rd and 7th Divisions, along with some Portuguese troops, to deal with Badajoz. Wellington then moved up some reinforcements to restart the siege of Badajoz on 29 May. Badajoz was now being held by some 3,000 French troops, under General Phillipon. Wellington considered the capture of Badajoz to be a priority.

By 3 June some twenty artillery pieces had been moved into position to begin firing at Badajoz Castle and San Cristobal. On 6 June Wellington threw elements of the 7th Division against San Cristobal. The attack was bloodily repulsed. Wellington launched another attack by the 7th Division at 2100 on 9 June. Once again the attackers were thrown back with heavy casualties. Wellington knew that time was not on his side and that the French would undoubtedly march to Badajoz's salvation.

PORTUGAL, RETREAT AND COUNTER INVASION

In fact Marmont was already on his way on 14 May. Wellington believed that upwards of 60,000 French could arrive at any time. Consequently, Wellington abandoned the siege on 10 June. He despatched 10,000 Spanish under Blake to move towards Seville in the hope that he could draw away some of the French. By 17 June Wellington was with Spencer at Elvas. On 18 June the French began massing at Merida and were ready to head west towards Badajoz.

French cavalry crossed the River Guadiana on 22 June, coming into contact with allied cavalry. The French cavalry could report that Wellington was dug in, in strength, between Elvas and Campo Mayor. As the French deliberated as to their next course of action, they found out that there were new insurrections in Granada and that Blake was moving on Seville. They did what they could to help Phillipon and then Marmont retired to the Tagus Valley.

Meanwhile Wellington began reorganizing his forces. More cavalry and infantry had arrived from Lisbon. He could now create two Anglo-Portuguese forces. He allocated 41,000 infantry and 5,000 cavalry to his own command, which would be used in the north. A further 9,000 infantry and 4,000 cavalry would be allocated to Hill, who would operate in the south.

Soult had begun marching east on 24 June in order to prevent Blake from attacking Seville. Soult discovered that the Spanish were around Niebla and on 2 July he arrived there and forced Blake to give up the siege. Blake now marched for the coast, where he was picked up by allied vessels. He then sailed to Cadiz. Frustrated, Soult then marched towards Granada.

Freire's forces, by mid-July, amounted to some 12,000 infantry and 1,500 cavalry. He was reinforced by troops from Cadiz and definitely had the upper hand against General Leval's French troops in Granada. On 9 August Soult arrived to reinforce Leval. He had 12,000 men with him and began counterattacking. In a few short days Freire's upper hand had been cancelled out and what remained of his force was fleeing into Murcia.

Soult now turned his attention on Ballesteros, who had landed at Algeciras from his base at Cadiz. Whenever the French had tried to corner the Spanish commander he had simply slipped away, either to Gibraltar or to Tarifa. As far as Soult was concerned Gibraltar was just too strong for him to contemplate. He therefore decided to attack Tarifa.

From around October 1811 there were 4,000 Anglo-Spanish troops at Tarifa and Soult sent General Leval at the head of 15,000 men to deal with them and take it. The French advanced in three columns. The roads were poor and the French were constantly harassed by guerrillas. They arrived at Tarifa on 20 December and dug in to bring up their siege equipment.

Tarifa was far from impregnable, but the only really vulnerable section of the wall was the northern one. If the French set up their guns to face any of the other walls they knew they would come under fire from the allied fleet. By 29 December the French batteries were in place and ready to fire at the 10ft-thick walls. Although the defence works seemed impressive, they were in fact crumbling and the first canon shot went straight through the wall and hit one of the buildings inside. By the middle of the afternoon there was a yawning gap in the north wall.

The British commander, Skerrett, wanted to evacuate, but the Spanish commander, Copons, believed that they could still hold Tarifa. His view was supported by General Campbell at Gibraltar. On 30 December the French offered the garrison the opportunity to surrender, but this was refused. So the French continued their bombardment. Soon the breach was around 20m wide. A French assault was now inevitable.

There was torrential rain and flooding, but this did not stop the French assault of some 2,200 men. The attack failed and 200 French were dead. Continuous poor weather added misery to the French besiegers. Everything was wet, including the ammunition and there was little food. Reluctantly, Leval lifted the siege on 4 January 1812.

With Marmont retiring to the Tagus Valley and Wellington heading for Ciudad Rodrigo, Hill was still around Badajoz and close by were 1,600 French, under D'Erlon. This theatre remained relatively inactive until 28 October 1811. Hill, having been reinforced by some Spanish troops, advanced with 11,000 men against a brigade of General Girard, which was based at Arroyo dos Molimos. Girard's men were swiftly overwhelmed. Having achieved his goal, Hill fell back towards Portalegre.

Hill patiently waited for another opportunity. A few weeks later he advanced on part of Dombrowski's division, which was at Merida. This time the attack failed and Dombrowski fell back to rejoin D'Erlon. Although Hill's actions were limited, they succeeded in their main goal of pinning down French troops.

Marmont was desperately trying to reorganize his troops in the Tagus Valley, so that he could quickly move to support any theatre in the peninsula, either as an entire force or as separate divisions or corps. Marmont then heard the alarming news that Wellington was threatening Ciudad Rodrigo.

In fact Wellington had also reorganised his forces at Elvas and then had marched north at the head of seven divisions. He had with him recently-arrived heavy guns and had set up at Ciudad Rodrigo by 11 August, patiently waiting for the French to react.

The French, however, considered Ciudad Rodrigo to be almost impregnable. But when they discovered that siege equipment was being brought up by barges, they began to concentrate at Salamanca on 23 September. The French had amassed nine divisions, some 58,000 men.

Wellington's reaction has been open to a great deal of debate. Some believe that he lost his nerve because he left just two divisions to surround the fortress and withdrew the bulk of his army into the hills to the west.

Marmont had a dual purpose in marching to Ciudad Rodrigo. Firstly he needed to ensure that the fortress could hold and secondly he was desperate to discover whether Wellington seriously intended to settle down for a long-term siege. Consequently, on 25 September Marmont launched cavalry probes to find out precisely where Wellington's forces were located.

The French soon ran into the British 1st, 3rd and 6th Divisions. It also appeared to the French that the British were quite unprepared for action, particularly Picton's 3rd Division, which was near El Boden. Marmont deliberated about sending infantry support to his cavalry. This gave Picton enough time to fall back on Fuenteguinaldo, followed by French cavalry.

Picton's movement now meant that Wellington had some 15,000 men concentrated in the area. But the French were advancing with 20,000 men in the lead and a further 30,000 following up. Had the French been more confident and determined they could easily have defeated Wellington. But once again they believed that he was simply luring them into a trap. This gave Wellington enough time to slip away and by the time the French had decided to do something about it, it was too late. By now winter was drawing in. Marmont withdrew to Almaraz.

The French believed that the Anglo-Portuguese army was far smaller than it actually was in reality. Consequently Napoleon ordered Marmont to transfer 12,000 of his men for operations under Suchet in Valencia.

Wellington had at his command some 63,000 men. He now knew that Marmont, weakened by the transfer, could not stop him from besieging Ciudad Rodrigo. Wellington's decision to press ahead with the siege and Napoleon's order that troops be transferred was to have serious repercussions for French efforts in the peninsula.

All of this activity came at a high cost; not just financially, but also for the population of both Portugal and Spain. Portugal, for example, with a population of around 2.5 million, had to support 59,000 regulars and 54,000 militia and reservists (January 1812). Added to this they had to find money for ammunition, munitions, food and clothing. The war was also a considerable drain on the British. In the period 1808 to 1810 the war had cost them an estimated £13.5 million.

If Portugal had financial difficulties, it was Spain, predominantly the battlefield, which had even greater challenges. Whole areas of the country were under foreign control. There were swathes of the country that sided with the French, others tried to remain neutral, whilst some areas were hotbeds of insurrection. Yet the war was far from being won by either side.

There were 230,000 French troops now in the peninsula. But many of these were in penny packets, scattered around the countryside. They were useless to the field armies and what is more they were vulnerable. The French proposed to try to draw in as many of those men as possible to create a reserve. By evacuating Andalucía, 70,000 men could be added to Marmont's army.

Whatever the French had in mind, it was not them that were going to determine the sequence of events over the next few months. Wellington was now ready. He would launch his offensive, having ensured that Portugal was safe and that the French were being worn down on every front.

Background to the Battle of Saguntum
Before we look at Wellington's grand offensive of 1812, there was one more battle in 1811 that would lead to the fall of Valencia to the French. It would be the last triumphant period for the French army.

Suchet had captured Tarragona in June 1811. He then began to prepare for his invasion of Valencia. You will recall that Marmont had been ordered to provide him with 12,000 troops. With these men, and reinforcements from France, Suchet had 70,000 men at his disposal. Unfortunately for Suchet he could not mass his 70,000 men into a single field army; there were too many other considerations. He had to allocate men to garrison Catalonia, under General Decaen, and Aragon, under General Musnier. This meant that when Suchet left Tortosa on 15 September he had just 20,000 men.

Facing him were some 36,000 Valencian troops. Admittedly most of them were recruits, whereas the bulk of Suchet's men were veterans. The

PORTUGAL, RETREAT AND COUNTER INVASION

only decent troops that the new commander in Valencia, General Blake, could count on were men that had fought with him at Albuera; these were the divisions of Zayas and Lardizabal.

Suchet's forces bypassed the Spanish garrisons at Oropesa and Peñiscola and took the bridge at Villareal. They crossed the River Mijares and by 23 September had reached Saguntum.

Blake had set to work on reinforcing this ancient fortress and had left a garrison there. Suchet launched an attack on the night of 27 September but he was thrown back. Suchet now moved up his siege guns and Blake, desperate to stop him from concentrating his attacks, sent troops out to harass the French columns.

Suchet managed to get his artillery pieces into action on 16 October and after forty-eight hours of artillery fire he decided to launch an assault. However once again the attack was driven back and Suchet now discovered that Blake was marching to Saguntum's aid at the head of 28,000 men. By this stage Suchet had around 14,000 men available. Suchet's left flank was protected by the coast. To protect his right flank he placed a sizeable force on the heights of Sancti Espiritus.

Blake was hoping to envelop Suchet by superior numbers. He would pin Suchet's front whilst he rushed 16,000 infantry, 1,700 cavalry and four artillery batteries around the French right flank.

The Spanish began to advance on the morning of 25 October. They outnumbered the French four to one. At first the flank attack went well, but at the crucial point Suchet's men counterattacked. Whole Spanish divisions fell apart. The Spanish cavalry was scattered and in a short space of time the entire Spanish left wing was in flight. The veteran units of Zayas and Lardizabal closed with the French left. Initially they did well, but the French counterattacked and they stalled. Massed Spanish cavalry moved in to deal with French horse that had been moved up. The French cavalry was routed.

Rapidly Suchet reorganised his lines and unleashed two squadrons of the 13th Cuirassiers against the Spanish cavalry. The attack worked and Suchet now brought up St Paul's battalions. A gradual Spanish retreat now turned into a rout. Zayas's men did what they could and it was only his Walloon Guards that saved his division from destruction.

By the end of the action the Spanish had lost 6,000 killed or wounded, in addition to several hundred being taken prisoner. Saguntum also surrendered, yielding another 2,500 prisoners. Suchet had bought this

WARGAME SCENARIOS

victory with 1,000 casualties. Blake's men fell back on Valencia, but Suchet was determined to press home his advantage.

The French were approaching Valencia by 24 December. Suchet could now muster 33,000 men. Blake was again outmanoeuvred and defeated outside the city and by the end of the day what remained of Blake's army was in Valencia, along with 100,000 civilians. Valencia had not been prepared for a siege and it was inevitable that the city would soon fall. Blake tried to break out but failed and by New Year's Day 1812 the French were beginning to position their batteries. The bombardment of the city began and on 8 January Blake finally surrendered. He turned over 16,000 prisoners of war and 370 guns.

Gaming the Battle of Saguntum: 25 October 181

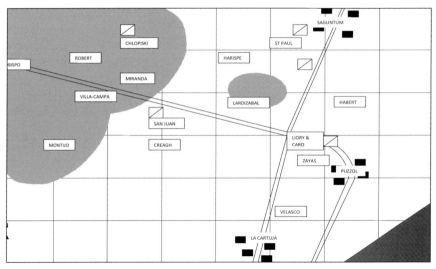

Saguntum Wargame Set Up

This was an unmitigated disaster for the Spanish, although they outnumbered the French by four to one. The battle begins with the Spanish advancing, but they can be very quickly checked and then put to flight due to the brittle nature of the units. This is a large engagement, but you may wish to cut down the numbers of troops by using a limited number of regiments to represent each of the divisions.

PORTUGAL, RETREAT AND COUNTER INVASION

Marshal Louis Gabriel Suchet's Armée d'Aragon

The order of battle is taken from 1 October. In the period leading up to the battle, Ficatier's Brigade, three battalions of Palombini's division and two squadrons of hussars had been detached from the army. On the morning of 25 October, Suchet had 20,000 men to maintain the siege and defeat Blake's relief force. This should be relatively easy if you take advantage of the inherent weaknesses of the Spanish. To win a decisive victory, there should be no unbroken Spanish units to the north of the line running from Puzzol; to win a minor victory there must not be more than one intact Spanish division to the north of this line. Two divisions to the north of the line would be a draw.

C-in-C: Marshal Louis Gabriel Suchet — Able
1st Division – Général de division (GdD) Musnier de la Converserie — Able

1st Brigade – Général de brigade (GdB) Robert — Able
114th Line (3 Btns) — Veteran Confident
1st Regt, Vistula Legion (2 Btns) — Veteran Confident

2nd Brigade – GdB Ficatier — Able
Not present at Saguntum
121st Line (3 Btns) — Veteran Confident
2nd Regt, Vistula Legion (2 Btns) — Veteran Confident

2nd Division – GdD Harispe — Able
1st Brigade – GdB Paris — Able
7th Line (4 Btns) — Veteran Confident
116th Line (3 Btns) — Veteran Confident

2nd Brigade – GdB Chlopicki de Necznia — Able
44th Line (2 Btns) — Veteran Confident
3rd Regt, Vistula Legion (2 Btns) — Veteran Confident

3rd Division – GdD Habert — Able
1st Brigade – GdB Montmarie — Able
5th Line (2 Btns) — Veteran Confident
16th Line (3 Btns) — Veteran Confident

WARGAME SCENARIOS

2nd Brigade – GdB Bronikowski   *Able*
117th Line (3 Btns)   Veteran Confident

4th Division (Italian) – GdD Palombini   Able
1st Brigade – GdB Saint Paul   *Able*
2nd Light (3 Btns), 1 btn detached   Experienced Steady
4th Line (3 Btns), 1 btn detached   Experienced Steady

2nd Brigade – GdB Balathier   Able
5th Line (2 Btns)   Veteran Confident
6th Line (3 Btns), 1 btn detached   Veteran Confident

5th Division (Neapolitan) – GdB Compère   Able
1st Light (1 Btn)   Experienced Steady
1st Line (1 Btn)   Experienced Steady
2nd Line (1 Btn)   Experienced Steady

Cavalry – GdB Boussart   *Able*
4th Hussars (4 Sqns), 2 Sqns detached   Veteran Confident
24th Dragoons (2 Sqns)   Veteran Confident
13th Cuirassiers (4 Sqns)   Veteran Confident
Italian *Napoleone* Dragoons (4 Sqns)   Veteran Confident
Neapolitan Chasseurs à Cheval (1 Sqn)   Veteran Confident

Capitán General Joaquin Blake y Joyes' Spanish Army
In addition there were Colonel Luis Andriani's garrison of Saguntum: five battalions of foot (2 each from the Savoya & don Carlos regiments, and 1 from the Cazadore de Orihuela). These battalions, together with gunners and sappers, made a total of around 2,600 men. A victory is possible, but probably at enormous loss. Your army is brittle and not well led. Strength is in numbers and you need to be careful to remove weak units from the line as when they break the whole lot could go! A decisive victory is won if you manage to retain an intact division either on or parallel to the road that runs west-to-east through the high ground. Alternatively, you achieve a decisive victory if you have managed to extract your army without having lost a broken or destroyed division after Game Turn 10. You may not issue retrograde orders to your units which mean they retreat off the table before Game Turn 10. A minor victory is won if you manage to have unbroken units on the table by Game Turn 15.

PORTUGAL, RETREAT AND COUNTER INVASION

C-in-C: Cap. Gen. Joaquin Blake y Joyes — *Poltroon*

Vanguard Division, 4th Army – Mariscal de Campo de Lardzábal — Able

Vanguard – Col Salbany — Cautious
Campomayor Light Battalion (1 Btn) — Green Cautious

1st Brigade – MdC de Lardzábal — Able
Regt. de Murcia (2 Btns) — Green Cautious
2nd Regt. de Badajoz (2 Btns) — Green Cautious
Foot Artillery bty (1×4pdr, 1×8pdr) — Green Cautious

2nd Brigade – Col Prieto — Cautious
Regt. de Africa (2 Btns) — Green Cautious
Tiradores de Cuenca (1 Btn) — Green Cautious
Artillery – Ten. Col. Saravia — Cautious
Foot Artillery bty (2×4pdr, 2×8pdr, 2×howitzer) — Green Cautious

4th Division, 4th Army – MdC de Zayas — Able

Vanguard – Brig. Favré d'Aunoy — Cautious
Combined Cazadores (1 Btn) — Green Cautious

1st Brigade – MdC de Zayas — Able
2nd Spanish Royal Guard (1 Btn) — Green Cautious
4th Spanish Royal Guard (1 Btn) — Green Cautious

2nd Brigade – Brig. Polo — Cautious
Voluntarios de Ciudad Roderigo (1 Btn) — Green Cautious
Voluntarios de la Patria (2 Btns) — Green Cautious
Regt. Imperial de Toledo (1 Btn) — Green Cautious

Reserve – Brig. De Hautregard — Cautious
1st Royal Walloon Guard (1 Btn) — Green Cautious
Legion Estrangera (1 Btn) — Green Cautious

Cavalry – Col. del Rio — Cautious
Regt de Cuenca (1 Sqn) — Green Cautious

WARGAME SCENARIOS

Artillery – Sgt. Mayor Gómez — Cautious
Foot Artillery bty (2×4pdr, 2×8pdr, 2×howitzer) — Green Cautious

Reserve Corps – Mariscal de Campo Caro y Sureda — Cautious

1st Reserve Brigade, 2nd Army – Brig. Velasco — Cautious
Voluntarios de Castilla (1 Btn) — Green Cautious
Regt de Avila (1 Btn) — Green Cautious
Provisional Line Regt (4 coys. Rgt. de Valencia, 3 coys. Rgt. de Savoya) (1 Btn) — Green Cautious
Foot Artillery Bty (2×4pdr, 1×8pdr, 1×Howitzer) — Green Cautious

2nd Reserve Brigade, 2nd Army – Col. Ruiz de Liory — Cautious
Regt Infante Don Carlos (1 Btn) — Green Cautious
Provisional Light Regt (4 coys. Caz. de Valencia, 2 coys. Caz. de Orihuela) (1 Batt) — Green Cautious
Foot Artillery Bty (2×8pdr) — Green Cautious

Cavalry Division – MdC Caro y Sureda — Cautious

Vanguard, 4th Army – Brig. Loy — Cautious
Granaderos a caballo (2 Sqn) — Green Cautious
Regt del Rey (1 Sqn) — Green Cautious
Husares de Castille (1 Sqn) — Green Cautious
Horse Artillery Bty (1×4pdr, 1×Howitzer) — Green Cautious

1st Brigade, 2nd Army – Col. Chacón — Cautious
Dragones de Numancia (4 Sqn) — Green Cautious
Regt de Alcántara (1 Sqn) — Green Cautious
Husares Españoles (1 Sqn) — Green Cautious
Husares de Granada (1 Sqn) — Green Cautious

2nd Brigade, 2nd Army – Col Salcedo — Cautious
Regt de Cuenca (2 Sqn) — Green Cautious
Caz. a caballo de Montaña (1 Sqn) — Green Cautious

PORTUGAL, RETREAT AND COUNTER INVASION

Left Wing – Teniente General Mahy	Cautious
Right Flank – Mariscal de Campo O'Donnell	Cautious
Division O'Donnell, 2nd Army – MdC O'Donnell	*Cautious*
Vanguard – MdC Sanjuán	*Cautious*
Cazadores de Caballo de Valencia (1 Sqn)	Green Cautious
Dragones del Rey (3½ Sqn)	Green Cautious
Voluntarios de Molina (1 Btn)	Green Cautious
Foot Artillery Bty (2×4pdr)	Green Cautious
1st Brigade – MdC Villacampa	Cautious
2nd Regt de la Princesa (2 Btns)	Green Cautious
2nd Regt de Soria (2 Btns)	Green Cautious
Artillery – Lt. Col. Luengo	Cautious
Foot Artillery Bty (2×8pdr, 2×howitzer)	Green Cautious
1st Division, 2nd Army – MdC Miranda	Cautious
Vanguard – Brig. Gasca	Cautious
Combined Column of Cazadores (Coys. from Regts. Castilla, Valencia & Ávila) (1 Btn)	Green Cautious
Cazadores a caballo de Valencia (1 Sqn)	Green Cautious
Cazadores de Valencia (2 coys)	Green Cautious
Foot Artillery Bty (2×pdr)	Green Cautious
Main Body – MdC Miranda	Cautious
Cazadores de Valencia (1 Btn)	Green Cautious
Regt. de Valencia (2 Btns)	Green Cautious
Voluntarios de Castilla (2 Btns)	Green Cautious
Rearguard – Brig. Casimira de la Valle	Cautious
Regt de Avila (1 Btn)	Green Cautious

WARGAME SCENARIOS

Left Flank – Mariscal de Campo Obispo	*Cautious*
2nd Brigade, Division O'Donnell – Col. O'Ronan	**Cautious**
2nd Btn, Voluntarios de Aragon (1 Btn)	Green Cautious
1st Btn, Cazadores de Valencia (1 Btn)	Green Cautious
Dragones del Rey (½ Sqn)	Green Cautious
4th Division, 2nd Army – MdC Obispo	**Cautious**
Tiradores de Doyle (1 Btn)	*Green Cautious*
Cazadores Campo de Cariñena (2 Btns)	*Green Cautious*
2nd Btn, Regt de Ávila (1 Btn)	*Green Cautious*
1st Btn, Voluntarios de Aragón (1 Btn)	*Green Cautious*
Voluntarios de Daroca (1 Btn)	*Green Cautious*
Dragones de la Reina (1 Sqn)	*Green Cautious*
Húsares de Aragón (2 Sqn)	Green Cautious
Reserve Corps (Expeditionary Corps, 3rd Army) – Ten. General Mahy	**Cautious**
Vanguard – Col. Terreros	**Cautious**
Tiradores de Cadíz (1 Btn)	Green Cautious
Voluntarios de Burgos (1 Btn)	Green Cautious
Dragones de Madrid (1 Sqn)	Green Cautious
1st Division – Brig. de Montijo	**Cautious**
1st Regt de Badajoz (2 Btns)	Green Cautious
Regt de Cuenca (2 Btns)	Green Cautious
2nd Division – Brig. Creagh de Lacy	*Cautious*
Regt de Corona (1 Btn)	*Green Cautious*
Regt Alcázar de San Juan (1 Btn)	*Green Cautious*
Dragones de la Reina (1 Sqn)	*Green Cautious*
2nd Dragoon Division – Brig. Osorio	**Cautious**
Dragones de Pavia (2 Sqn)	Green Cautious
Dragones de Granada (2 Sqn)	Green Cautious
Húsares de Fernando VII (1 Sqn)	Green Cautious

PORTUGAL, RETREAT AND COUNTER INVASION

Artillery – Brig. Ibarra *Cautious*
Foot battery (2×4pdr, 2×8pdr, 2×howitzer) *Green Cautious*

	Btns	Sqns	Guns
Vanguard Division, 4th Army	8		8
4th Division, 4th Army	9	1	6
Reserve Corps	5	14	8
Right Flank	12	5½	8
Left Flank	8	3½	
Reserve Corps	8	7	6
Spanish Army Total	50	31	36

Chapter 4

Wellington Takes the Offensive

In early January 1812 Wellington concentrated seven Anglo-Portuguese divisions at Agueda. He had with him siege equipment ready to take on Ciudad Rodrigo. By 8 January Wellington had moved into position.

Ciudad Rodrigo itself had received little attention since the siege that Ney had initiated in 1810. What had been done is that a series of new earthworks, or redoubts, had been constructed to prevent the same line of attack being used by the allies. The garrison consisted of just 2,000 men, under General Barrié. The fortress had a large number of guns and sufficient ammunition and food to hold out for a substantial period of time.

Wellington knew that the longer he hung around besieging Ciudad Rodrigo, the more likely it was that Marmont would march to its aid. As a result Wellington determined to make short work of the fortress. On the very first night he sent elements of his light division against the Renaud redoubt. The men crept up on the position. French sentries were shot from the parapet and the British rushed the redoubt. The allies now began to bombard the fortress itself. Wellington had new trenches dug and the batteries were in place by 11 January. A second set of parallels began on 13 January and on the same night a British raiding party dealt with the French garrison that was holding the Convent of Santa Cruz. The British were now within 200 metres of the fortress walls.

The French commander, however, was planning a counterattack. He decided he would raid the allied earthworks at around 1100. He had noted that at that time the first working party of the day left the earthworks and shortly afterwards they were replaced by a second group of men. As the night workers left at 1100, the French attacked, not only overrunning the earthworks, but also recapturing Santa Cruz.

WELLINGTON TAKES THE OFFENSIVE

Wellington was furious. The allies began by bombarding the San Francisco Convent with twenty-seven siege guns. The convent was stormed during the night and by this stage the French had all pulled back into the city itself. Making the damage good that the French had caused on 14 January, the allies managed to finish the second parallel on 18 January. They could now bring devastating fire onto the walls of the fortress.

It soon became clear to the French that the British would launch an assault and they began to prepare inner defences. Wellington had already decided that he would launch the third division at the main breach at 1900 on 19 January. Craufurd's men would try to storm a smaller breach. Whilst these attacks were going, in two columns under O'Toole and Pack would try to climb the south wall and draw the garrison to them.

As it was, O'Toole and Pack's men managed to get into the city and Craufurd's light division was also successful. However Picton's men faced an entirely different prospect. They managed to get up to the main breach, but found it barricaded and beyond that there was a 25ft drop. The French had positioned large cannons, which were tearing the attackers to pieces.

Whilst the French could hold Picton back they could do nothing to stop the other allied troops from surging through the town. The French tried to fall back, house by house, but the siege was over. What remained of the garrison became prisoners of war. The allies took many artillery pieces and other weapons. Craufurd had been lost, as had General Mackinnon. For the cost of 1,300 casualties Wellington had achieved in just twelve days what he had expected to take him twice that length of time.

By the time Marmont had discovered that Ciudad Rodrigo was under threat it was too late to send help. Marmont, by this stage, was based around Almaraz. He had received reinforcements but his commitments were still enormous and in fact of the eight divisions he technically had available to him only four could be brought together as a field army. As soon as he heard that Wellington was at Ciudad Rodrigo he pulled together three divisions and marched for Salamanca. He then heard the dreadful news on 21 January that the fortress had fallen.

It was here that Marmont received instructions from Napoleon to begin an advance on Beira; in other words the Portuguese frontier. Whatever information Napoleon was working on was clearly out of date. It was now obvious that Wellington was making for Badajoz. Consequently Marmont ignored Napoleon's instructions and determined to pull together as much of his force as was possible at Almaraz and then try to intercept Wellington en route to Badajoz.

WARGAME SCENARIOS

Napoleon clearly disagreed with Marmont's belief that Badajoz was Wellington's target. As a consequence, now with four divisions, Marmont marched towards Ciudad Rodrigo, arriving close by on 30 March. Here Wellington had left a garrison of 3,000 Spaniards, after having made some attempt to repair the fortress. Without siege equipment all Marmont could do was to blockade the place and move west towards Almeida. Behind him guerrillas quickly cut off his communication routes.

Marmont had no greater luck at Almeida, finding it well defended. He then headed down the River Coa towards Sabugal. He arrived at Guarda on 14 April. Here he managed to rout Portuguese militia under Generals Trant and Wilson.

In actual fact Marmont was achieving very little and this had suited Wellington perfectly well, who, as Marmont had predicted himself, had stormed Badajoz on 6 April. Wellington had been determined to take Badajoz, as he saw it as a pivotal position from which he could operate either in southern or northern Spain. He had assembled his force of some 60,000 men, including fifty-eight siege guns, between Elvas and Badajoz. With him were eight Anglo-Portuguese divisions, four independent infantry brigades, a large number of cavalry, including Dragoons just arrived from Britain, and 1,000 artillery men. Wellington had brought together a force that could not only deal with Badajoz once and for all, but see off anything that Soult might be able to throw at him.

The allied army began crossing the River Guadiana on 14 March. On 16 March Wellington despatched Hill and Graham to deal with D'Erlon's men and General Villemur at the head of 5,000 Spaniards towards Seville, whilst the bulk of his army marched with him towards Badajoz.

Badajoz was still held by Phillipon. He had repaired the damage done by the second siege; he had improved the defence works around San Cristobal and had dug tunnels and filled them with explosives. He had also dammed and flooded the Rivillas brook. It was a far more formidable position than ever before.

Wellington's first target was the Picurina Fort, to the southeast of Badajoz. He began by digging a parallel, despite four days of torrential rain. The River Guadiana did not help matters when it burst its banks due to the torrential rainfall. The weather improved on 24 March and by 25 March Wellington had some twenty-eight guns firing at the Picurina Fort and the eastern walls of Badajoz. He launched a storming party that night and despite heavy casualties the fort was taken. Wellington now aimed to move artillery into the fort so that he could fire on Badajoz.

By 31 March the guns were in place and bombarding the eastern side

WELLINGTON TAKES THE OFFENSIVE

of Badajoz. Still the defenders could be relatively content, as the brook was flooded. The allies had tried to overrun the San Roque Lunette on the eastern side of Badajoz, but had been beaten off. More allied guns were brought up to fire on the steadily enlarging breaches in the east wall.

The French did everything to try to repair the damage. Time, however, was not on Wellington's side. He discovered that both Soult and D'Erlon were on their way. Wellington could not delay any further and he determined to storm Badajoz on 6 April.

Wellington decided that the breaches would be assaulted by the Light and the 4th Divisions. The 3rd Division would launch an attack on the eastern side, as a diversion. The 5th Division would launch a similar diversion against the western wall and another diversion would be targeted at the San Roque Lunette. Wellington had hoped that the attack would commence at 2200, but at around 2145 French sentries spotted Picton's men forming up in the trenches. They brought down heavy shell fire on Picton's men, who were forced to begin their attack prematurely. Meanwhile the 5th Division, consisting of some 4,000 men, was not ready to attack until 2300.

The Light and the 4th Division began their advance. They had to move to the left to find a safe route across a 12ft-deep water-filled ditch. This brought them in front of the Santa Maria bastion, a dry part of the moat. But it was booby trapped. The French lit the fuses and killed or wounded 1,000 attackers in one enormous explosion. There was understandable chaos, which the French gunners and infantry took full advantage of. After two hours of achieving very little Wellington ordered his men to withdraw. He had taken 2,200 casualties.

Elsewhere, however, things were going rather better. Picton's men found themselves facing just 300 French troops. Picton's first two attacks were beaten off, but he gambled his last brigade and this time his men scaled the walls and routed the defenders. In the attack Picton was seriously wounded and he had lost 700 killed or wounded. But the defences had been breached.

The 5th Division managed to overwhelm the San Vincente bastion. The sign that allied troops were inside Badajoz gave the Light and 4th Division new heart and they too stormed into Badajoz. A handful of French cavalry escaped to take the bad news to Soult.

Soult had desperately tried to pull his forces together as soon as he had realised that Badajoz was under threat. He had managed to muster 13,000 men and had marched to join up with D'Erlon's corps. By 4 April he had 25,000 men at Llerena, but even with this army he would be outnumbered

WARGAME SCENARIOS

by at least two to one. He could not risk his command unless Marmont could assist him. But Marmont of course was engaged in his useless invasion of Portugal. Soult had enough to cope with, with the Spanish forces in his area of operations. All he could hope to do was to protect Seville.

Wellington could be sure that Soult would be remaining on the defensive and, as a consequence, he was free to move back towards Ciudad Rodrigo. Wellington now determined to deal with Marmont's Army of Portugal. First he needed to make sure that Soult could not march with his troops to aid Marmont. The obvious target was to destroy the pontoon bridge that was weakly held by the French at Almaraz. Wellington despatched Hill with 7,000 men to destroy the target. He also sent Graham with a pair of divisions to cover Hill.

Hill arrived at Trujillo on 15 May. By 17 May he was at the pass of Miravete, just a mile and a half to the south of the bridge. Realising that an attack on the three French-held forts overlooking the pass of Miravete and then having to tackle Fort Napoleon on the south bank of the River Tagus and Fort Ragusa on the north bank would end in disaster, he decided to launch a decoy assault. He sent Howard's brigade through the pass of Cueva. This bypassed the three French forts and by dawn on 18 May Howard's men were approaching the pontoon bridge.

The French in Fort Napoleon opened up but in a few minutes, despite some initially high British casualties, the French garrison commander, Colonel Aubert, found that his command had been overwhelmed. There was one further redoubt before the pontoon bridge could be reached. This was held by 360 Prussians, but as soon as they saw that Fort Napoleon had fallen they routed across the bridge. Howard's men followed them and only when part of the pontoon bridge collapsed were the French saved from absolute disaster. The British opened fire on Fort Ragusa with the captured guns from Fort Napoleon. In short order the Ragusa garrison panicked and began to retreat. Hill's men destroyed Ragusa and Napoleon, along with the bridge. By the time General Foy's division arrived all that was left was a small garrison sitting in Fort Miravete.

Soult was now certain that Wellington was planning a major offensive against him. He could not have been more incorrect. All Wellington had hoped to achieve was to isolate Soult so that he could hit the French in the north.

With Hill and Ballesteros pinning down Soult, and Santocildes's Army of Galicia mounting diversionary attacks, Wellington was now ready to move in strength against Marmont. Wellington sent what aid he could to

WELLINGTON TAKES THE OFFENSIVE

Spanish guerrillas and also urged the Royal Navy to mount a series of operations along the coast. Meanwhile another force under General Maitland was being assembled in Majorca. This would be conveyed to Catalonia to deal with Suchet. At the head of eight infantry divisions, four cavalry brigades and fifty artillery pieces Wellington crossed the Agueda on 13 June. His lead elements were heading for Salamanca.

The French could see the allied force approaching, but dared not close. Marmont was desperately trying to buy time to bring his scattered forces together. By 19 June, although still outnumbered, he had 36,000 infantry, 2,800 cavalry and eighty guns. He was desperately sending requests for reinforcements to Madrid and to Soult. King Joseph had no idea what was really going on. He was receiving similar pleas for help from both Marmont and Soult, both of whom believed that Wellington was bearing down upon them with at least 60,000 men.

Background to the Battle of Salamanca

Rather than trying to scoop up Marmont's forces as they began to converge, Wellington was determined to deal with Marmont once and for all in a single engagement. He chose Salamanca deliberately, setting up his army to the east and determined to fight a defensive battle.

In Salamanca the French held three fortified convents. Inside was a garrison of 800 men and thirty-six guns. The one thing that Wellington had neglected to bring with him was a significant siege train. In fact all he had was four heavy guns with 100 rounds each. Undaunted, the attack against the convents of Salamanca began on the night of 17 June. The target was San Vincente.

A trench was dug from the hospital towards the convent. But the French artillery soon put paid to this attempt. Wellington had a pair of cannons dragged up to the roof of the San Bernado convent to bring San Vincente under fire. Later he added 300 snipers to the building. Over the next couple of days another two batteries were brought into action against the French position. At last San Vincente was showing signs of damage.

Marmont had not been idle and by 20 June he was close to the heights of San Cristobal. After an artillery duel the French probed towards Morisco. The French were now concerned that they were being drawn into a trap. They were still relatively weak, with 30,000 men and by the evening of 22 June Marmont had pulled back to a defensive position around six miles away.

With the imminent prospect of a major engagement receding Wellington turned his attention back to Salamanca. He had decided to now focus on San Cayetano. He launched 400 men from the 6th Division against it on 23 June but over a quarter of them were killed, including their commander, General Bowes.

Meanwhile Marmont had sent a force across the River Tormes at Huerta. They attacked Dragoons of General Bock's command. Wellington immediately responded by sending the 1st and 7th Divisions, supported by cavalry, to assist. The French simply retreated back across the river.

Much-needed artillery ammunition arrived for the allies on 26 June. They used it to good effect and set the roof of San Cayetano on fire. This was to mark the end of the defence of the strongholds. As the allied assault columns formed up the French surrendered.

It was a major blow for the French, but Marmont was still waiting for additional troops to arrive before he could risk all in a major battle against Wellington. Marmont fell back to the Douro River. He was hoping that Bonnet's division was on its way, along with reinforcements under General Caffarelli. Marmont sent Foy's division towards Toro, in the hope that he would link up with Bonnet. The only news he could bring Marmont was bad: a Spanish force under Santocildes was besieging Astorga and Benavente, and Portuguese troops under Silveira were besieging Zamora. Finally on 7 July Bonnet arrived. Marmont could now muster 43,000 infantry, 2,200 cavalry and seventy-eight guns.

Wellington, meanwhile, had also moved up towards the Douro River, which meant that if Marmont wanted to take the initiative he would have to cross the river. On 15 July Marmont pushed two divisions across the river at Toro. It was a feint. Wellington rushed to face the crossing, only to discover that the French army had in fact slipped across at Tordesillas. Marmont now swung west, pushing through Nava and closing on Wellington's rear. Wellington had been outmanoeuvred and he began to retreat towards the Guarena River, with French cavalry close on his tail. Wellington stopped his troops on the western bank of the river, but the French were close at hand and launched an assault on Castrillo. They threw the allied troops out of the village, but then ran into steady lines of troops belonging to Anson and Stubbs. The French advance faltered. To the south French cavalry had crossed the river, but were bounced by light cavalry from Anson's command.

The French vanguard, under Clausel, had failed in both of their attempts to roll up Wellington's rearguard. Wellington's men were still dug in and Marmont realised the folly of launching an all out assault. Marmont's army drifted south, trying to work around Wellington's position, but Wellington simply responded by doing the same. The two armies shadowed one another until they reached Cantalpino and here Marmont deployed for a major assault, but Wellington slipped away, heading towards Salamanca.

The French continued south, still hoping to work their way around Wellington. They marched into Huerta and then crossed the River Tormes once again on 21 July. With the constant marching and counter-marching neither Wellington nor Marmont could have expected that there would be a major engagement on 22 July. In fact the battle of Salamanca seems to have erupted more by chance than by design. Neither side knew with absolute certainty the precise location of the enemy. The terrain was wooded and hilly.

Marmont received news that the allied 7th Division had been spotted. He believed that this was the rearguard and he pushed troops forward to try to roll them up. Foy's men were in the lead and they came into contact with a pair of allied regiments near Nuestra Senora de la Peña. With Foy's men approaching head on, Marmont sent Bonnet's division to work around the 7th.

Wellington could see the French advancing and immediately drew up his army into defensive positions. Cole's division formed up opposite Bonnet. Broadly the allied army had adopted an L shape.

Marmont was still convinced that the allies were withdrawing. He sent Maucune's division to take the village of Arapiles. The attack came in at 1400. Marching behind Maucune was Thomières's division. They slipped across the rear and headed towards the village of Miranda. Between Maucune and Bonnet's division Clausel's division formed up, making an unbroken line.

Wellington watched the French movements and was already redirecting his own army. The 7th Division moved to support the allied right wing, which just left the Light Division to check Foy at Nuestra Senora de la Peña. Next to them, on the northern part of the L-shaped line, was the 1st Division. Wellington was swiftly reinforcing the front near the Arapiles village, realising that the main weight of the French army was being concentrated against it. In fact Wellington managed to mass five infantry divisions and five cavalry brigades.

Suddenly, Wellington noticed that Thomières's men, marching towards Miranda, had left a yawning gap on Maucune's left flank. As he pondered his decision for a few moments the French infantry seemed to still be moving to the west. Wellington realised that he had the chance to roll up the whole of the Army of Portugal and destroy it piece by piece. Immediately Wellington decided to attack.

WARGAME SCENARIOS

Wellington launched D'Urban's Portuguese cavalry, which ploughed into Thomières's 101st line. Pakenham's 3rd Division moved up to support the cavalry. Thomières's right flank was collapsing, but Curto's untrained French cavalry tried to ride to the rescue of the French infantry; they were easily beaten off by Pakenham. In a matter of minutes Thomières was dead, half of his men were gone and his artillery was overrun. To compound French misery Marmont, standing on the south Arapiles hill, was wounded by an enemy shell. He was injured badly enough to be replaced by Bonnet, who minutes later was also seriously wounded. French command now fell to Clausel.

As far as the French were concerned, these three incidents sealed the fate of their army, as Foy later wrote:

> 'The Duke of Ragusa [Marmont] committed us to the action – he brought it on contrary to Clausel's advice. The left was already checked when he received his wound, by which time it was impossible either to refuse to fight or to give the fight a good direction. All that could be done was to attenuate the disaster – that Clausel did. There was no gap in the command – we should have been no better off if the marshal had never been hurt.'

The allied 4th and 5th Divisions now moved against the French centre. There was vicious fighting, as Cole's division locked horns with Clausel's division. Leith's brigades surged forward to deal with Maucune's division. Allied cavalry moved up and Maucune's regiments withdrew and formed squares. The British line infantry advanced towards the squares. Leith was hit, along with 300 of his men, but well drilled volleys smashed into the squares. Allied cavalry under Le Marchant smashed into Maucune's left flank. Maucune's battalions were shattered by the 4th and 5th Dragoon Guards. Le Marchant brought up the 3rd Dragoons and together his command ploughed into the emerging columns of Brennier's division. There was great slaughter, but Brennier's men managed to rally at the edge of the woods and then began to advance again. Once again Le Marchant charged. The French were broken and this time for good, but Le Marchant was killed.

The French now desperately tried to present a solid rearguard, supported by Curto's cavalry. The French cavalry managed to redeem themselves by scattering what was left of Le Marchant's command.

Clausel and Bonnet launched a counterattack. They had inflicted enormous casualties on Pack's Portuguese troops and as the French infantry moved forward, Cole's men began to waver and fall back. Clausel was now in a dilemma: he had broken the 4th Division, should he now use this success as a springboard to assault Wellington's line, or use the success to cover the retreat of the army?

Clausel decided on the former. He brought up Boyer's Dragoon division and threw them at Cole's faltering men. Clausel and Bonnet continued forward. Wellington was forced to thrown in all of his reserves. The 6th Division moved to check Bonnet, whilst the 3rd and 7th tackled Clausel. Wellington threw Campbell's 1st Division on the southern Arapiles, overrunning the French battery that had set up there. Both Bonnet and Clausel were halted and then began to retreat.

The only unscathed French division was Sarrut's, which was desperately trying to hold off the allied advance as the other French divisions fell back in disorder. In the nick of time Ferey's division arrived. Ferey deployed seven of his nine battalions in a line and posted the remaining two battalions in square on his flanks. He was formed up on the edge of the Pelagarcia Wood. As the allied 6th Division closed with him his men volleyed into their ranks, bringing down over 800 men.

Wellington's divisions began to converge on Ferey, the only active French force left. Allied artillery was brought up and Wellington threw Rezende's Portuguese troops and what remained of Clinton's division against them. By the time Ferey's men finally fell back in disorder 1,000 of them were dead, including Ferey. But Clinton's brigades had been shattered. Ferey's men continued to fight a rearguard action through the woodland, linking up with Foy and then crossing the Alba Bridge.

As subsequent events would reveal, Wellington mistakenly believed that Alba was being held by the Spanish. He had not been told that the Spaniards had abandoned Alba on 20 July. As a result Wellington did not press his pursuit too strongly, believing that the French were trapped in any case. Some believe that Wellington actually failed to take advantage of the situation; he could have completely destroyed the French army. To cover his own back he simply blamed the Spanish for having abandoned Alba.

The battle of Salamanca had been a bloody one. Allied losses amounted to 4,800. The French had lost 6,000 killed and wounded and 7,000 French had been taken prisoner. Ferey and Thomières were both dead, Marmont, Clausel and Bonnet had been wounded and the French had also lost twenty artillery pieces.

WARGAME SCENARIOS

Gaming the Battle of Salamanca: 22 July 1812

Salamanca Wargame Set Up

The two opposing armies marched on Salamanca, crossing the River Tormes on 21 July. Wellington wanted to avoid action unless it was under the most advantageous of circumstances. Marmont was keen not to engage in full battle but felt obliged to fight some sort of engagement. On 22 July Marmont thought he had an ideal opportunity. Dust clouds to the south of Salamanca suggested that Wellington was retreating. The Allied troops that could be seen appeared to be the Allied rearguard. Marmont thought that he could engage this small force and win a cheap victory, thus complying with the wishes of King Joseph. The true situation could not have been more different.

Wellington's Army
During the day Wellington moved his hidden divisions into positions facing south. At around 1400, Wellington could see that Marmont was attempting to move around his flank. The French divisions were marching along the British and Portuguese front. They were dangerously strung out and exposing their flanks. It was time to attack. This is an ideal opportunity to destroy the French army. A decisive win is achieved if you manage to destroy or break four or more of the French divisions. If you manage to break or destroy three of the French divisions, then you win a minor victory. Anything less is a draw.

WELLINGTON TAKES THE OFFENSIVE

C-in-C: Lieut. Gen. the Earl of Wellington — *Gifted*

Cavalry: commanded by Lieutenant General Sir Stapleton Cotton — *Able*

1st Brigade: commanded by Major General Gaspard Le Marchant: — *Able*
– 5th Dragoon Guards, 3rd and 4th Dragoons — *Experienced Arrogant*

2nd Brigade: commanded by Major General George Anson: — *Able*
– 11th, 12th and 16th Light Dragoons — *Experienced Confident*

3rd Brigade: commanded by Major General Victor von Alten: — *Able*
– 14th Light Dragoons and 1st Hussars, King's German Legion — *Experienced Confident*

4th Brigade: commanded by Major General Baron Bock: — *Able*
– 1st and 2nd Dragoons, King's German Legion — *Experienced Confident*

Portuguese Brigade: commanded by Brigadier General D'Urban: — *Able*
– 1st, 11th and 12th Portuguese Dragoons. — *Experienced Steady*

1st Division: commanded by Major General Henry Campbell — *Able*

1st Brigade: commanded by Colonel Fermor: — *Able*
– 1/Coldstream, 1/3rd Guards, and Coy. 5/60th Foot — *Elite Confident*

2nd Brigade: commanded by Major General Wheatley: — *Able*
– 2/24th, 1/42nd, 2/58th, 1/79th Foot and Coy. 5/60th Foot. — *Veteran Confident*

WARGAME SCENARIOS

3rd Brigade: commanded by Major General Baron Löw: — Able
– 1st, 2nd and 5th Line Battalions, King's German Legion. — Experienced Steady

3rd Division: commanded by Colonel (local Major General) Pakenham — Able

1st Brigade: commanded by Lieutenant Colonel Alexander Wallace: — Able
– 1/45th, 74th, 1/88th and 3 Coys 5/60th Foot. — Veteran Confident

2nd Brigade: commanded by Lieutenant Colonel James Campbell: — Able
– 1/5th, 2/5th, 2/83rd and 94th Foot. — Veteran Confident

Portuguese Brigade: commanded by Colonel Manley Power: — Able
– 1 and 2/9th, 1 and 2/21st Portuguese Line and 12th Caçadores. — Experienced Steady

4th Division: commanded by Major General (local Lieutenant General) Lowry Cole — Able

1st Brigade: commanded by Major General William Anson: — Able
– 3/27th, 1/40th, Coy 5/60th Foot. — Veteran Confident

2nd Brigade: commanded by Lieutenant Colonel Ellis: — Able
– 1/7th, 1/23rd, 1/48th and Coy Brunswick Oels. — Veteran Confident

Portuguese Brigade: commanded by Colonel George Stubbs: — Able
– 1 and 2/11th and 1 and 2/23rd Portuguese Line, and 7th Caçadores. — Experienced Steady

5th Division: commanded by Major General (local Lieutenant General) Leigh. — Able

WELLINGTON TAKES THE OFFENSIVE

1st Brigade: commanded by Lieutenant Colonel Greville:
– 3/1st, 1/9th, 1 and 2/38th Foot and Coy Brunswick Oels.

Able

Veteran Confident

2nd Brigade: commanded by Major General Pringle:
– 1 and 2/4th, 2/30th, 2/44th Foot and Coy Brunswick Oels.

Able

Veteran Confident

Portuguese Brigade: commanded by Brigadier General Spry:
– 1 and 2/3rd, 1 and 2/15th Portuguese Line, and 8th Caçadores.

Able

Experienced Steady

6th Division: commanded by Major General Clinton.

Able

1st Brigade: commanded by Major General Hulse:
– 1/11th, 2/53rd, 1/61st and Coy 5/60th Foot.

Able

Veteran Confident

2nd Brigade: commanded by Colonel Hinde:
– 1 and 2/32nd and 1/36th Foot.

Able
Veteran Confident

Portuguese Brigade: commanded by Brigadier General de Rezende:
– 1 and 2/8th, 1 and 2/12th Portuguese Line, and 9th Caçadores.

Able

Experienced Steady

7th Division: commanded by Major General Hope.

Able

1st Brigade: commanded by Colonel Colin Halkett:
– 1st and 2nd Light Battalions King's German Legion, 7 Coys Brunswick Oels.

Able

Experienced Steady

2nd Brigade: commanded by Major General von Bernewitz:
– 51st, 68th Foot and Chasseurs Britanniques.

Able

Experienced Steady

WARGAME SCENARIOS

Portuguese Brigade: commanded by Colonel Collins: — Able
– 1 and 2/7th, 1 and 2/19th Portuguese Line, and 2nd Caçadores. — Experienced Steady

Light Division: commanded by Lieutenant General Charles, Baron von Alten. — Able

1st Brigade: commanded by Lieutenant Colonel Barnard: — Able
– 1/43rd Foot, 2/95th Rifles (4 Coys), 3/95th Rifles (5 Coys), and 3rd Caçadores. — Elite Confident

2nd Brigade: commanded by Major General Vandeleur: — Able
– 1/52nd Foot, 1/95th Rifles (8 Coys) and 1st Caçadores. — Veteran Confident

Independent Brigades
1st Brigade: commanded by Brigadier General Pack: — Able
– 1 and 2/1st, 1 and 2/16th Portuguese Line, and 4th Caçadores. — Experienced Steady

2nd Brigade: commanded by Brigadier General Bradford: — Able
– 1 and 2/13th, 1 and 2/14th Portuguese Line, and 5th Caçadores. — Experienced Steady

Spanish Division: commanded by Major General De España: — Able
– 2/Princesa, Tiradores de Castilla, 2/Jaen, 3/1st Seville, and Caçadores de Castilla. — Experienced Steady

Artillery: Lieutenant Colonel Hoylet Framingham: — Able
– 54 guns: Troops of Ross, Bull and Macdonald, Royal Horse Artillery; and batteries of Lawson, Gardiner, Greene, Douglas, May and Arriaga (Portuguese). — Veteran Confident

WELLINGTON TAKES THE OFFENSIVE

Marmont's Army

You have been caught on the hop here and there are far more Allies present than you could have possibly guessed. In order to win a decisive victory you must destroy or break two Allied divisions and then retire with all of your divisions intact. You may not begin retirement until Game Turn 10. To win a minor victory, you must destroy or break one Allied division and then retire with all of your divisions intact; again you may not start a retirement until Game Turn 10. If you manage to break or destroy an Allied division, but lose a division in the process, then this is a draw.

C-in-C: Marshal Marmont, Duke of Ragusa	*Poltroon*
Light Cavalry Division, commanded by General Curto:	*Able*
– 18 squadrons (*6 squadrons*)	*Experienced Steady*
Heavy Cavalry Division, commanded by General Boyer:	*Able*
– 8 squadrons (*3 squadrons*)	*Experienced Steady*
1st Division: commanded by General Foy:	*Able*
– 8 battalions (*3 battalions*)	*Experienced Steady*
2nd Division: commanded by General Clausel:	*Able*
– 10 battalions (*3 battalions*)	*Experienced Steady*
3rd Division: commanded by General Ferey:	*Able*
– 9 battalions (*3 battalions*)	*Experienced Steady*
4th Division: commanded by General Sarrut:	*Able*
– 9 battalions (*3 battalions*)	*Experienced Steady*
5th Division: commanded by General Maucune:	*Able*
– 9 battalions (*3 battalions*)	*Experienced Steady*
6th Division: commanded by General Brennier:	*Able*
– 8 battalions (*3 battalions*)	*Experienced Steady*

WARGAME SCENARIOS

7th Division: commanded by General Thomières:
– 8 battalions *(3 battalions)*

Able

Experienced Steady

8th Division: commanded by General Bonnet:
– 12 battalions *(4 battalions)*

Able

Experienced Steady

Artillery, commanded by General Tirlet:
– 78 guns *(7 guns)*

Able

Experienced Steady

Shortly after dawn on 23 July Wellington despatched cavalry, under Bock and Anson, to chase the French. Bock's men spotted some of Curto's cavalry near Garcia Hernandez and immediately charged. Unbeknown to them Foy's infantry division lay hidden in a dip. A French infantry regiment appeared in front of Bock's Dragoons, forming a square. They fired at the oncoming Dragoons. To the great fortune of the German cavalry a horseman was shot down close to the square and his mount rolled into the square, flattening dozens of Frenchmen. The Dragoons poured into the gap and cut up the 76th Line.

The Dragoons now spotted another French regiment, the 6th Léger, moving off to the east. The Dragoons chased the French infantry and before the French had a chance to form square the cavalry had ploughed into them. Foy's two remaining regimental squares now beckoned. The Dragoons charged, but this time they were driven off. The French had lost around 1,000 men and the Dragoons 130.

Foy marched on and linked up with a cavalry brigade that had been sent by Caffarelli from the Army of the North. Foy's men and the cavalry retreated towards Penaranda.

King Joseph heard the shattering news of Marmont's defeat at Salamanca on 23 July. King Joseph had been desperately trying to scrape together as many men as possible to support Marmont and had in fact mustered some 14,000 men. Made aware of the situation, King Joseph decided that rather than marching to join up with Clausel, now in command of the Army of Portugal, he would be better served trying to protect Madrid.

Wellington was also soon appraised of this situation and he determined to destroy Clausel's army as his main priority. He started heading towards Valladolid, which the French abandoned on 30 July. Wellington also requested that Silveira and Santocildes close in on Clausel. Wellington left

WELLINGTON TAKES THE OFFENSIVE

a Spanish force at Valladolid and 18,000 men, under Clinton, to keep an eye on Clausel. By this stage Wellington had seen the opportunity to seize Madrid. By 10 August Wellington's troops had reached Guadarrama. Wellington pushed on towards Madrid. Ahead of his army were seven Portuguese cavalry squadrons, under D'Urban, heavy Dragoons of the King's German Legion, some light infantry and some horse artillery. They were camped at Majalahonda.

Suddenly they came under attack from French cavalry. It was a disaster for the Portuguese horse and the Dragoons, but the light infantry managed to hold the cavalry off long enough for Wellington's main force to arrive.

By now King Joseph realised that there was nothing that could save Madrid. He headed for Ocaña, leaving his wounded in the city. Wellington marched in on 12 August unopposed.

The reason why Madrid fell so easily was that other French commanders and their forces were under extreme pressure in all of the other theatres. D'Erlon had just 12,000 men facing 19,000 Anglo-Portuguese and 4,000 Spaniards under Hill in Estremadura. Ballesteros, at the head of 9,000 men, was operating in the south and had attacked a French division under Conroux at Bornos. The Spanish had been defeated, but it had tied down valuable French troops.

Hill was now ready to launch diversionary attacks on D'Erlon, which meant that Soult would have to support him. On 11 June lead elements of Hill's army had clashed with the French at Llerena. Hill now pulled back, having drawn Soult to assist D'Erlon and prevented him from supporting Marmont.

Ballesteros had attacked Malaga. The French chased him and the Spaniard, rather than heading back towards Gibraltar, plunged into Andalucía and attacked Osuna.

It seemed clear by the middle of August, with the defeat at Salamanca and the threat against Madrid, that the south would have to be abandoned. Soult and D'Erlon began retiring east.

In the north Admiral Popham had at his disposal two ships of the line, five frigates, a number of transport vessels and 11,000 Anglo-Spanish Marines. In addition he could call on the support of Spanish guerrillas. Facing him in the north-eastern provinces of Spain was Caffarelli's Army of the North, which amounted to some 35,000 men. Caffarelli's men, however, were spread out in innumerable garrisons. Popham set sail from Corunna and on 21 June had begun raiding the coast. He aimed to tie down as many of the French as possible. Popham was able to seize

WARGAME SCENARIOS

Santander and use this as his new base. This now meant that supplies and reinforcements coming from Britain could make the far-shorter trip to Santander than Lisbon.

On 13 August Popham attacked Bilbao. The French evacuated it. Caffarelli was forced to send 7,000 men to recapture the city. This all played into Popham and Wellington's hands; yet more French were unavailable to help Marmont.

Far to the east, in Catalonia, similar diversionary tactics were underway. Suchet had managed to seize Valencia, but his troops were strung out all along the east coast. There were pockets of British or Spanish troops all over this sector and there was always the danger of additional forces landing from the Balearic Islands. There was no way that Suchet, the French commander, could afford to send Marmont a single man.

General Lacy, at the head of 8,000 men, struck against French garrisons across Catalonia. Towards the end of July 11,000 men, under Maitland, landed at Palamos.

It had not all gone the allies' way in this theatre. On 21 July José O'Donnell's 12,000 strong Army of Murcia had attacked French positions at Castalla. O'Donnell had made a huge mistake when he had split his army into three groups. The French commander, Harispe, had just 5,000 men, but he struck against the central column whilst the other two Spanish formations were too far away. As soon as O'Donnell's other formations saw that their centre column had been overwhelmed they fled towards Alicante. The Spanish had lost 3,000 men. As soon as Maitland found out about this defeat he embarked and sailed for Alicante, as he could ill-afford to lose the Spanish troops. It was here that Maitland heard the rumour that Soult was marching east towards him, at the head of 80,000 men. All Maitland could do was to dig in and await instructions.

There were many options open to Wellington, now firmly in control of Madrid. He knew that the mauling that Clausel had taken at Salamanca would put him out of action for several weeks. He also knew that even if Soult was marching to join up with Clausel that this would take some time and in any case the French might not be inclined to launch an offensive. Wellington firmly believed that it was possible that they would try to retake the capital and consequently he ordered Hill to join him in Madrid. By 3 September Wellington, along with 21,000 men, had linked up with Clinton, to the north at Arevalo.

Clausel had been hard at work. He had swiftly re-equipped his force from his depot at Burgos and then had marched west at the head of 25,000 men as early as 13 August. His target was to extract the French garrisons at Astorga, Toro and Zamora.

The sudden French movement had taken the allies by surprise. Clinton's 7,000 men had been forced to pull back from Cuellar to Arevalo. The Spanish under Santocildes had been panicked into abandoning Valladolid.

Foy's French division had already reached Toro. He had taken out the garrison and destroyed the fortifications. He now marched towards Astorga, but the fortress had already fallen and instead he chased Santocildes and relieved Zamora on 26 August. Foy destroyed the fortifications and then rejoined Clausel at Valladolid on 4 September. Clausel then retreated and fell back beyond Burgos, where he left a sizeable garrison.

Wellington, thrown by the sudden French activity, decided to give chase. By the morning of 19 September his army was around Burgos. The fortress itself was fairly strong and protected by 2,000 infantry, under General Dubreton. In truth Wellington lacked the fire power to reduce the fortress, as he had only eight heavy guns. Before he had a chance of being able to take Burgos he had to overwhelm the outlying defence works. He threw part of the 1st Division and Pack's Portuguese Brigade against the outer defence works. Pack's main body was beaten back, but some of the 1st Division managed to get into the defences. The French panicked and the position was overrun.

Wellington now set about positioning his artillery, but rather than wait for the guns to demolish the walls, he decided to launch an infantry assault. It was beaten off with heavy casualties. Wellington began the building of a parallel on 23 September. A further trench was dug and a 1,000lb mine was placed below the walls' foundations. The mine was detonated on 29 September and infantry unleashed to storm through the breach. Unfortunately there was no breach. All the mine had succeeded in doing was to destroy some ancient stonework from an older fortress. Burgos Castle's walls were still intact.

A new sap was constructed and artillery moved up to cover the assault point. The French responded by destroying two of the cannons that were set up. Wellington, in desperation, requested that more guns be sent from Santander. Meanwhile the sap and new mine were set, which was detonated on 4 October. This time it worked and a huge gap was torn in the northwest wall. The allies managed to establish a foothold and work began on digging towards the inner walls of the castle. The French launched a counterattack, which held up allied progress then they launched a second, unexpected attack, which delayed Wellington even more. With the weather getting worse and ammunition becoming short, Wellington determined to carry Burgos by storm. He had also learned that Souham was marching to assist Burgos. Souham had recently replaced Clausel.

On 18 October the British set off a mine under the Church of San Roman and using this as a diversion an infantry assault was sent in. It was beaten off with heavy casualties. This was Wellington's last throw of the dice at Burgos. Souham and Caffarelli were close and the siege had to be abandoned.

The French troops arrived to relieve Dubreton on the morning of 22 October. Wellington had lost over 2,000 men and an enormous amount of equipment. The garrison had lost around 300. Even worse for the allies, the French had mustered a new force and were determined to retake Madrid.

The French had, in fact, mustered a potential field army of 110,000 men. Caffarelli had brought 12,000 men and had linked up with troops from Bayonne and Souham's Army of Portugal to create 53,000 men. Meanwhile King Joseph had linked up with Soult, giving them a total of 60,000 men. This was a particularly difficult set of circumstances for the allies. The allied troops were scattered and many of them in retreat.

Immediately available to Wellington were 24,000 Anglo-Portuguese, 11,000 Spaniards under Santocildes, and a further 20,000 at Toledo under Hill and 18,000 at Madrid, under Alten. Wellington desperately needed to draw the French away. He instructed Maitland to make for Valencia, and Ballesteros and troops from Cadiz to advance into La Mancha. Unfortunately Suchet could easily deal with Maitland and Ballesteros was not yet ready to march.

With Wellington retreating from Burgos, Souham, at the head of his 6,000 cavalry supported by his infantry, was in pursuit. Sanchez, Anson and Bock, along with light infantry of the King's German Legion and horse artillery, held the French off as best they could. There was a major engagement at Venta Del Pozo when British Dragoons tried to hold back the French, as the tail end of the allied army passed through Villadrigo.

By now the bulk of Wellington's army had reached the River Carrion. Here Wellington determined to stand and fight. The French were hot on their heels. Foy's division was thrown at the Spanish troops on Wellington's left on 25 October and Maucune's division stormed over the river at Villamuriel. In short order the allied left wing faced encirclement and Wellington threw four brigades in to stop Maucune. Wellington's men retook Villamuriel but it was now clear that the river line was compromised and he would have to pull back. Instead of heading west Wellington swung east and now had the River Pisuerga in front of him.

The French desperately tried to discover where Wellington was concentrating. Part of Foy's division crossed the River Douro at Tordesillas on 29 October, once again turning Wellington's left flank. Wellington fell back on Valladolid to link up with Hill, but by now it was too late for the French to continue their pursuit. A new rebellion had broken out in the northeast and Caffarelli's 12,000 men were needed there.

Hill had received an instruction from Wellington on 29 October that he should abandon Madrid and head west. He left Skerrett and Cole with 4,000 men to deny the French an easy crossing of the River Jarama. Soult arrived at the bridge on 30 October. His initial probes were beaten back and he began to bombard the British positions. By dawn the following day he had discovered that the British had slipped away and Soult could recommence his march towards Madrid.

Hill had indeed abandoned Madrid by noon on 31 October. His troops had made for Villacastin. New orders told him to make for Alba de Tormes and from there meet up with Wellington to the south of Salamanca. By this time the French had marched into Madrid and they were now determined to chase Wellington and defeat him.

Harried by French cavalry, the allied army retreated west. The march claimed thousands of lives and almost as many desertions. By this stage Wellington had been named Commander in Chief of the Spanish Army. In theory he now had to also deal with the reorganisation of the Spanish regular troops, amounting to 160,000 men. Reforms and training were much needed but Spanish officers were reluctant to implement them.

On other fronts things were not so rosy for the French. They had suffered an absolute disaster in Russia and now faced the prospect of fighting the combined strength of Russia, Prussia, Austria and Sweden. Although Soult was called to assist Napoleon in his hour of need and a number of French troops were pulled out of the peninsula, there were still 200,000 French in Spain. The French were determined to make good any of their losses, but not at the expense of the peninsula. Things were by no means settled, even though Wellington and his battered forces were now in Portugal.

In the north 14,000 guerrilla troops were operating in Navarre alone. Popham was making raids all along the coast; Caffarelli could barely hold onto the garrisons let alone keep communications open with France.

Napoleon had new instructions for his brother, King Joseph. He believed that only a small garrison should be kept in Madrid and that a new capital should be established at Valladolid. He suggested that Caffarelli should be replaced by Clausel and that the Army of Portugal should be sent north to deal with the continuing problems, particularly in Biscay and Navarre. He also suggested that Gazan, who had replaced Soult, take up defensive positions between Valladolid and Salamanca to prevent Wellington from making incursions into Spain.

The Spanish guerrillas were in no hurry to succumb to French pressure. One of the guerrilla leaders, Mina, overran Tafalla in February 1813. A French attempt to regain Tafalla failed. Clausel despatched Barbot's division to destroy Mina. Barbot's lead elements were ambushed at Lodosa on 30 March and Mina killed 1,000 Frenchmen and then melted away into the Pyrenees. Clausel was not finished. He pressed on and attacked on 12 May, overrunning Mina's main camp and killing 1,000 guerrillas.

Meanwhile, on the same day, the Anglo-Spanish garrison at Castro-Urdiales was forced to evacuate when they were attacked by Foy, supported by three other divisions. Despite the successes, the struggle for the Biscay region was not over.

Chapter 5

Collapse and Defeat

Background to the Battle of Vitoria

On 11 May 1813 Wellington, writing to Lord Bathurst, had determined to drive the French out of northern Spain, taking full advantage of Spanish regular- and guerrilla-actions in Biscay. He proposed to turn the French position on the River Douro. By this stage, in addition to all of the detachments scattered around the countryside, some operating as garrisons, he could pull together 81,000 Anglo-Portuguese and 21,000 Spanish troops. En route from Cadiz was O'Donnell's corps of some 14,000. There was also another 12,000 troops available to him that was already fighting against Clausel in the north. Added to this, facing Suchet was another 50,000 troops.

Wellington needed to make sure that Suchet was in no position to march to the aid of King Joseph. He impressed upon allied troops in Catalonia that they must do their utmost to pin Suchet and prevent him from moving west.

By the end of May 1813 Wellington was ready to launch a major offensive. 30,000 men under General Hill were already underway. Another major army under Graham had marched into Salamanca on 26 May.

The French were perfectly well aware of Hill's force and believed it to be the only major enemy field army in operation. They completely missed Graham's force. As soon as the French division under General Daricau that was at Zamora did discover it they fled east. Graham marched into Zamora on 2 June and began marching along the River Douro to link up with Hill at Toro on 3 June. By the time the two armies had been united Wellington had 90,000 men on the north bank of the River Douro.

The French had been concentrating their forces around Valladolid, Medina and Tordesillas. King Joseph could muster around 51,000 men. He had considered giving battle but now he realised he was massively outnumbered. He began to retreat towards Burgos and sent urgent despatches to Clausel to send him men.

WARGAME SCENARIOS

Wellington immediately despatched his cavalry to pursue and shadow the French. His main force took a north-easterly direction, aiming to work around the French flank. The French did not fall for it and they pulled out of Burgos on 13 June to take up defensive positions behind the River Ebro. All they could do now was hope that Clausel would march to support them. The French also believed that Wellington was marching into impossible countryside, with little in the way of supplies. What they did not know was that Popham, operating from Santander, had already established a supply route. By mid-June Wellington's army was approaching Vitoria and elements were closing in on Bilbao.

On 17 June the French discovered their dreadful mistake, as they ran into lead elements of Wellington's army. King Joseph was all for retreating once again. His generals had mixed opinions; some believed that they should immediately link up with Suchet and face Wellington, whilst the King himself believed that the most important objective was to hold open the road to France.

Consequently French troops began to concentrate around Vitoria on 19 June. It was not a great position and in any case the French had not taken any steps to destroy bridges, which would be invaluable to Wellington. In addition to this, the French drew up along a twelve mile front, which once again would play into Wellington's hands.

By the end of 20 June Wellington had brought 80,000 men to the battlefield. He could immediately see that the French were vulnerable and proposed launching four dense columns at the French positions. Hill, at the head of 20,000 men, would attack via the Heights of Puebla. Two more columns with 30,000 men would attack between Mendoza and Nanclares. Finally 20,000 men, under Graham, would hit the French rear and flank at Yurre.

Hill's men were the first to get into action at 0800 on 21 June. They drove the French back despite enemy attempts to reinforce their position. The situation was becoming quite desperate and it was at this point that Graham launched his assault. Once again the French began to withdraw, first from Aranguiz and then back to the Zadorra River. Graham's troops were also trying to force the French away from the bridgeheads near Durana.

The French had failed to defend Tres Puentes and elements of the Light Division crossed the River Zadorra. The French had also failed to protect the crossing at Mendoza and Picton's 3rd Division crossed. There was now an enormous rupture in the French lines and the French were forced to retreat northwards. As they fell back more and more Anglo-Portuguese troops poured over the river. Arinez fell and this meant that the French had to abandon Margarita.

The Anglo-Portuguese now focused on capturing Lermanda, also on the south bank of the river. The French hung on for as long as they could, but relentless assaults forced them out. The French tried to form a new line between Crispijana, close to the riverbank, and Esquivel, just below the Puebla Heights.

To the north the French were still stubbornly holding onto the bridgehead at Gamma Mayor. They were still just holding on by their fingertips at Durana against Spanish pressure. However, the fact that Durana was now in allied gun-range effectively cut the road to Bayonne, one of the key objectives of the allied offensive.

At around 1600 just six French infantry divisions were holding the line between Crispijana and Esquivel. They were, however, supported by seventy-five artillery pieces and 4,500 cavalry. The end, however, looked inevitable, as bearing down on them were 30,000 allied troops and some thirteen batteries of artillery.

Hill's men were still making progress through the Puebla Heights. On the French flank alongside the heights the French General Gazan, terrified that his flank was about to be turned, began to withdraw. This left just D'Erlon's men facing Wellington's new assault. Allied troops poured through the gap left by Gazan, overrunning Gomecho.

At the same time a determined effort pushed the French out of Crispijana. The French line had been obliterated. All that remained was for the French to try and extricate themselves.

Reille's divisions to the north, trying to hold back Graham, now found that with D'Erlon's men in retreat, the Anglo-Portuguese units surging towards Vitoria were falling on their flank. Reille began to withdraw. He posted troops at Betona to cover his retreat. The French were desperately trying to escape up the road, towards Salvatierra, but it was chaos.

Once again the allied pursuit was mismanaged and the men seemed more interested in looting the wagons that the French had had to abandon. By the end of the battle the French had lost 5,000 killed or wounded, 3,000 prisoners had been taken and 150 guns lost. Allied casualties amounted to some 5,000 killed or wounded.

WARGAME SCENARIOS

Gaming the Battle of Vitoria: 21 June 1813

Vitoria Wargame Set Up

This is an enormous and complicated battle that could easily be fought as a series of actions rather than attempting to squeeze all of the phases of the engagement on to one table. Certainly, the engagement involving Hill's forces against Gazan and D'Erlon could be fought as a separate battle as could the fight between Graham's army and Reille. The Allied order of battle is fairly complete, but the one for the French indicates the split of the forces into the different components. It was an overwhelming victory for the Allies and the expectations of the French as far as victory conditions are concerned, are limited.

Wellington's Army

You must crush the French army with your superior numbers and better positioning. In order to win a decisive victory you will need to destroy or break two of the three French armies and have possession of all of the towns on the battlefield. To win a minor victory, you must destroy or break one of the French armies and capture all of the towns on the battlefield. Any other result will count as a draw.

Lieutenant General the Marquess of Wellington	*Gifted*	–

COLLAPSE AND DEFEAT

Right Column: commanded by   Able
   Lieutenant General Sir Rowland Hill

1st Brigade: commanded by Major   Able
   General Victor von Alten:
– 14th Light Dragoons and 1st Hussars,   *Experienced Confident*
   King's German Legion

2nd Brigade: commanded by   Able
   Lieutenant General Fane:
– 3rd Dragoon Guards and 1st Royal   Experienced Confident
   Dragoons

2nd Division: commanded by Lieutenant   Able
   General William Stewart

1st Brigade: commanded by Colonel   Able
   Cadogan:
– 1/50th, 1/71st and 1/91st Foot, 1 coy   *Veteran Confident*
   5/60th Foot

2nd Brigade: commanded by Major   Able
   General Byng:
– 1/3rd, 1/57th Foot, 1st Provisional Btn.   Veteran Confident
   (2/31st and 2/66th Foot) and 1 coy
   5/60th Foot

3rd Brigade: commanded by Colonel   Able
   O'Callaghan:
– 1/28th, 2/34th, 1/39th Foot and 1 coy   Veteran Confident
   5/60th Foot

Portuguese Brigade: commanded by   Able
   Brigadier General Ashworth:
– 1 and 2/6th, 1 and 2/18th Portuguese   Experienced Steady
   Line, and 6th Caçadores

Portuguese Division: commanded by   Able
   Major General Silveira, Conde de
   Amaranthe

WARGAME SCENARIOS

1st Brigade: commanded by Brigadier General de Costa:
– 1 and 2/2nd, 1 and 2/14th Portuguese Line

Able

Experienced Steady

2nd Brigade: commanded by Brigadier General Archibald Campbell:
– 1 and 2/4th, 1 and 2/10th Portuguese Line and 10th Caçadores

Able

Experienced Steady

Spanish Division: commanded by Major General Morillo:
– Regimiento de Leon, Regimiento de Union, Regimiento del Legion

Able

Novice Steady

Artillery: commanded by Major Carncross:
– Beane's Troop Royal Horse Artillery, Maxwell's Battery Royal Artillery and 2 Portuguese batteries under Major Tulloh

Able

Veteran Confident

Right Centre Column: commanded by the Marquess of Wellington

1st Brigade: commanded by Lieutenant Colonel Sir Robert Hill:
– 1st and 2nd Life Guards and Royal Horse Guards

Able

Veteran Confident

2nd Brigade: commanded by Colonel Colquohon Grant:
– 10th, 15th and 18th Light Dragoons (Hussars)

Able

Experienced Steady

3rd Brigade: commanded by Major General William Ponsonby:
– 5th Dragoon Guards, 3rd and 4th Dragoons

Able

Veteran Confident

Portuguese Brigade: commanded by Brigadier General D'Urban:
– 1st, 11th and 12th Portuguese Dragoons

Able

Experienced Steady

COLLAPSE AND DEFEAT

4th Division: commanded by Major General Lowry Cole	Able
1st Brigade: commanded by Major General William Anson:	Able
– 3/27th, 1/40th, 1/48th, Provisional Btn. (1 and 2/53rd Foot) and 1 coy 5/60th Foot	Veteran Confident
2nd Brigade: commanded by Major General Skerrett:	Able
– 1/7th, 20th, 1/23rd, and 1 coy Brunswick Oels	Veteran Confident
Portuguese Brigade: commanded by Colonel George Stubbs:	Able
– 1 and 2/11th and 1 and 2/23rd Portuguese Line, and 7th Caçadores	Veteran Confident
Light Division: commanded by Lieutenant General Charles, Baron von Alten	*Able*
1st Brigade: commanded by Major General Kempt:	*Able*
– 1/43rd Foot, 1/95th Rifles (8 coys), 3/95th Rifles (5 coys) and 3rd Caçadores	*Veteran Confident*
2nd Brigade: commanded by Major General John Ormesby Vandeleur:	Able
– 1/52nd Foot, 2/95th Rifles (6 coys) and 1st Caçadores	Veteran Confident
Artillery: commanded by Major Augustus Simon Frazer:	Able
– Ross's, Gardiner's and Ramsay's Troops, Royal Horse Artillery, Sympher's Battery, King's German Artillery	Experienced Steady
Left Centre Column: commanded by Lieutenant General the Earl of Dalhousie	Able

WARGAME SCENARIOS

3rd Division: commanded by Lieutenant General Sir Thomas Picton	Able
1st Brigade: commanded by Major General Thomas Brisbane:	Able
– 1/45th, 74th, 1/88th and 3 coys 5/60th Foot	Veteran Confident
2nd Brigade: commanded by Major General Colville:	Able
– 1/5th, 2/83rd, 2/87th and 94th Foot	Veteran Confident
Portuguese Brigade: commanded by Major General Manley Power:	Able
– 1 and 2/9th, 1 and 2/21st Portuguese Line and 11th Caçadores	Experienced Steady
7th Division: commanded by Lieutenant General Lord Dalhousie	Able
1st Brigade: commanded by Major General Barnes:	Able
– 1/6th Foot, 3rd Provisional Btn (2/24th and 2/58th Foot), and Brunswick Oels (7 coys)	Veteran Confident
2nd Brigade: commanded by Colonel William Grant:	Able
– 51st, 68th, 1/82nd Foot and Chasseurs Britanniques	Experienced Steady
Portuguese Brigade: commanded by Major General Le Cor:	Able
– 1 and 2/7th, 1 and 2/19th Portuguese Line, and 2nd Caçadores	Experienced Steady
Artillery: commanded by Major Buckner:	Able
– Batteries of Cairnes and Douglas	Experienced Steady
Left Column: commanded by Lieutenant General Sir Thomas Graham	Able

COLLAPSE AND DEFEAT

1st Brigade: commanded by Major
   General George Anson: *Able*
– 12th and 16th Light Dragoons   Veteran Confident

2nd Brigade: commanded by Major   *Able*
   General Baron Bock:
– 1st and 2nd Dragoons, King's German Legion   *Experienced Steady*

1st Division: commanded by Major   *Able*
   General Kenneth Howard

1st Brigade: commanded by Major   *Able*
   General Kenneth Stopford:
– 1/Coldstream, 1/3rd Guards, 1 coy   *Veteran Confident*
   5/60th Foot

2nd Brigade: commanded by Colonel   *Able*
   Collin Halkett:
– 1st, 2nd and 5th Line Battalions, 1st and   Veteran Confident
   2nd Light Battalions, King's German Legion

5th Division: commanded by Major   *Able*
   General Oswald

1st Brigade: commanded by Major   *Able*
   General Hay:
– 3/1st, 1/9th, 1/38th Foot and 1 coy   *Veteran Confident*
   Brunswick Oels

2nd Brigade: commanded by Major   *Able*
   General Robinson:
– 1/4th, 2/47th, 2/59th Foot and 1 coy   Experienced Steady
   Brunswick Oels

Portuguese Brigade: commanded by   *Able*
   Brigadier General Spry:
– 1 and 2/3rd, 1 and 2/15th Portuguese Line,   Experienced Steady
   and 8th Caçadores

Independent Portuguese Brigades   *Able*

WARGAME SCENARIOS

1st Brigade: commanded by Brigadier General Pack:	Able
– 1 and 2/1st, 1 and 2/16th Portuguese Line, and 4th Caçadores	Experienced Steady
2nd Brigade: commanded by Brigadier General Bradford:	Able
– 1 and 2/13th, 1 and 2/24th Portuguese Line, and 5th Caçadores	Experienced Steady

French Army

Outright victory is probably a forlorn hope, but there is a possibly that you could inflict sufficient casualties on them for the Allies to think twice about pressing the issue. To win a decisive victory you must hold all of the towns and villages on the French side of the river: you may lose Gamarra Mayor only. To win a minor victory you must hold the line Arinez-Magarita-Lermanda-Crispijana-Vitoria at Game Turn 15. If you still have an intact army on the battlefield at the end of Game Turn 15, but have not achieved any of the other objectives, then the game is a draw.

C-in-C: Prince Joseph Napoleon, King of Spain	Able
Chief of Staff: Marshal Jean Baptiste Jourdan	Able
Army of the South: commanded by General Gazan	Able
1st Cavalry Division: commanded by General Soult:	Able
– 4 regiments	Experienced Steady
2nd Cavalry Division: commanded by General Tilly:	Able
– 6 regiments	Experienced Steady
3rd Cavalry Division: commanded by General Digeon:	Able
– 4 regiments	Experienced Steady

COLLAPSE AND DEFEAT

1st Division: commanded by General Leval:
– 14 battalions

Able
Experienced Steady

3rd Division: commanded by General Villatte:
– 12 battalions

Able

Experienced Steady

4th Division: commanded by General Conroux:
– 12 battalions

Able

Experienced Steady

6th Division: commanded by General Daricau:
– 10 battalions

Able

Experienced Steady

General Maransin's brigade:
– 6 battalions

Able
Experienced Steady

Army of the Centre: commanded by General Count D'Erlon

Able

1st Cavalry Division: commanded by General Treillard:
– 4 regiments

Able

Experienced Steady

2nd Cavalry Division: commanded by General Avy:
– 2 regiments

Able

Experienced Steady

1st Division: commanded by General Darmignac:
– 11 battalions

Able

Experienced Steady

2nd Division: commanded by General Cassagne:
– 12 battalions

Able

Experienced Steady

Army of Portugal: commanded by General Reille

Able

WARGAME SCENARIOS

1st Cavalry Division: commanded by General Mermet:
– 5 regiments

Able

Experienced Steady

2nd Cavalry Division: commanded by General Boyer:
– 4 regiments

Able

Experienced Steady

4th Division: commanded by General Sarrut:
– 6 battalions

Able

Experienced Steady

6th Division: commanded by General Lamartinière:
– 9 battalions

Able

Experienced Steady

King Joseph's Spanish Army
Guard, Cavalry and Infantry – 2 regiments of cavalry, 3 battalions infantry

Able

Experienced Steady

The French had abandoned Salvatierra at around dawn on 22 June. Little wonder that Wellington, having begun his pursuit at 1000 hours, failed to catch up with them. There were many options open to Wellington. It was clear that what remained of King Joseph's army was heading for the Pyrenees. Clausel was some distance away and Foy was abandoning Biscay. By 25 June Wellington had surrounded Pamplona and had sent Graham off to chase Foy. The bulk of his troops, however, were heading for the River Ebro.

Foy was in fact retiring towards Villafranca; Graham got there before him, only to discover that Maucune's division was already holding it. The French held Villafranca long enough for Foy to pass through it and then Maucune retired. Graham continued to pursue.

On 27 June the French had mustered around 16,000 men at Tolosa. Against them Graham could muster 26,000, including Spanish troops under Giron. Foy, however, was more than a match for Graham. The allied assault was beaten back, but Graham had prudently sent large numbers of troops around the flanks and this encouraged Foy to pull back towards the River Bidassoa, destroying the bridges to prevent Graham from following. Instead, Graham marched on San Sebastian, which he surrounded.

Clausel had actually been en route to Vitoria to reinforce King Joseph, but when he discovered that the battle had been lost he marched towards Saragossa and linked up with what remained of King Joseph's army at St Jean-Pied-De-Port on 15 July.

COLLAPSE AND DEFEAT

Background to the Battle of Castalla
Events in central Europe could well have an enormous impact on the Peninsular Campaign. The rumours were that Napoleon had won some major battles and that he was demanding peace on his own terms. This would free up enormous numbers of French troops. In the short term it would mean that Wellington could not invade southern France and in the longer-term the French could be back in the peninsula in significant numbers. Consequently Wellington held back, waiting for confirmed news. He decided that Pamplona and San Sebastian should be besieged and that the French should be dislodged from any positions they might hold along the River Bidassoa.

As it transpired, Napoleon blamed his brother entirely for the string of defeats, both on the battlefield and for the loss of territory. Joseph was recalled from Spain and Soult was despatched to try and salvage the situation. News of the French defeat at Vitoria had also weakened the French hand at the negotiating table.

Wellington, therefore, resolved to try to make any French return to the peninsula as difficult as possible. He focused initially on San Sebastian, feeling that he could starve out the French garrison of Pamplona.

By the first week of July allied troops had cut off San Sebastian by land and forty heavy guns had been brought up. The problem was that there was only a narrow causeway leading to the fortress itself. This would prove only too easy for the French to rake with gun and musket fire. The allies noticed that at low tide the River Arumea's estuary was virtually dry. It would be possible to slip troops along it and attack the fortification from the east. The allies began their attempts to reduce the monastery of San Bartolomé, which protected the causeway to the fortress. An attempt to storm it was beaten off on 15 July. Two more days of shelling followed and then another assault and this time the defenders withdrew through San Martin, towards the breastworks that protected San Sebastian's southern approach. The allies now set up batteries on the Heights of Ayete and began firing at the eastern wall. The allies managed to place a mine under the breastworks and continued their bombardment; finally a breach appeared.

On 25 July the allies launched two assaults; the first against the breastworks was beaten off, but the other was a far more serious attempt via the estuary and almost immediately it ran into difficulties. The French slaughtered 600 men in a matter of minutes. The dead and the wounded were scattered all over the sand and many of the latter would die as the tide came in. The attack was an absolute disaster for the allies.

As Wellington pondered his options, he heard that the French had reorganised their field armies and there was already heavy fighting at the

WARGAME SCENARIOS

Maya Pass and the Roncesvalles Pass. Graham was ordered to abandon the siege of San Sebastian. It was obvious to Wellington that the French attacks aimed to relieve both San Sebastian and Pamplona.

Although Wellington had hoped that allied forces on the south-east coast would tie down and threaten Suchet's men, nothing much happened until Sir John Murray got underway in March 1813. Murray was not really suited for an independent command. On paper he had a force of some 52,000 men, outnumbering what Suchet could scrape together by at least three to one. He had begun to stir and move northwards, but he cancelled his plans to attack Valencia and instead set up around Castalla. Suchet was amazed and decided that he would take the offensive.

At dawn on 11 April Suchet attacked General Elio's Murcian army. Elio was at the head of some 15,000 men but the blow fell on his vanguard at Yecla. The French attack was entirely successful; 1,500 Spaniards were either killed or wounded and what remained of Elio's force was falling back on Jumilla. Suchet turned east. By the time the day was out Suchet had overrun Villena and by the following morning he was clashing with the forward elements of Murray's force at Biar.

Biar was held by Colonel Adam, commanding just over 2,000 troops and a battery of artillery. Adam's men were driven out and Suchet despatched cavalry to complete the rout. However they were held off by elements of the 27th Foot. Adam's men managed to retreat to rejoin Murray at Castalla.

By the morning of 13 April Suchet had determined to tackle Murray. Suchet could muster 11,000 infantry, 1,250 cavalry and twenty-four artillery pieces. Against him Murray had 17,000 infantry, 1,000 cavalry and thirty guns. Murray's men were set up along high ground to the west of Castalla. His right flank rested on Castalla and was protected by vineyards and flooded ground. Suchet decided that this was not the ideal position to launch his assault. He simply left cavalry, under Boussard, to keep an eye on Castalla. Instead Suchet concentrated the bulk of his troops on Murray's left, whilst Habert's men kept Murray's centre occupied.

The attack was led by General Robert. He closed on Whittingham's Spanish troops. Part of Robert's force also collided with Adam's battalions. The steady musketry fire from the British and the Spanish ripped into the advancing French columns. The 121st Regiment, on the far left of Robert's division, broke and this signalled a wholesale retreat.

Suchet realised that the attack had failed. Boussard and Harispe covered the withdrawal. In all, the French lost 1,300 men and the allies just short of 450. The French withdrew towards the River Xucar, whilst Murray linked up with Elio's army.

COLLAPSE AND DEFEAT

Gaming the Battle of Castalla: 13 April 1813

Castalla Wargame Set Up

Allied forces totalled some 18,716 and the French 13,564. By some standards this is a fairly small battle and it can be fought with a single regiment or two representing each of the divisions. Cavalry numbers are quite low.

Sir John Murray's Forces

Hold the ridge line and beat off the French attacks to win a minor victory. To win a decisive one, you must break or destroy one of the French infantry divisions. If you have not achieved these objectives but still have all of your divisions intact at the end of Game Turn 12, then you have achieved a draw.

C-in-C: Sir John Murray — *Cautious*
Advanced Guard under Adam: — *Able*
– 3 battalions *(1 battalion)* — *Veteran Confident*

1st Division under Clinton: — *Able*
– 5 battalions *(2 battalion)* — *Veteran Confident*

2nd Division under Mackenzie: — *Able*
– 5 battalions *(2 battalion)* — *Veteran Confident*

133

WARGAME SCENARIOS

1st Spanish Division under Whittingham: *Able*
– 6 battalions *(3 battalion)* *Veteran Confident*

2nd Spanish Division under Roche: *Able*
– 5 battalions *(2 battalion)* *Green Confident*

Cavalry: – 5 squadrons *(2 squadrons)* *Veteran Confident*

Artillery: – 30 guns *(3 guns)* *Veteran Confident*

Marshal Suchet's Forces
Push the enemy from the heights and seize Castalla to win a decisive victory. To win a minor victory, destroy or break two of the Allied divisions. To gain a draw, destroy one of the enemy divisions.

C-in-C: Marshal Suchet *Able*
1st Division under Robert: *Able*
– 8 battalions *(4 battalions)* *Experienced Steady*

2nd Division under Harispe: *Able*
– 6 battalions *(2 battalions)* *Experienced Steady*

3rd Division under Habert: *Able*
– 4 battalions *(2 battalions)* *Experienced Steady*

Cavalry under Boussard: *Able*
– 8 squadrons *(4 squadrons)* *Experienced Steady*

Artillery: – 30 guns *(3 guns)* *Experienced Steady*

Background to the Battle of Sorauren
Wellington was still pressing Murray for more positive action, bearing in mind that this was the period immediately before the battle of Vitoria. Wellington wanted Murray to attack Tarragona and draw Suchet away from Valencia. This would give the Spanish a golden opportunity to take Valencia.

The centre of activity was Alicante. Murray withdrew his British troops from Yecla and replaced them with Elio's men. More troops arrived at Alicante and before the armada set off on 31 May Murray had assembled 15,000 infantry, 800 cavalry, twenty-four artillery pieces and siege artillery.

COLLAPSE AND DEFEAT

Two days later the force disembarked just eight miles from Tarragona.

General Copons, at the head of 7,000 Catalan troops, covered Murray's landing and together they marched against Tarragona. Tarragona was held by General Bertoletti and a 1,600 man garrison. However, even with an armada of 180 enemy vessels and 20,000 men threatening to overrun his position, Bertoletti did not panic. Had Murray ordered an immediate assault he would undoubtedly have carried the position. Instead he dug in and began to create parallels. By 7 June the outer walls were badly damaged. Once again Murray had the opportunity to assault, but turned it down. This was all giving Suchet valuable time to respond.

Suchet had indeed left a small shadow force to cover the Spanish and his main army was marching towards Tarragona. Equally, other French troops were now also responding and reinforcements had been sent to Barcelona. General Mathieu, the governor of Barcelona, had managed to pull together 6,000 troops. He began moving towards Tarragona. As soon as he realised the strength of the enemy forces he pulled back and waited for reinforcements near Vilaneuva.

Working on false information, Murray now panicked. He believed that the French had massed 20,000 men and were at Reus, ready to strike. Consequently, he ordered his siege equipment to be evacuated and abandoned his attacks on Tarragona. Ultimately he embarked all of his troops, but then suddenly changed his mind and decided to land a large force to tackle the lead elements of Suchet's army.

The vanguard of Suchet's troops was led by General Pannetier. As soon as he saw Murray's men marching towards him he fell back to rejoin Suchet. Murray marched against Mathieu, demanding that Copons march to his aid. Bizarrely Murray now seemed to have changed his mind once again and re-embarked his force without telling Copons. It could have been absolute disaster for the Spaniards, but Suchet, having believed that he had saved Tarragona, now marched back to face Elio and Del Parque, leaving just his vanguard to keep an eye on the British. Mathieu probed towards Reus, reaching there on 17 June. By then Copons had withdrawn, realising that he was on his own.

As a result of his muddled behaviour Murray was not only replaced by Lord Bentinck, but he also faced court martial. Although Murray had been singly unsuccessful in bringing Suchet to battle, apart from the engagement at Castalla, he had in fact achieved his primary objective of preventing Suchet from sending help to King Joseph.

Deployed along the River Xucar was General Harispe with some 14,000 men. He was holding back the Spanish forces of Elio and Del Parque.

WARGAME SCENARIOS

Between them the Spaniards had 33,000 men. At the beginning of June they had begun advancing as ordered by Wellington. But Harispe got in the first strike, falling on Del Parque and killing and wounding 1,500 men. Del Parque fell back to Castalla. He would have to wait until July before Bentinck came to reinforce him.

However the situation for the French in this part of the peninsula was far from rosy. They now knew that King Joseph had been defeated at Vitoria and that Clausel was retreating through Saragossa. It now meant that they could be cut off and would have very little hope of salvation. Suchet was left with no real option. He had to evacuate Valencia and Aragon. Suchet first led his men back towards Tarragona. Continuously he was harassed by Spanish guerrillas under Mina.

Meanwhile, Decaen and Mathieu withdrew on Barcelona. Bentinck pushed towards Tarragona, with the plan to join up with Copons. Meanwhile, Elio and elements of Del Parque's force surrounded Valencia and Tortosa, which still had small French garrisons.

As Suchet continued to retreat Bentinck followed him. By now Bentinck had some 28,000 men at his disposal. The French, however, would not give up without a fight and Suchet planned an immediate counter offensive. Advancing from Molins de Rey, at the head of 12,000 men, Suchet smashed into the allied vanguard under Colonel Adam at Ordal. Meanwhile, Decaen, at the head of 7,000 men, struck out from Martorel and attacked Villafranca.

Suchet hit the allied camp at 1100 hours on 13 September. The allied force was completely unprepared and the fighting was over in a matter of minutes. In the confused fighting over 600 allies were killed or wounded, including Adam.

Suchet then despatched his cavalry to join up with Decaen's men at Villafranca. They had hoped to fall on Bentinck's force there, but he had fallen back to Tarragona.

In July 1813 Soult created the Army of Spain by pulling together the remnants of the four armies that had existed up until that point. He now had 73,000 infantry in some nine divisions, 7,000 cavalry in two divisions, 140 artillery pieces and a sizeable reserve force. Soult performed miracles in reorganising the force and it was ready for operations by 20 July. The fact that Wellington had not crossed the River Bidassoa had bought the French valuable time to reorganise.

Wellington's troops were spread out along the front. His own headquarters was at Lesaca, the Light Division was based at Vera, the 2nd

COLLAPSE AND DEFEAT

Division at Maya, the 6th at San Testeban and the 7th was at Echalar. If the French were to try to thrust through to relieve Pamplona, Wellington had Picton's division at Olague, Cole's division at Viscarret and elements of the 2nd Division at Altobiscar (along with Spanish troops).

Soult had decided to leave Villatte with 20,000 men to cover the lower River Badassoa. He would indeed make a thrust towards Pamplona. D'Erlon, Clausel and Reille were each given three infantry divisions. D'Erlon headed for Maya and the other two generals began to advance from St Jean-Pied-du-Port.

The lead division of Clausel's force ran into the forward positions of Byng's brigade of the 2nd Division at 0600. Clausel found that the allied troops were too well dug in and he tried to work around them. Reille's men had also run into allied outposts, this time the lead elements of the 4th Division. The troops under General Ross held off the French columns as they tried to enter and deploy onto the Linduz Plateau. Meanwhile D'Erlon's troops were closing on the bulk of the 2nd Division around Maya. Initially the advance went well and the allied outposts were overwhelmed. The French then began to form up in expectation of a counterattack.

It was on its way in the shape of the 7th Division. The counterattack by the British troops failed and soon the British were falling back. As more British troops began to arrive the French advance faltered.

So far Soult's probes had been contained, but Stewart's 2nd Division was in a poor state and could easily be overwhelmed. Consequently, the division began to retreat towards Zubiri. Wellington began to reshuffle his forces; he sent the majority of the 6th Division to Irurita, Graham was told to evacuate San Sebastian and the Light Division was ordered to move up from Vera. Wellington then headed for Irurita himself to link up with Hill. D'Erlon seemed unwilling to advance any further south for fear of being outflanked.

Wellington, working on out-of-date information, learned that Cole was retreating and being chased by a large French force. Cole's intention was to link up with Picton at Zubiri. Wellington ordered the 3rd and 4th Divisions to hold Zubiri at all costs. Meanwhile Wellington would send as much help as possible, including Hill, the 6th Division and elements of O'Donnell's force near Pamplona. By the time Wellington was issuing these orders Cole had in fact already linked up with Picton and they had fallen back to Sorauren, where they had joined O'Donnell.

The French, led by Clausel, were following them. Reille's force was somewhat behind, having lost their way in fog. The French finally found the new allied line at 0900 on 27 July.

By the time Wellington reached Ostiz he discovered that Cole and Picton had fallen back to Sorauren. He immediately sent word to Hill and to the 6th Division, appraising them of the new situation.

Had Soult now launched an assault on the allied lines he would undoubtedly have overwhelmed them, but instead he waited and only in the afternoon did he authorise a limited assault. Admittedly the French troops were still moving up and they had not yet fully concentrated. There was also hope that D'Erlon would be able to reach the battlefield in time. As it was, the French were not ready to begin offensive actions until midday on 28 July. By this time the 6th Division, along with Hill's troops, were beginning to arrive. The longer Soult waited the more allies they would have to fight.

Soult ordered Foy to engage the enemy around Huarte. The bulk of the army under Clausel and Reille would attack the centre of Wellington's army. Conroux was given the job of holding off the 6th Division and preventing it from deploying. Conroux's force was woefully inadequate for the job and soon he was falling back towards Sorauren.

The British centre was positioned on top of 1,000ft tall hills. The French had to climb to reach the allied lines. Here and there they made some progress and some British battalions broke. Anson's men faced the massed columns of Maucune. Devastating volleys ripped into the French columns and Maucune's force fell back down the hill in great disorder. This freed up Anson and Byng to support Ross and Campbell against Vandermaesen. The added force was strong enough to make this French division pull back and also the supporting division, led by Tupin.

Meanwhile, nearer Zabaldica, Lamartiniére's division was advancing against Spanish troops and the 40th Foot. The French were initially held off, but as they regrouped for a second attack the Spanish fled, leaving the 40th alone. Despite losing 130 men the 40th beat the French back and the attack ran out of steam.

By this stage the French had lost around 3,000 killed or wounded and the allies slightly less, with 2,650. As yet neither Hill nor D'Erlon had arrived on the battlefield. In fact on the night of 28 July the weather had been so poor that Hill had made a temporary stop at Lizaso. D'Erlon was, of course, close by. He was trying to shadow Hill when he discovered that Soult was already at Sorauren.

By this stage Soult had realised that the bulk of Wellington's army had now concentrated and his opportunity to push through to Pamplona had

COLLAPSE AND DEFEAT

been lost. He now proposed an entirely different objective, realising that if the bulk of Wellington's forces were now around Sorauren there could only be a handful of allied troops covering San Sebastian. He decided to swing north: pushing D'Erlon's corps ahead the French would now make for the Biscay coast. In doing so he hoped to cut straight through Hill's force and then relieve San Sebastian.

Wellington was concerned that Soult would try to work around him and then drive on Pamplona. Hill was ordered to remain at Lizaso. He directed the 7th Division to cover Hill's right flank and for the Light Division to make for Lecumberri (they were presently at Zubieta). The rest of his troops dug in.

By dawn on 31 July Clausel's men had slipped away from the Sorauren battlefield, heading along the east bank of the River Ulzama. The bulk of the rest of the French army was still in plain view, moving across Wellington's front. Wellington decided that this was too good an opportunity to miss and launched a major attack.

The 2nd Division approached Sorauren from the west and Pakenham from the south. The French holding the village came under enormous artillery fire. Conroux ordered a withdrawal, but by now it was virtually too late. His men were being cut to pieces by the artillery and ever-closer musket volleys. Nearly 3,000 French would fall or be taken prisoner.

Gaming the Battle of Sorauren: 28 July 1813

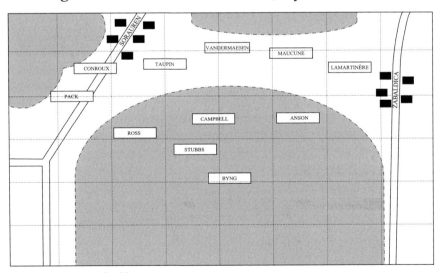

Sorauren Wargame Set Up

WARGAME SCENARIOS

Rather than trying to recreate the sprawling battle of Sorauren, we have focused on the action around Sorauren and Zabaldica in the north. Here, the French attempted to dislodge the Allied formations from the high ground between the two settlements. Further to the south was another line held by Picton, Morillo and O'Donnell in front of Huarte. This scenario therefore looks at the French attacks on the Allied centre.

Allied Army

It is imperative to hold the high ground and to shuffle the supporting brigades to deal with any threat by the French columns. A decisive victory is won if the ridge has not been penetrated by a French division by Game Turn 10. A minor victory is achieved if the high ground is held by Game Turn 10, but one Allied brigade has been broken or destroyed. If two or more brigades have been broken or destroyed and the high ground is held by Game Turn 10, then this is a draw.

Wellington — *Gifted*

1st Brigade: commanded by Brigadier General Pack: — *Able*
– 1 and 2/1st, 1 and 2/16th Portuguese Line, and 4th Caçadores — *Experienced Steady*

2nd Brigade: commanded by Ross: — *Able*
– 1/7th, 20th, 1/23rd, and 1 coy Brunswick Oels — *Veteran Confident*

2nd Brigade: commanded by Brigadier General Archibald Campbell: — *Able*
– 1 and 2/4th, 1 and 2/10th Portuguese Line, and 10th Caçadores — *Experienced Steady*

Portuguese Brigade: commanded by Colonel George Stubbs: — *Able*
– 1 and 2/11th and 1 and 2/23rd Portuguese Line, and 7th Caçadores — *Veteran Confident*

2nd Brigade: commanded by Major General Byng: — *Able*
– 1/3rd 1/57th Foot, 1st Provisional Btn. (2/31st and 2/66th Foot) and 1 coy 5/60th Foot — *Veteran Confident*

COLLAPSE AND DEFEAT

1st Brigade: commanded by Major *Able*
  General William Anson:
– 3/27th, 1/40th, 1/48th, Provisional Btn.   *Veteran Confident*
  (1 and 2/53rd Foot) and 1 coy 5/60th Foot

Give 1 battery of field guns per brigade (Veteran Confident)

Soult's Army

The simple task is to take the high ground and sweep the Allied formations to the south. If you have three French divisions on the high ground by Game Turn 10, then you have won a decisive victory. If you have one French division on the high ground by Game Turn 10, then this is a minor victory.

Soult *Able*
Conroux: *Able*
– 9 battalions *(4 battalions)* *Experienced Steady*

Taupin: *Able*
– 10 battalions *(4 battalions)* *Experienced Steady*

Vandermaesen: *Able*
– 7 battalions *(3 battalions)* *Experienced Steady*

Maucune: *Able*
– 7 battalions *(3 battalions)* *Experienced Steady*

Lamartinière: *Able*
– 10 battalions *(4 battalions)* *Experienced Steady*

Give 1 battery of guns per formation (Experienced Steady)

The French were now pushed back, with Clausel trying to hold off the 7th Division. Reille was desperately trying to escape and Foy was separated and lost his way entirely. He eventually ended up at Iragui. In fact Foy lost all chance of linking up with Soult and under pressure from Picton he retreated all the way back into France. Soult, meanwhile, was with D'Erlon at Lizaso, formulating the attacks against Hill. It was clear from the sound of gunfire that the rest of his army was now engaged against Wellington. There was no time to lose and the urgency of the situation was reinforced when Soult heard that Dalhousie's division was marching to support Hill.

WARGAME SCENARIOS

Soult threw D'Erlon's troops against Hill. The pressure against Hill began to tell and he was forced back, with the loss of around 1,000 men. French casualties in this engagement were around 800. With Lizaso cleared, the route was now open for the French to strike north, as Soult had intended, but by now it was too late. The rest of Soult's army had been mauled at Sorauren and the only option was to use Lizaso as a route back into France. D'Erlon's men held Lizaso whilst the remnants of the French army slipped away.

At 1000 hours Hill tried to dislodge D'Erlon's rearguard. Three assaults failed. Once again the pursuit fell into confusion. Wellington believed that the bulk of the French army was in fact retreating through Maya, but he was wrong and this did not become apparent until 1 August.

By now the lead elements of the retreating French army had crossed the River Bidassoa in the region of Yanzi and Echalar. They were being pursued by the Light Division. Alten's men encountered Darmagnac's division bringing up the rear of the French force near Yanzi. The French were unable to deploy along the track near the river and had to abandon their wounded.

By 2 August Wellington had reinforced Alten with the 4th Division and Dalhousie's troops and had pushed the French back as far as Sarre. This ended the campaign, which had cost the French 13,000 casualties and the allies 7,000. But as Wellington would discover, Soult was not yet finished.

The on-off, off-on siege of San Sebastian recommenced on 26 August. Eight days before sixty-three heavy guns had been brought up to pound the position, but the bombardment could not begin until the ammunition arrived. This was finally delivered on 23 August. The artillery began to pound San Sebastian and by 30 August the bulk of the garrison's guns had been put out of action and there was a 300m gap in the south-eastern wall. There was also a smaller breach further to the north. Additional allied guns had also been installed near the horn work in front of the fortress and as a battery on Santa Clara Island. Wellington again favoured using the low tide in the estuary to launch the assault. Low tide on 31 August was calculated to be at around noon and the attack would begin just an hour before. Elements of the Light and 1st Division would deliver the assault on the main breach, whilst Portuguese troops, under Bradford, would try their luck on the smaller breach.

The garrison commander, Ray, now with a surfeit of artillery crew, handed out as many as three muskets to each of his 2,500 men. He had also directed the burial of mines all along the breach.

Five minutes before the assault was due to go in the allied artillery

COLLAPSE AND DEFEAT

ceased fire. 750 men led by General Leith scrambled towards their start positions. Portuguese troops also began to move into position. It was now immediately apparent that the assault was going to take place. As Leith's men tried to storm the breach the mines were detonated and hundreds of muskets were fired at the dense column. Leith's men managed to get as far as the breach, but no further. Hundreds were killed. The Portuguese had no more luck and they too were beaten off with heavy losses.

Wellington was determined that he would not be beaten and with what remained of the storming parties crouching for cover, the artillery opened up again. Little-by-little the returning fire from the garrison eased and the allied infantry surged forward again.

Leith's men managed to work their way in and then there was a massive explosion, followed by a chain of explosions. There had been an accidental detonations of bombs and cartridges. The 2nd Brigade of the 5th Division tried to storm the smaller breach, but they were held back by bayonets. The British pushed more and more men into the vicious hand to hand combat and little by little the French were pushed back.

The garrison, now realising that they were in danger of being overwhelmed, began to fall back. Wellington threw in Bradford's Portuguese. There was more vicious hand to hand fighting as what remained of the garrison fled towards the Castle of La Mota. It would take until 8 September to force Ray and his remaining 1,300 men to surrender. They had been under fire from sixty heavy guns.

Before San Sebastian fell Soult was organising an attempt to break through to the beleaguered garrison. Soult proposed to hit allied positions between Irun and Vera with seven divisions. D'Erlon would protect their flank with four brigades. In order to carry out this audacious attack, Soult had concentrated his troops between Ainhoue and St Jean-de-Luz.

The offensive got underway on 31 August, with the French being able to establish bridgeheads across the Bidassoa before they were spotted. 16,000 men under Freire, the Spanish Army of Galicia, awaited them at San Marcial. The advancing lead brigades of Reille's corps ran into determined opposition, forcing the French back. The French massed for another attack at midday and once again were beaten off. The offensive was grinding to a halt and they had not yet even run into Wellington.

Clausel, at the head of four divisions, was trying to turn Freire's flank. He had pushed allied units away from Vera, but had now run into Anglo-Portuguese troops that seemed to be increasing in number by the hour. D'Erlon, who had worked around the flank, was now at Urdax and he too was under severe pressure.

Rather than lose his army in this piecemeal fashion, Soult ordered a withdrawal. Clausel's men fell back on the River Bidassoa, but the constant rain that day had swollen the river and the fords were now unusable. The only way across the river was at the small bridge at Vera. The salvation of 10,000 Frenchmen relied on this rickety structure. At the eastern end of the bridge there were some fortified houses, held by a company of the 95th Rifles. It would cost the French 200 killed and wounded to force the riflemen out. The French filed across the bridge. The offensive had been an utter disaster; 4,000 men had been lost and the allies had lost around 2,500, most of them from Freire's command.

Soult could confidently expect that Wellington would now launch an offensive against him, with the intention of penetrating into southern France. All Soult could hope for was that time would be on his side and that he would have sufficient opportunity to prepare. The French set about building fortified positions along the River Bidassoa. Soult considered that the most likely line of approach would be between Vera and Ainhoue. He despatched Foy to cover St Jean-Pied-du-Port, which would cover the passes into the Pyrenees. Reille was given the task of holding the lower River Bidassoa, Clausel and D'Erlon, with six divisions, would hold his central position. Soult's line stretched for twenty-three miles. He had tried to cover all eventualities, but in reality he was not strong in any position at all and if the allies achieved a breakthrough there was little chance that many of his men would get out alive.

Wellington discovered that at low tide the lower Bidassoa could be crossed, as there were a number of fords. The best option appeared to be at Béhobie. At this point the estuary was a mile and a half wide and only protected by Maucune's division. Against it Wellington mustered 24,000 infantry. During the night of 6 October Wellington's troops moved up to the river. By dawn the following day the French could see enemy troops beginning to cross the mudflats. Maucune tried to form his troops up, but he was completely outnumbered and after holding for just a short while his men began to fall back. More troops crossed closer to Béhobie. The French began to fall back towards Croix de Boquets.

At Vera, Alten's Light Division, supported by Spanish troops under Giron, launched a frontal assault. The allies faced 4,700 French under Conroux and Taupin. The allies could muster 6,500. It was actually a very short-lived engagement and the French began to withdraw.

Soult, meanwhile, was actually at Ainhoue with D'Erlon. By the time Soult arrived the situation was out of control. Reille's men had been scattered and Wellington's allied force was across the river in considerable

COLLAPSE AND DEFEAT

numbers. Soult had no option but to pull back towards the River Nivell, having lost some 1,700 men. Wellington's losses amounted to some 1,600.

Having dislodged Soult from his positions Wellington did not push on into France. There were other matters that needed to be resolved. The first was the enormous battles taking place in central Europe. The Austrians had just been beaten at the battle of Dresden and closer to home Wellington wanted to take Pamplona.

Pamplona was held by around 3,000 men under the command of General Cassan. It had been blockaded since 25 June. There had been hope for the garrison in late-July when Soult had seemed to be on the verge of breaking through to them, but that hope had disappeared. Cassan resolved to hold for as long as he possibly could, until the food ran out. At that stage he would destroy what he could of the fortifications to deny them to the allies and then surrender. He was informed that if any damage was done to the fortifications Wellington would order his execution, along with those of his officers and one in ten of his men. Cassan finally gave in and surrendered on 31 October.

With the fall of Pamplona, Wellington was now free to consider his options in another offensive against Soult. The French had taken up positions along a twenty-mile front, running from St Jean-de-Luz to Ainhoue. Reille's men held the lower Nivelle River, Clausel, at the head of three divisions, held the central position, and D'Erlon's pair of divisions covered Ainhoue. Foy's men, with the onset of winter, had abandoned the passes and were now covering D'Erlon's left flank.

By the beginning of November Wellington had massed 82,000 infantry and was ready to launch them against Soult's 62,000 defenders. Soult's men were not of the same calibre as those that had fought in innumerable engagements across the peninsula. The huge losses that the veteran divisions had suffered over the years had been replaced with raw conscripts.

Wellington considered his options and decided on launching diversionary attacks on Soult's flanks and deploying the bulk of his force against Soult's centre. General Hope and General Hill would launch the diversionary attacks. Hill was given 22,000 men to demonstrate in front of D'Erlon and Foy. Hope was allocated 25,000 and he would pin Reille. Beresford was given the task of leading the 33,000 men for the central assault.

Hope moved up toward the lower Nivelle on 10 November, drawing Reille's command to him as Wellington had hoped. Hill launched an attack on D'Erlon. Foy, trying to draw the enemy away, attempted to force his way towards Maya, but found his route blocked by Spanish troops. Beresford's men made excellent progress against Clausel's divisions. Little

WARGAME SCENARIOS

by little the French were giving way. Clausel's battalions had taken the bulk of the casualties and in all Soult had lost 4,300 men against the allied losses of 3,400. The only option open to Soult was to fall back once again, this time to the River Nive and his supply base at Bayonne.

Once again Wellington did not press the pursuit. He had heard that Napoleon had just been defeated at Leipzig. There was a chance that France might surrender and there was no way of telling how the French population would react to enemy forces operating on their home soil. As it transpired, Napoleon chose not to abdicate. An invasion of France was, therefore, essential and in order to ensure that Britain held a powerful place at the negotiating table, Wellington was urged to thrust into France at the earliest opportunity. But Wellington was reluctant to take his Spanish allies with him for fear that they would seek retribution against the French population for the atrocities and slaughter that they had suffered at French hands for all these years.

With the Spanish sent south, Wellington's force now barely outnumbered Soult's command. Soult could muster some 63,000 effectives, but even more of them were raw conscripts than before. Wellington's 64,000 men would be organised into three columns for the new campaign, which he launched on 9 December.

Hope, commanding four divisions, was to advance from St Jean-de-Luz along the coast road towards Bayonne. Beresford, commanding the 3rd and 6th Divisions, would march towards Ustaritz and then construct pontoon bridges over the River Nive before moving on Bayonne from the south. Beresford's column would be supported by the 7th and 4th Divisions. Hill, with a pair of cavalry brigades and three infantry divisions, would make for Cambo. He too would attempt to cross the River Nive and then move on Bayonne. The Light Division would be scattered across the front in an attempt to ensure that lines of communication and supply were maintained.

Hope's troops marched out at dawn and passed through Barrouillet and then encountered French units at Anglet. After a brief fight the French withdrew towards Bayonne. Beresford had been able to approach the River Nive near Ustaritz without opposition and had put a pontoon bridge across the river. By dark on 9 December the bulk of the 3rd and 6th Divisions were across the river and the 4th and 7th Divisions were moving up. Hill had also reached Cambo without a great deal of opposition. He too had crossed the river but had then run into D'Erlon's divisions. Soult, however, had a surprise for Wellington. D'Erlon's men had slipped away during the night and Soult had massed his troops to attack Hope. The French troops were in position by dawn on 10 December.

COLLAPSE AND DEFEAT

Suddenly Clausel's three divisions fell on the forward positions of the Light Division encamped to the north of Arcangues. Hope meanwhile had also come under attack, from Reille, at the head of a pair of infantry divisions and a Dragoon brigade. Hope's troops were stretched out all the way back to the River Nivelle. The lead units of Reille's formations overwhelmed the outer defences of the 5th Division. Campbell's brigade, however, provided stiffer opposition, holding the French back whilst Hope desperately organised a defence. French Dragoons overwhelmed the 1st Portuguese Line Infantry and Campbell's men withdrew towards Barrouillet. Here they were reinforced by Bradford's Portuguese and a brigade led by Robinson from the 5th Division.

The French, however, were also moving up reinforcements. Part of Foy's division, commanded by Villatte, combined with Leval's men to continue the attack. Greville's brigade of the 5th Division now appeared and attacked Foy, but they made little headway and they too were pushed back.

Hope's force was in grave danger of being surrounded, but the lead elements of the 1st Division now appeared, in the guise of Lord Aylmer's brigade. They engaged the French and gradually pushed them back until they finally retired.

This surprise engagement had cost Wellington 1,500 men and the French approximately 1,000. It had been a brave decision by Soult, but now other problems arose. Three of Soult's German battalions deserted to Wellington once they heard about the Leipzig defeat. In order to prevent further desertions the rest of his German troops were disarmed.

Despite these unwelcome losses, Soult attacked again on the afternoon of 11 December. Barrouillet was once again the target. Reille led the attack, supported by one of Clausel's divisions. Once again Hope was caught unawares. Wellington had ordered Beresford to re-cross the Nive and come to Hope's assistance. Beresford's men moved rapidly through the countryside, toward Barrouillet. Soult now realised that he had lost the race to destroy Hope's command.

Soult determined to try his luck against Hill now that the bulk of Wellington's forces were on the west bank of the Nive. Soult left three divisions to hold Bayonne and concentrated the rest of his troops to attack Hill. Hill had deployed his 14,000 men and twelve guns in a defensive position, stretching from the River Adour through St Pierre to the River Nive. Wellington had warned him of the chance that Soult would concentrate against him.

The French started massing shortly after dawn on 13 December. Hill had deployed his men well; they were on three heights, but each of the heights was separated by deep ravines. The tightness of the terrain also favoured Hill. Soult had managed to scrape together 40,000 infantry, but there was no way that he could deploy them all against Hill. All he could hope was that by mounting enormous pressure on one of Hill's positions that he could break through.

The first attack came in at 0800. Abbé's division, with twenty-two artillery pieces, struck against Hill's central position. Other French units probed against Hill's left. As the French infantry closed in the centre they came under heavy fire, since Hill had deployed ten of his guns in the centre. Soult threw elements of Darmagnac's division and Foy's men at Hill's right. They managed to push back Byng's units and for a moment it looked as if they would break through.

Hill was throwing all of his reserves into the centre and Soult was also reinforcing the attack, applying more and more pressure. Hill could see that at any minute his command would break, so he rallied as many men around him as possible and personally led a charge against the French centre. The French began to give way and as they did so the French attack on the allied left petered-out.

Moments later, at the head of the 3rd and 6th Divisions, Wellington appeared. The French immediately withdrew to Bayonne. The seven-hour struggle for St Pierre had been won. The French had lost around 2,400 men and Hill's command some 1,800. This would effectively end operations for the year.

Whilst political manoeuvring took place between France and the allied coalition, Napoleon attempted to cut the ground out from under Wellington by negotiating peace directly with the Spanish. Indeed Ferdinand signed a treaty, which precipitated the withdrawal of French troops, notably the bulk of Suchet's forces.

Background to the Battle of Orthez
By the middle of February 1814 Soult, despite the loss of troops to the eastern front, the loss of his German units, and of his allied Spanish, could still muster 60,000 men and seventy-seven artillery pieces. Against him were ranged 70,000 men under Wellington.

In order to protect southern France Soult had placed the bulk of his forces along the River Bidouse. He believed that Wellington intended to try to cross the River Adour and push into France.

Wellington launched his troops against Soult's positions along the River Bidouse and managed to cross at St Palais. Promptly Soult pulled back to the River Saison. The pressure was unrelenting and on 17 February

COLLAPSE AND DEFEAT

Anglo-Portuguese troops under Hill began crossing the River Saison at Arriverayte. Once again Soult pulled back, taking up positions on the east bank of the River Gave D'Oloron. This was precisely what Wellington had hoped for. He had not intended that his main thrust would be across the rivers; instead he proposed to cross the River Ardour to the west of Bayonne, in order to seize the city.

On 23 February the lead elements of General Hope's 31,000 men began crossing the River Ardour using rafts. On 24 February an allied naval force arrived and began to ferry more and more of Hope's troops across the river. At the same time a massive pontoon bridge was being constructed. The French had believed that this was simply a diversionary assault and had paid little attention to it and had barely tried to prevent it. The pontoon bridge was completed by the evening of 26 February and by the end of the day Hope had pushed 15,000 men across the river. His lead elements were already in Bayonne's suburbs.

Throughout 27 February Anglo-Portuguese infantry fought for possession of the outskirts of Bayonne. Slowly but surely the French withdrew until they were surrounded and the siege for Bayonne could now begin.

Meanwhile, to the east, a new allied offensive had opened on 24 February. French positions between Sauveterre and Navarrenx were under pressure from Picton and Beresford. Hill had managed to cross the River Gave d'Oloron at Viellanave. By the end of the day some 20,000 Anglo-Portuguese troops had crossed the river. Once again Soult was forced to withdraw, this time heading for Orthez.

Wellington despatched Hill towards Orthez, whilst he instructed Beresford to swing around through Lahonton to fall on Soult's right flank. Soult, however, was determined not to be dislodged once again. He took up positions on a ridge close to Orthez. He still had with him a considerable force, not having lost too many men over the past fortnight. He could deploy 33,000 infantry, 3,000 cavalry and fifty-four artillery pieces. Against him Wellington could deploy 40,000 infantry, 3,000 cavalry and forty-four guns.

Wellington came up with a complex battle plan. It would see Hill attacking Orthez and then trying to work his way around the French left. Beresford would be thrown at Soult's right; Picton would then move up in front of Orthez and take up Hill's positions. With both of Soult's flanks in peril Picton would force his way forward and as Soult fell back Beresford and Hill would cut him off.

The attack got underway at 0830 on 27 February. The first attack came in from Cole's 4th Division, assaulting French positions on high ground at

WARGAME SCENARIOS

St Boes. The French, commanded by Taupin, held off the attack, pushing back two serious attempts. Even though a regiment from the Light Division was sent to help Cole his men fell back.

The 3rd and the 6th Divisions were making little headway in the centre. They had gained the lower slopes defended by the French, but by 1045 French troops under D'Erlon had made their position untenable.

Wellington threw Walker's 7th Division and elements of the Light Division in against St Boes to help Cole. Picton, in the centre, also pushed his troops forward once again. The most exposed French division in the centre was Foy's and once Foy himself was wounded his men began to fall back. To Foy's left was Harispe's command. Harispe was covering Orthez and preventing Hill from becoming involved in the main engagement. As Foy fell back, in order to prevent himself from being cut off and slaughtered Harispe also fell back. This gave Hill the opportunity to push his 12,000 men across the Gave De Pau River and attack the French left flank.

Foy's retreat had turned the battle. Picton could now press Darmagnac's division and once they began to withdraw he could focus on Rouget's men. Slowly but surely Taupin, still holding out at St Boes, became isolated. The British 52nd Foot moved into the gap. This settled the issue. Taupin had no choice but to fall back or be surrounded.

Gaming the Battle of Orthez: 27 February 1814

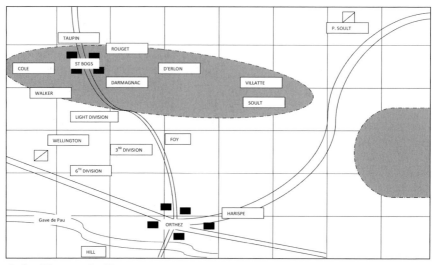

Orthez Wargame Set Up

COLLAPSE AND DEFEAT

Wellington's army mustered some 44,402 men and fifty-four guns against a French army of around 37,000 with forty-eight guns. At the beginning of the battle, Beresford's divisions attacked Taupin's and Paris's men in St-Boes. They managed to capture the church but were unable to force their way into the village. The French right-wing commander, Reille, launched a counterattack, driving the British out. Wellington threw the Light Division into the fight; the division drove a wedge between Reille's right wing and D'Erlon's divisions. Hill's men then crossed the river and enveloped the French left. Picton's force stormed over the ridge; at that point Soult was forced to withdraw.

Wellington's Forces
The primary objective is to seize the ridge and push the French out of St Boes. To win a decisive victory, no unbroken French unit must be occupying the ridge by the end of Game Turn 12. To win a minor victory, this has to be achieved by Game Turn 15.

C-in-C: Wellington — *Gifted*
2nd Division – Stewart — *Able*

Byng's Brigade: — *Able*
– 3 battalions — *Veteran Confident*

Barnes's Brigade: — *Able*
– 3 battalions — *Veteran Confident*

O'Callaghan's Brigade: — *Able*
– 3 battalions — Veteran Confident

Harding's Portuguese Brigade: — *Able*
– 5 battalions — Experienced Steady

3rd Division – Picton — *Able*

Keane's Brigade: — *Able*
– 4 battalions — *Veteran Confident*

Power's Brigade: — *Able*
– 5 battalions — Veteran Confident

WARGAME SCENARIOS

4th Division – Cole *Able*

Anson's Brigade: *Able*
– 4 battalions Veteran Confident

Ross' Brigade: Able
– 3 battalions Veteran Confident

Vasconcello's Portuguese Brigade: Able
– 5 battalions Experienced Steady

6th Division – Clinton *Able*

Pack's Brigade: *Able*
– 3 battalions Veteran Confident

Lambert's Brigade: Able
– 4 battalions Veteran Confident

Douglas's Brigade: Able
– 5 battalions Veteran Confident

7th Division – Walker *Able*
Inglis' Brigade: *Able*
– 4 battalions Veteran Confident

Gardiner's Brigade: Able
– 3 battalions Veteran Confident

Doyle's Brigade: Able
– 5 battalions Veteran Confident

Light Division – Alten *Able*

British – 3 battalions Veteran Confident

Portuguese – 9 battalions Experienced Steady

Portuguese Division – Le Cor *Able*

COLLAPSE AND DEFEAT

Da Costa's Brigade: Able
– 5 battalions   Experienced Steady

Buchan's Brigade: Able
– 4 battalions   Experienced Steady

Fane's Light Cavalry Brigade: *Able*
– 2 regiments   *Experienced Confident*

Vivian's Light Cavalry Brigade: *Able*
– 2 regiments   *Experienced Confident*

Somerset's Light Cavalry Brigade: Able
– 3 regiments   Experienced Confident

Artillery:
– 54 guns (5 guns)   *Experienced Confident*

Soult's Army
It is fairly unlikely that the army will be able to withstand a wholehearted assault on ridge, so holding the ridge for as long as possible without endangering the army is the priority. If you have an intact division operating on the ridge by Game Turn 12 then this is a decisive victory, as is having broken one Allied division by this time. You may only give retirement orders to your units after Game Turn 12. If you manage to extricate all of your divisions from the table (routing units do not count), then you will win a minor victory.

C-in-C: Soult   *Able*
D'Erlon's sector   *Able*

Foy's Division: *Able*
– 9 battalions (4 battalions)   *Experienced Confident*

Darmagnac's Division: *Able*
– 10 battalions (5 battalions)   *Experienced Confident*

Reille's sector   *Able*

Rouget's Division: *Able*
– 9 battalions (4 battalions)   *Experienced Confident*

WARGAME SCENARIOS

Taupin's Division: *Able*
– 9 battalions *(4 battalions)* *Experienced Confident*

Clausel's sector *Able*

Villatte's Division: *Able*
– 6 battalions *(3 battalions)* *Experienced Confident*

Harispe's Division: *Able*
– 13 battalions *(6 battalions)* *Experienced Confident*

P Soult's Cavalry Division: *Able*
– 6 regiments *(2 regiments)* *Experienced Confident*

Artillery: – 48 guns *(5 guns)* *Experienced Confident*

The French began to withdraw towards the River Luy de Bearn and the town of Sault de Navailles. Soult had once again been dislodged. Wellington had suffered 2,200 casualties and the French some 4,000.

Soult did not end his retreat. He made for Aire on the River Adour and on 2 March his rearguard, commanded by Harispe, held off Hill's columns to allow the rest of Soult's army to withdraw.

This now left Bordeaux fatally exposed. Beresford, at the head of a sizeable contingent, began his march into the city on 7 March. They were not opposed and they marched in on 12 March.

Background to the Battle of Tarbes

There were still, of course, French troops in the peninsula, concentrated now in upper Catalonia. By this stage Suchet had 17,000 men, barely enough to hold Barcelona, the fortress of Llobregat and Figueras. Bizarrely, it was to be treason that would seal the fate of most of Suchet's men. One of his own staff officers, Van Halen, forged Suchet's signature informing the garrisons at Tortosa, Lerida, Mequinenza and Monzon to surrender. Some 1,900 men were lost to Suchet; all except the garrison at Tortosa, who suspected that something was amiss.

With the exception of a small garrison left at Barcelona, Suchet's men began their slow and dangerous retreat towards the Pyrenees. Apart from a handful of isolated garrisons the French occupation of the peninsula was now over.

Wellington brought up 10,000 Spanish troops and assembled a force of some 50,000 men in the Aire region, ready for a new offensive on 18 March.

COLLAPSE AND DEFEAT

Ahead of his force of infantry and artillery were 8,000 cavalry, shielding and screening the force from prying enemy eyes. Against him Soult could now only muster 35,000 men, the vast majority of which had little or no battle experience and understandably he was reluctant to risk them.

Soult began to withdraw towards Tarbes. On the evening of 20 March his rearguard force fought an action against the pursuing allied 6th and Light Divisions. Having achieved this Soult continued his march towards Toulouse. Wellington led the main force through Trie whilst Hill, at the head of 13,000 men, pushed through St Gaudens. The poor roads allowed Soult to slip away and he managed to get to Toulouse on 24 March.

Gaming the Battle of Tarbes: 20 March 1814

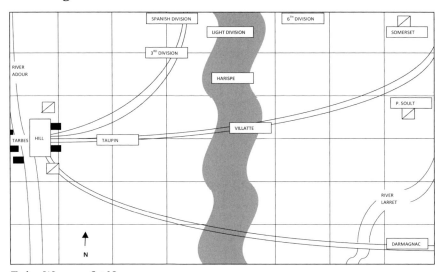

Tarbes Wargame Set Up

This is an action fought by the lead elements of Wellington's Army as they pursued Soult. This engagement involves the French rearguard as their positions on the River Adour were turned. This is a delaying action and, as such, the French should not expose themselves to a full battle: simply they need to hold long enough for the rest of the army to slip away, but not at the expense of being overwhelmed.

Allied Army
With Hill pinning Taupin at Tarbes, the Allies have a chance of

WARGAME SCENARIOS

overwhelming the French rearguard and rolling them up. To win a decisive victory, there should be no unbroken French units on the ridge by Game Turn 12. If an Allied unit has managed to cross the River Larret by Game Turn 12 then this is also a decisive victory. A minor victory is won if both of the roads running west-to-east are held by the Allies and there are still some unbroken French units that have not passed over the River Larret.

Hill's Column: commanded by Lieutenant General Sir Rowland Hill	Able
1st Brigade: commanded by Major General Victor von Alten:	Able
– 14th Light Dragoons and 1st Hussars, King's German Legion	Experienced Confident
2nd Brigade: commanded by Lieutenant General Fane:	Able
– 3rd Dragoon Guards and 1st Royal Dragoons	Experienced Confident
2nd Division: commanded by Lieutenant General William Stewart	Able
1st Brigade: commanded by Colonel Cadogan:	Able
– 1/50th, 1/71st and 1/91st Foot, 1 coy 5/60th Foot	Veteran Confident
2nd Brigade: commanded by Major General Byng:	Able
– 1/3rd, 1/57th Foot, 1st Provisional Btn. (2/31st and 2/66th Foot) and 1 coy 5/60th Foot	Veteran Confident
3rd Brigade: commanded by Colonel O'Callaghan:	Able
– 1/28th, 2/34th, 1/39th Foot and 1 coy 5/60th Foot	Veteran Confident
Portuguese Brigade: commanded by Brigadier General Ashworth:	Able

COLLAPSE AND DEFEAT

– 1 and 2/6th, 1 and 2/18th Portuguese Line, and 6th Caçadores	Experienced Steady
Portuguese Division: commanded by Major General Silveira, Conde de Amaranthe	Able
1st Brigade: commanded by Brigadier General de Costa:	Able
– 1 and 2/2nd, 1 and 2/14th Portuguese Line	Experienced Steady
2nd Brigade: commanded by Brigadier General Archibald Campbell:	Able
– 1 and 2/4th, 1 and 2/10th Portuguese Line, and 10th Caçadores	Experienced Steady
Spanish Division: commanded by Major General Morillo:	Able
– Regimiento de Leon, Regimiento de Union, Regimiento del Legion	Novice Steady
Artillery: commanded by Major Carncross:	Able
– Beane's Troop Royal Horse Artillery, Maxwell's Battery Royal Artillery and 2 Portuguese batteries under Major Tulloh	Veteran Confident
3rd Division: commanded by Lieutenant General Sir Thomas Picton	Able
1st Brigade: commanded by Major General Thomas Brisbane:	Able
– 1/45th, 74th, 1/88th and 3 coys 5/60th Foot	Veteran Confident
2nd Brigade: commanded by Major General Colville:	Able
– 1/5th, 2/83rd, 2/87th and 94th Foot	Veteran Confident
Portuguese Brigade: commanded by Major General Manley Power:	Able

WARGAME SCENARIOS

– 1 and 2/9th, 1 and 2/21st Portuguese Line, and 11th Caçadores	Experienced Steady
Light Division: commanded by Lieutenant General Charles, Baron von Alten	*Able*
1st Brigade: commanded by Major General Kempt:	**Able**
– 1/43rd Foot, 1/95th Rifles (8 coys), 3/95th Rifles (5 coys), and 3rd Caçadores	Veteran Confident
2nd Brigade: commanded by Major General John Ormesby Vandeleur:	**Able**
– 1/52nd Foot, 2/95th Rifles (6 coys), and 1st Caçadores	Veteran Confident
Sixth Division – Clinton	*Able*
Pack's Brigade:	**Able**
– 3 battalions	Veteran Confident
Lambert's Brigade:	**Able**
– 4 battalions	Veteran Confident
Douglas's Brigade:	**Able**
– 5 battalions	Veteran Confident
Somerset's Light Cavalry Brigade:	*Able*
– 3 regiments	*Experienced Confident*

Soult's Rearguard

The primary objective is to buy time for the rest of the army to slip away. This is a dangerous position that has already been compromised by the arrival of the Allied 6th Division and the Light Division. To win a decisive victory, all of your divisions must safely pass across the River Larret or they may exit on the north road running west-to-east. You may not order a general retirement until Game Turn 8. You will need to extricate Taupin, Harispe and Villatte in order to win a decisive victory. If you manage to extricate two infantry divisions (not Darmagnac) then this counts as a minor victory.

COLLAPSE AND DEFEAT

No overall commander
Division Villatte — Able
Brigade Saint-Pôl: — Able
– 21st Léger (1 btn), 86th Line (1 btn), 96th Line (1 btn), 100th Line (1 btn) — Experienced Steady

Brigade Lamorandière: — Able
– 28th Léger (1 btn), 103rd Line (1 btn), 119th Line (2 btns) — Experienced Steady

Division Harispe — Able
Brigade Dauture: — Able
– 9th Léger (2 btns), 34th Line (2 btns), 45th Line (1 btn) — Experienced Steady

Brigade Baurot: — Able
– 25th Léger (2 btns), 115th Line (1 btn), 116th Line (1 btn), 117th Line (1 btn) — Experienced Steady

From the Army of the Centre: Comte Drouet D'Erlon
Division Darmagnac — Able
Brigade Gruardet: — Able
– 31st Léger (2 btns), 51st Line (1 btn), 75th Line (1btn) — Experienced Steady

Brigade Menne: — Able
– 118th Line (3 btns), 120th Line (3 btns) — Experienced Steady

From Comte Reille's Army
Division Taupin — Able
Brigade Rey: — Able
– 12th Léger (2 btns), 32nd Line (2 btns, 43rd Line (2 btns) — Experienced Steady

Brigade Racant: — Able
– 47th Line (2 btns), 55th Line (2 btns), 58th Line (2 btns) — Experienced Steady

Cavalry: Général Baron Pierre Soult. Division Soult — Able

WARGAME SCENARIOS

Brigade Berton:
– 2nd Hussars (2 squadrons), 13th Chasseurs (3 squadrons), 21st Chasseurs (3 squadrons)

Able
Experienced Steady

Brigade Vial:
– 5th Chasseurs (2 squadrons), 10th Chasseurs (3 squadrons), 15th Chasseurs (3 squadrons), 22nd Chasseurs (3 squadrons)

Able
Experienced Steady

Wellington slowly moved up and constructed a pontoon bridge over the River Garonne. He began to cross on 3 April. Wellington managed to push 19,000 men across the river before the bridge was swept away. The French missed a golden opportunity to destroy the isolated troops. For four days the men had to fend for themselves until Wellington had taken the bridge at Croix d'Aurade and then moved the rest of his troops across the river. Wellington could now assault Toulouse from three directions.

The city was well fortified and had 42,000 men in its garrison. Against them were arrayed Wellington's force of 49,000 and fifty artillery pieces. Wellington selected the eastern wall as the main point of assault. This attack would be left to Beresford at the head of the 4th and 6th Anglo-Portuguese Divisions and the Spanish Division. They would have to storm the Monte Rave ridge, which had two main redoubts protecting its flanks. Once this had been captured the city would lie well within range and at the mercy of the allied artillery.

Hill, meanwhile, would assault the suburb of St Cyprien, to the west of the river. Attacks would also be made against the northern side of the city, by the 3rd and the Light Divisions.

Wellington's assault on the city began at 0500 on 10 April. Hill kept the 3,700 men of Maranisn's division busy in San Cyprien. Picton threw his men against Daricau's command, protecting the northern side of the city. Picton could not get across the Royal Canal and fighting concentrated around the Petit Granague Farm and the bridgehead at Ponts Jumeaux.

The approach to Monte Rave was not easy for Beresford. It was covered by the marshland around the River Ers. This meant that his troops had to march south for two miles before they could turn to face the ridge.

General Freire's Spanish troops had been given the unenviable task of storming the northern edge of the ridge, including the Great Redoubt. They got into position and patiently waited whilst the 4th and the 6th Anglo-Portuguese divisions continued to march south to their start line. In

COLLAPSE AND DEFEAT

the confusion and the gunfire they thought they had been given the signal to begin their assault. They charged, pushing back the French troops until they came under close-range fire from the Great Redoubt. They were pinned down and the French took full advantage, inflicting massive casualties on them. The bulk of the Spanish routed, leaving just one regiment holding on, which they continued to do until they were ordered to withdraw.

Finally Beresford got his men into position. The redoubt at the far southern end of the ridge, the Sypière, was the target of Anson and Lambert. Defending it was Taupin's division. Taupin immediately counterattacked, but once again the columns were no match for the steady lines of British Redcoats. The French infantry was beaten back and began rapidly reforming on the reverse slope of the ridge.

It took two hours for Beresford to get his artillery into position in the redoubt that he had just captured. But he now began to open up on Harispe's division. Freire had rallied his Spanish troops and his two divisions made another attempt to storm the Great Redoubt. They were beaten back by sheer weight of fire, losing 1,000 men and playing no further part in the engagement.

Beresford was pushing troops along the ridge towards the Great Redoubt. Harispe was under enormous pressure, but he launched counter assaults. By now Beresford's men had suffered 1,600 casualties and Harispe 1,000. Harispe now fell back towards the Great Redoubt.

The French held on until the guns could be rescued and then they withdrew across the Royal Canal. By 1800 the major engagement had ended. French casualties had amounted to 3,200 and Wellington had lost 4,600 killed or wounded. Wellington's men would not be ready for more action for some time.

Soult, unaware of the casualties he had caused, chose to slip away from Toulouse during the night of 11 April. By the following evening allied officers were dining with civic dignitaries in the city. It was only then that it became clear that Paris had actually fallen on 31 March and that Napoleon had abdicated.

This was not however the final drops of blood spilled in the Peninsular War. Hope was still besieging Bayonne and in fact on 14 April the French Commander Thouvenot launched a sudden counterattack, with 6,000 infantry against the suburb of St Etienne. The besieging force was caught completely unawares and amongst the 5th Division's casualties were General Hay and 800 others. The French even managed to capture a wounded General Hope. Bayonne continued to defy the allies and it was not until Soult gave Thouvenot a direct order to surrender that they complied on 26 April.

The Peninsular War was now officially over. Napoleon was on his way to Elba. In many respects the peninsula had become Napoleon's Vietnam. He had never managed to win the hearts and minds of the Spanish people. As importantly, he had given the allies the opportunity to bleed him dry in a theatre that he never gave his full attention to, yet which proved to be so important. At a time when he could have used 200,000 veteran troops in central Europe they were tied down in the peninsula. Whilst the French had lost the war a far deeper and more painful legacy was to remain on the peninsula; both Spain and Portugal's economies had been ruined, hundreds of thousands of civilians had either been killed or had starved to death and for years, in Spain in particular, there would be social unrest and political upheaval.

Chapter 6

Armies of the Peninsular War

In this section we will look at the nature of the four key protagonists in the Peninsular War, attempt to identify their key characteristics and look at how typical formations can be created in order to wargame the maximum number of different campaigns.

The Spanish army
The Spanish present particular problems from the outset. Of course there was a regular Spanish army of dubious value. However, even though the Spanish regular forces were not as well trained or competent as the British and Portuguese that fought alongside them, without doubt the Allies would have lost the war in the Peninsula without the Spanish regulars. In innumerable cases both the Spanish commanders and their soldiers performed well below what could reasonably be expected of a national force. However on other occasions, such as Alcaniz, Baylen, San Marcial and Tamames, Spanish forces proved themselves perfectly capable of dealing with the French on their own. Towards the latter part of the Peninsular War Spanish troops, under General Freire, were especially good and were involved in the thick of the fighting in and around Toulouse.

When the Peninsular War broke out there were around 100,000 Spanish regulars. Despite their huge losses, poor supply situation and high desertion rate, they could still field 160,000 men in 1812. This needs to be put into context, as 160,000 men represented a force far larger than the British and Portuguese troops combined.

The Spanish were not ideal for pitched battles. They lacked the training and they lacked the equipment to effectively operate in the field. The Spanish troops, however, were invaluable in sieges and in blockades, where they were perfectly happy to dig in and hold the line, applying pressure here and there as necessary, allowing British and Portuguese troops to take more offensive action. Undoubtedly it was the availability of Spanish troops that allowed the British and Portuguese to concentrate for the battle of Salamanca.

Regardless of the fact that the Spanish, man-for-man and even regiment-for-regiment, were no match for the French, the sheer size of their forces meant that the French could not ignore them. The French went to considerable trouble in trying to corner Spanish forces and defeat them, but often they slipped away, which meant that the French, in fear of their lines of supply and communication being cut, would have to detach valuable troops. A prime example of this is Massena's invasion of Portugal in 1810. On paper the French Imperial forces in the Peninsula amounted to a massive 325,000 men. In practice, however, in order to ensure that Spanish guerrillas and regulars were not given free reign to rampage across the Peninsula, barely a quarter of the available French forces could be deployed for the invasion.

The regular Spanish army itself in 1808 had managed to avoid or ignore the majority of military innovations that had taken place. In effect, it was an outdated 'royal army'. There were just two regiments of foot guards and two cavalry regiments, each with five squadrons, that comprised the household troops. On paper there were thirty-five, three-battalion line-infantry regiments. There were also foreign regiments in service; six Swiss, three Irish and a Neapolitan. On average line infantry battalions could muster around 700 men.

In 1808 there were just twelve light-infantry battalions. The battalions would average around 1200 men each. The situation for the cavalry was even worse. In May 1808 the cavalry force amounted to around 15,000 men but there were only 9,000 mounts available. A lack of decent mounts was to be a major problem throughout the war. There were twenty-four cavalry regiments, each with around five squadrons. Twelve of these regiments were heavy, six were Hussars and the balance were light Dragoons. Each of the regiments was supposed to have 800 men but this figure was largely reliant on the availability of horses.

The artillery and the engineer situation was no better. The Spanish could field four field artillery regiments, each with ten batteries. A battery would normally have around 120 men. Only six of the forty batteries were horse artillery. There were additional artillery units in fortresses: in fact twenty-one batteries with 2,000 gunners supported by just 1,000 engineers and sappers.

Supplementing the Spanish regular army were the militia units. Each of the forty-three battalions had some 600 men. In addition to this there were four, two-battalion provincial grenadier regiments. Each of these regiments had 1,600 men.

No one who has read even the broadest outline of the Peninsular War or glanced at a Sharpe book or dramatisation will fail to have noticed that an integral part of the resistance force that the Spanish put up against the French were in fact gangs of guerrillas. The size of these units varied enormously, from just a handful of men to several thousand. The French found them slippery, resourceful, tough fighters and merciless with stragglers. The guerrillas would use hit-and-run tactics. They would strike at isolated detachments, supply wagons, messengers, suspected collaborators and other targets of opportunity. They did not tend to involve themselves in stand up battles with French regulars. They would prefer to deal a number of tiny blows against the French than risk all in a single action. They were supplied and assisted by the British and they provided in return invaluable information about French movement and would pass on intercepted messages. In some cases virtually no communication between French armies got through. A prime example was at the Battle of Salamanca. Marmont fought the battle prematurely as he was unaware of the fact that King Joseph was marching towards him with 14,000 reinforcements. Another prime example was just after the Battle of Talavera. Wellington had around 18,000 men and he had decided to march to engage what he believed to be 10,000 French troops. In fact Wellington was marching towards three French army corps, amounting to 50,000 men; without doubt he would have been soundly beaten. In the nick of time the guerrillas provided him with vital intelligence to allow him to retreat.

There was another, third Spanish force at work during the Peninsular War. These were Spaniards who had chosen to cooperate or collaborate with the French. They were known as Afrancesados. Broadly speaking they were from the Spanish upper classes. To the majority of the Spanish population the Afrancesados were traitors and these men and their families were often the first targets for assassination by guerrillas.

Overall the anti-French forces of Spain were instrumental in ensuring victory in the theatre. On average over the four years of the Peninsular War the French were losing 100 men every day. In other words, this was upwards of 164,000 men. Many of these did not fall in the pitch battles expertly won by Wellington. Instead they were lost due to guerrilla raids, lack of medical supplies, fresh water, food and shelter.

The Portuguese army
The other indigenous force in the Peninsular War was of course the

WARGAME SCENARIOS

Portuguese. Their performance in 1808 was less than glorious, but by September 1809, stiffened by the British, they had started to become a formidable force. By September 1809 the Portuguese could muster twenty-four line regiments, each with two battalions and a paper strength of 770 men per battalion. In practice, however, the regimental strength was usually no more than 1300. They could also muster six battalions of Caçadores, or light infantry. There were seven companies of just over 100 men and one of these companies was designated as marksmen. These are the troops that are distinguished by the fact that they were given brown uniforms and used rifles instead of muskets.

Sir Robert Wilson raised the Loyal Lusitania Legion, which consisted of three battalions each with 1,000 men. Attached to the legion were a battery of artillery and a handful of cavalry. In 1811 the legion was disbanded and became the 7th, 8th and 9th Caçadores.

The Portuguese had twelve regiments of medium cavalry. On paper there should have been 600 men but in practice this was usually 500. They also had four regiments of artillery and it is not believed that they deployed any horse artillery at all. There was a tiny engineer corps of a handful of men.

Supporting the regular Portuguese army were the militia units. Portugal itself was broken up into forty-eight conscription areas or districts. Each district was required to provide a two-battalion regiment with a paper strength of 1,500 men. These were particularly useful between 1810 and 1812. In practice the situation was often that the two battalions would take it in turns to serve in the field.

For internal defence, rather like a home guard, the Portuguese could call up their reservists, or Ordenanza. Many of them lacked firearms and instead used the pike. They could be useful as they were virtually self-sufficient and would be handy holding fortified lines and in siege situations. It was not a puny force and in May 1810 the Portuguese could muster 329,000 Ordenanza.

The British army

The British army during this period consisted of around one-hundred infantry regiments and just over twenty cavalry regiments. During the period 1808 to 1814 some fifty-one British line infantry regiments saw action in the Peninsula. In theory, a British infantry battalion consisted of around 1,000 men, and a regiment could consist of several battalions, so this meant that on occasion more than one battalion of a regiment would serve in a particular theatre, although this was relatively unusual.

ARMIES OF THE PENINSULAR WAR

Three foot guard regiments also saw action in the Peninsular War. However of particular use during the war were the British light infantry. They were a comparatively-new force in the British army. The men were armed with short muskets and by 1814 there were six light regiments. The British also deployed riflemen, notably the 95th Rifles. These men were used in relatively-small numbers but were excellent in rough terrain and for sniping.

British cavalry regiments tended to have up to four squadrons, each with around 100 men. The British Lifeguards and the Horse Guards saw service in the Peninsular War. Alongside them three regiments of Dragoon Guards and three regiments of Dragoon were also used. Some eight Light-Dragoon regiments were deployed in the theatre, along with four Hussar regiments.

The British deployed eleven brigades or batteries of foot artillery during the war, along with several horse artillery batteries. Most British batteries consisted of six guns. In addition to the British infantry, cavalry and artillery units, the King's German Legion, Brunswickers and French Emigres also saw service. The King's German Legion had five cavalry regiments, and a number of line- and light-infantry battalions, as well as foot- and horse-artillery. Brunswick troops provided riflemen and some cavalry. The French Emigres were of dubious value and when used were deployed as skirmishers.

The French army
The French troops that were used during the Peninsular War varied enormously in quantity and in quality. Initially, conscripts with little or no experience were used in 1808. In fact the majority of the cavalry used by Bessières were very inexperienced: only around ten percent of the 12,000 men had ever seen action.

The army of Portugal, led by Junot, could boast around fifty-percent veterans out of a total of 30,000 men. When Napoleon marched into Spain most of his force was experienced, but it must be remembered that even so-called veteran regiments now had ranks filled with inexperienced replacements, due to the enormous attrition rate in the central-European battles and campaigns. Despite the fact that many of the French were conscripts, they could still give a good account of themselves and this was even the case when experienced Peninsular-War soldiers were replaced with less experienced men after 1812.

Around sixty-four different French line regiments saw service during the Peninsular War. In theory, each of the line regiments could have up to five battalions of men. Each of the battalions was split down into six companies; four of the companies were fusiliers, and there was one Grenadier company and one Voltigeur company. The paper strength of each company was 140 men.

French light infantry regiments had a very similar structure to the line infantry. The principle difference was the description of the men by company. The fusilier companies were known as Chasseurs and the Grenadiers as Carabiniers.

The terrain did not favour the deployment of heavy French cavalry. Consequently, French Dragoons were the most commonly-used heavy cavalry by the French. In all some sixteen regiments saw service in the Peninsula. Some Cuirassiers saw limited service. The French also used eleven regiments of Chasseurs à Cheval. They also deployed Lancers and seven Hussar regiments. In theory a French cavalry regiment consisted of up to four squadrons of 100 men.

A shortage of horses restricted the use of French artillery during the war. The enormous French guns used in central Europe were rarely deployed. In fact the heaviest artillery used by the French was 8pdrs. Most of the French guns were in fact 6pdrs or 4pdrs. A French horse artillery battery would have six guns and a foot battery would have eight guns.

It was not just regular French troops that were used by Napoleon in the Peninsula: he made use of Imperial troops from across Europe. These included men from Italy, Switzerland and Poland. King Joseph tried to raise a number of Spanish units, as did other French commanders, but these Juramentados were generally more of a liability than an asset.

Towards the end of the Peninsular War, when the conflict had spilled into southern France, French National Guard units, or reservists, were brought into action. Unlike the regular army they were organised into cohorts, which were broadly the equivalent of battalions. Several of these cohorts would be put together to create a legion. Although the men fought well, they fought at a grave disadvantage. They had inexperienced officers and obsolete equipment.

Tactics and weapons

The nature of the war and the terrain of the Peninsula did not favour the mass tactics and large armies that were such a feature of the campaigns in central Europe. Initially the French deployed full army corps, which consisted of several divisions and brigades. In 1812 the French did away with their corps structure and from then on in the Peninsula the largest tactical unit was the division. This meant that a typical French or Spanish division would consist of around 4,000 men plus artillery. Facing them on the same tactical scale would be two British brigades, with some Portuguese troops attached to them. Their strength would be around 6,000 men plus artillery.

Infantry regiments could consist of up to five battalions, although the most common number was two. The fusilier- or centre-companies were usually made up of men who had some experience, but the bulk of the infantry would have little or no battlefield history. More agile and seasoned troops would be assigned to the light companies and the most experienced and larger men to the grenadier companies.

Cavalry was used sparingly and usually several squadrons of a regiment would have a horse battery attached to them. The most useful cavalry during the war were Hussars, Chasseurs and Lancers. They could not only make a significant contribution on the battlefield, but they were also perfect for screening a larger force, pursuing a broken enemy and carrying out reconnaissance patrols.

The only shock cavalry used during the Peninsular War were the Dragoons. In effect they were medium cavalry and theoretically trained to fight as well on foot as on a horse. They could be used to deliver charges against wavering infantry, but lacked the weight and the impetus for much else. The British also deployed heavy cavalry, although these were not armoured men.

The bulk of the infantry was armed with smoothbore, muzzle-loading flintlock muskets. The weapon was around 1m long and could weigh up to 15lbs. In addition to this there was a 40cm bayonet, which could be attached to the end of the musket. The muskets fired a lead ball weighing around an ounce. The firing procedure was complicated and time consuming and consisted of around twenty actions. It needed a solid and steady man to ensure that he performed all of the actions in the correct order. Any number of problems could interfere with the effectiveness of the fire from an infantry regiment. Inadequate training, poor maintenance of the weapon, damp powder, worn-out flints and simply forgetting to take the ramrod out before firing were all regular problems.

In theory the musket had an effective range of around 1,000 yards but in practice the effective range was ten-percent of this and even then picking out an individual target often meant a miss. As with the rest of the Napoleonic Wars, the tactic was to open fire on a target with a hail of shot and pepper the target with hits. Consequently, the main tactic was to try to ensure that the firing regiment was in an ideal position and formation to deliver a series of crashing volleys. The men, therefore, formed up in close order, usually in three ranks. Any more ranks than this and the subsequent ranks could not fire. The problem with additional ranks was that they could not contribute to the fire fight, yet at the same time they presented a better target to the enemy. The idea was that men from the third rank would step into gaps left in the front two ranks as casualties were taken. This would ensure continued fire power.

The French, however, had slightly different ideas. They liked to use the column as their primary manoeuvre formation. They could move faster than a line and maintain their cohesion. It was also easy for the column to quickly deploy into line or into square. A line would take longer to make these adjustments.

The French tended to use a mixture of line and column. The line would provide the fire power and the screen whilst the columns moved up at speed. This was known as mixed-order, but, in fact, looking at the battles, this tactic was rarely used during the Peninsular War and columns were far more common. The trouble was that as the columns moved to within effective musket range of an enemy line only a handful of the men in the column could return fire. Not only that, the column was an excellent target of closely-packed men. Time after time the French columns were shot to pieces by the British line.

The French never really intended for the columns to be used as battering rams to break through enemy lines. Instead they were designed to move up quickly following an artillery bombardment and protected by skirmishers. They would also only really be unleashed when the enemy line was wavering. It had worked for the French on countless occasions in central Europe. Time-after-time the line, or linear tactics, had been shattered by surging French columns following up after an artillery bombardment.

The terrain in the Peninsular War favoured counter-column tactics. On the whole, the British adopted defensive tactics on the battlefield. They only ever showed part of their force, so that the French could not be entirely certain where the bulk of the British forces were deployed. This meant that the target for the artillery and consequently the columns was uncertain and limited. On several occasions the French thought they were delivering a decisive column attack against a flank only to find it was the British centre. The consequences were inevitable.

Wellington in particular had refined the tactics of dealing with the French to an art. He would deploy light companies from the British battalions supported by Portuguese Caçadores and British riflemen. These would create a screen that would prevent the French Voltiguers from approaching the main British lines and identifying the key concentrations. In a number of cases the number of allied skirmishers deployed led the French to believe that this was in fact the main allied line. The French columns would then advance and as they did so they would come under artillery fire. As they approached they would be hit by riflemen first then the muskets of allied skirmishers. The allied skirmish screen would melt away and the French columns would be faced with an unbroken line of British infantry in front of them. There were three choices: continue in a column and risk being shot to pieces, redeploy under fire and take the consequent casualties, or pull back. In many cases it was already too late and the French infantry were fired-up and wished to get to grips with the British that had been torturing them throughout their whole advance. All the French officers could do was to join the charge.

General Thomas Bugeaud wrote:

> 'The men became excited, called out to one another, and increased the speed of their march; the column became a little confused. The English remained quite silent with ordered arms, and from their steadiness appeared to be a long red wall. Very soon we got nearer, crying "Vive l'Empereur! En Avant! A la Baionnette"! Shakos were raised on the muzzles of muskets, the march became a run, the ranks fell into confusion, the agitation became a tumult; shots were fired as we advanced. The English line remained silent, still and unmoved, with ordered arms, even when we were no more than 300 yards distant, and it appeared to ignore the storm that was about to break. The contrast was striking; in our innermost thoughts, we all felt that the enemy was taking a long time in firing, and that this fire, held for so long, would be very unpleasant when it came. Our ardour cooled. The moral power of a steadiness which nothing can shake overcame our minds. At this moment of painful expectation, the English wall shouldered arms; an indescribable feeling would fix many of our men to the spot; they began an uncertain fire. The enemy's steady, concentrated volleys swept our ranks; decimated, we turned round seeking to recover our equilibrium; then three formidable cheers broke the silence of our opponents; at the third they were on us, pushing our disorganised flight.'

The surprising failure of French light troops in the tactical sense was remarkable given their successes before the Peninsular War. Prior to this they had been extremely capable and numerous and a French division would be able to deploy 100 skirmishers for every battalion. In practice this meant around 800 men in the Peninsular War, but this was fewer than the men available to a British division.

Many have suggested that the major reason for the French failures on the battlefield were down to the quality of the troops themselves. Just a decade before, lines and columns and skirmishers would have acted in perfect concert with one another. But now, with different men and different terrain, they seemed incapable of adapting to situations. When they had a chance to show their true tactical abilities they did well, such as at Salamanca or at Albuera, when mixed-order French units nearly shattered the allied lines. Yet the French seemed wedded to clumsy, unwieldy and ultimately doomed tactics on the battlefield. Despite the French defeat in the Peninsular War they would continue to make the same mistakes, even up to the First World War.

The common tactic for infantry dealing with cavalry was to try to form some sort of square. The term square is actually something of a misnomer as it was often a rectangle, which could comprise of just a handful of men or anything up to a division. If the infantry had managed to form a square and were just facing cavalry it was extremely rare for the cavalry to be able to make any kind of impact on the infantry formation. However if the cavalry was supported by infantry and artillery the squares would prove vulnerable.

At Garcia Hernandez, infantry squares were broken by unsupported cavalry, but in most cases the cavalry would be roughly handled by an unbroken mass of bayonets and musketry fire. The French were as capable as the British of fending off unsupported cavalry, as 200 Frenchmen engaged in foraging near Ciudad Rodrigo on 9 July 1810 discovered. They were set upon by six British cavalry squadrons. The French infantry rapidly formed a square and waited until the last minute before delivering a devastating volley, which forced the British cavalry, a part of General Craufurd's command, to retreat and allow the French to march back to their main force.

If cavalry caught infantry in any other set of circumstances they could usually inflict enormous damage. This was particularly true if they fell on the infantry from either the flanks or the rear. At the battle of Albuera the British brigade under General Sir John Colborne was cut to pieces by French cavalry. Even columns were not safe from cavalry attack, but at least the men could more easily turn and present a solid, if unconvincing, face to the cavalry.

ARMIES OF THE PENINSULAR WAR

The natural inclination of the infantryman was to try to form a square whenever they felt threatened by cavalry. This often played into the hands of the enemy, who would then not attack using cavalry but would open fire with artillery and send in an infantry assault.

Artillery used during the period consisted of essentially either cannons or howitzers. A howitzer would fire in a high arc, whilst the cannon shot would speed directly towards the target on a horizontal path. The cannons could fire one of three different types of projectile. Round shot was essentially a ball, which was ideal for longer range shots. The other two types of projectile were essentially shorter-range weapons. Grape shot consisted of either metal shot, nails, and/or pebbles and glass in a bag, whereas canister tended to be metal balls fired in tins.

The howitzer had a fused shell, essentially a hollow, metal ball with explosives inside. The idea was that the shell would fall and explode over its target, sending fragments of metal in all directions. In the vast majority of cases, rather than exploding midair, the shell hit the ground and then fragmented.

The Peninsula itself, as a theatre of war, was not ideal. Large areas of Spain and Portugal lacked the resources needed in order to sustain large field armies. Not only that, but the supply chains were enormously long and vulnerable. The British and their allies relied on food, ammunition, weapons and clothing coming into ports. The Royal Navy played an important role, not only in protecting merchant shipping, but also bringing in vital supplies for the troops and for the civilian population.

The supply situation was difficult enough with the allies based in and around Portugal, but once they began to penetrate into Spain, seeking out the French, the logistical situation became almost impossible. The roads were dreadful and even worse in the winter. There were always too few draft animals.

The French also relied on supplies from outside of the Peninsula. But without a fleet that could protect itself from the Royal Navy, the vast majority of supplies had to be moved by land. The guerrillas and rebels claimed enormous quantities of French supplies. The French often lacked wagons and carts, horses or mules or sufficient men to protect the supply convoy. Time after time the French actions were impeded by the poor supply situation, rendering them incapable of movement, let alone offensive operations.

In other theatres the French had been pretty good at living off the land, but for the most part the Peninsula was not only incapable of yielding up sufficient food, but there was also the problem of a hostile local population. Consequently, in order for the French to find their own food the forces had to break up and forage, which made them easy prey for roving bands of guerrillas and pre-emptive attacks from the allies.

For the British, supplies were absolutely essential. They seemed to be hopelessly inept at foraging for themselves and if food was in short supply there could be major problems. The French on the other hand, without regular supplies and having to rely on their own wits to feed themselves, still managed to do so throughout the whole conflict.

If the supply situation was not a difficult problem to cope with in itself, an equal difficulty emerged with communications. We have to bear in mind that all information had to be passed either by word-of-mouth or by handwritten-despatches. Messages had to be physically relayed and this was in a country in which poor weather, extreme distances, dreadful roads and an unreliable local population had to be traversed. The French were especially vulnerable and guerrillas and armed peasants would make a point of ambushing French couriers.

Even on the battlefield communications tended to be by word-of-mouth or scribbled note. The problem was that both on the battlefield, and to a greater extent in the campaign, by the time information arrived at its destination it was often out of date. There was no way of checking precisely what was meant by a note that was unclear or a set of orders that were contradictory. Commanders had to make do with their best guess at what the instructions or orders meant and probably fulfil them even though they knew that the situation had radically changed and that the premise upon which the order had been written was now false.

Coordination was therefore rather difficult and in any case many of the military commanders and governors, as far as the French were concerned, seemed to be in competition with one another as much as at war with the allies.

Technically, Joseph was the new monarch of Spain, but to all practical purposes he was little more than a military governor; one of eight Frenchmen. It was not until 1812 that Napoleon allowed his brother to become the primary French representative in the Peninsula, but by this stage it was virtually too late. Military commanders still avoided complying with Joseph's instructions; his attempts to coordinate action. If they did not agree with him they simply referred the matter to Napoleon. This meant that vital decisions were not made, as messages and responses had to travel all the way to and then from Paris. If Napoleon took a position then he would be operating on information that could literally be weeks old.

At the beginning of the Peninsular War Napoleon had expected a swift and easy victory in the Peninsula. Portugal had fallen very easily, but, largely due to the command and control inadequacies of the French army, Napoleon's troops had failed to subdue and then control Spain. In Napoleon's defence he had confidently expected that his peninsular involvement would only last a matter of weeks, so setting up the necessary conditions for an efficient infrastructure had not entered his mind. He had no way of knowing in 1808 that his men would still be fighting on Spanish soil six years later.

Army Lists

There can never be truly comprehensive army lists to cover the six years of conflict, nor for that matter the changes that took place on a daily basis as regiments lost men, received replacements or had companies detached for other duties. In the *Wargamer's Guide to the Napoleonic Wars*, a series of relevant army lists were presented, as can be see below. These are perfectly acceptable generic forces, but for wargamers that wish to build their armies around specific campaigns there are two main options:

- Firstly, refer to the orders of battle related to specific engagements and build your armies around these lists
- Secondly, consider the composition of the army at the outset of a specific campaign and base your armies on these lists.

In the remainder of this chapter, we focus on the latter, as the specific engagement lists can be found in the relevant chapters.

Generic Army Lists

British in Portugal 1808

This is the early force that was used by Wellesley in the Peninsula when he won his first battle against the French. Note that it lacks cavalry and this is to some extent made up by the fact that there are elite light units. It can be used in conjunction with a Portuguese division or enlarged to represent the eight brigades that were actually available at the time.

WARGAME SCENARIOS

General of the Division	Gifted
1st Brigade commander	Gifted
5th Foot	Veteran Confident
9th Foot	Veteran Confident
38th Foot	Veteran Confident

2nd Brigade Commander	Gifted
36th Foot	Veteran Confident
40th Foot	Veteran Confident
71st Foot	Veteran Confident

3rd Brigade Commander	Gifted
5/60th Rifles	Elite Confident
2/95th Rifles	Elite Confident
Attached Foot Artillery – 2 medium guns and 1 medium Howitzer	Veteran Confident

Notes: The Rifle units are obviously armed with rifles and are considered light infantry

British in Portugal 1808-1809

This list aims to represent a British force that faced the French when they invaded Portugal. It can be used in conjunction with a Portuguese brigade. Unlike the 1808 list it now has cavalry.

General of the Division	Able
1st Brigade commander	Able
1st Line Regiment	Veteran Confident
2nd Line Regiment	Veteran Confident
3rd Line Regiment	Veteran Confident
60th or 90th Rifles	Elite Confident

Notes: The light infantry are rifle-armed and can operate in extended or skirmish order

2nd Brigade Commander	Able
4th Line Regiment	Veteran Confident
5th Line Regiment	Veteran Confident
6th Line Regiment	Veteran Confident
Light Regiment	Elite Confident

Notes: The light regiment is not rifle-armed but can operate in extended or skirmish order

ARMIES OF THE PENINSULAR WAR

Cavalry Brigade Commander	Able
Light Dragoon Regiment	Experienced Steady
King's German Legion Hussars	Veteran Confident
Attached Foot Battery – 2 medium guns and 1 medium Howitzer	Veteran Confident

British 1813-1814

This is the type of force that would have fought in the Peninsular War during this period and have also operated in the south of France. It was involved in the campaign in the Pyrenees and the invasion of southern France.

General of the Division	Gifted
1st Brigade commander	Able
1st Line Regiment	Elite Confident
2nd Line Regiment	Veteran Confident
3rd Line Regiment	Veteran Confident
2nd Brigade Commander	Able
4th Line Regiment	Veteran Confident
5th Line Regiment	Veteran Confident
6th Line Regiment	Veteran Confident
Portuguese Brigade Commander	Able
1st Portuguese Regiment	Experienced Steady
2nd Portuguese Regiment	Experienced Steady
3rd Portuguese Regiment	Experienced Steady
Caçadore Regiment	Experienced Steady

Notes: The Caçadore Regiment is light and may be armed with rifles

Attached Cavalry Brigade Commander	Able
Hussar Regiment	Experienced Arrogant
Attached Foot Battery – 2 medium guns, 1 medium Howitzer	

Notes: One British Rifle Regiment, graded as Elite Confident, should be split between the two British Brigades to simulate them operating as independent rifle companies. They would be armed with rifles and could operate as light-infantry skirmishers.

WARGAME SCENARIOS

French in Portugal 1808
This list is designed to match the British in Portugal 1808 and incorporates elite Swiss units. The complete army also had an additional infantry brigade and more Dragoons.

General of the Division	Able
1st Infantry Brigade commander	Able
1st Léger Regiment	Elite Confident
2nd Léger Regiment	Experienced Steady
1st Line Regiment	Experienced Steady
2nd Line Regiment	Experienced Steady

Notes: The Léger Regiments are classed as light infantry and in practice the line regiments were all capable of skirmishing.

2nd Infantry Brigade Commander	Able
3rd Line Regiment	Veteran Confident
4th Line Regiment	Veteran Confident
Swiss Regiment	Elite Arrogant

Notes: In practice the Swiss Regiment was capable of skirmishing

Reserve Brigade Commander	Able
1st Combined Grenadier Regiment	Elite Arrogant
2nd Combined Grenadier Regiment	Elite Arrogant
Cavalry Brigade Commander	Able
Chasseur Regiment	Trained Impetuous
Dragoon Regiment	Trained Impetuous
Foot Artillery Battery – 3 medium guns, 1 medium Howitzer	Experienced Steady

French in the Peninsular War to 1812
This is the force that fought against the Duke of Wellington and the Spaniards. In practice many of the regiments operated as skirmishers due to the nature of the warfare. The list lacks additional Hussars and Chasseurs that may also have been present at times.

General of the Division	Gifted
1st Brigade commander	Able
1st Léger Regiment	Experienced Steady
1st Line Regiment	Experienced Steady
2nd Line Regiment	Experienced Steady

ARMIES OF THE PENINSULAR WAR

3rd Line Regiment	Green Steady
4th Line Regiment	Green Steady
5th Line Regiment	Green Steady

Notes: The Léger Regiment is light infantry and the two Experienced line regiments can operate in skirmish order.

2nd Brigade Commander — Able

2nd Léger Regiment	Experienced Steady
3rd Léger Regiment	Experienced Steady
6th Line Regiment	Experienced Steady
7th Line Regiment	Experienced Steady
8th Line Regiment	Green Steady
9th Line Regiment	Green Steady

Notes: The two Léger regiments are light infantry and the two Experienced line regiments can operate in skirmish order.

Cavalry Brigade Commander — Able

1st Dragoon Regiment	Experienced Steady
2nd Dragoon Regiment	Experienced Steady
Field Artillery Battery – 3 medium guns, 1 medium Howitzer	Experienced Steady

France 1814

This is a mixed French force that fought against a number of allied armies. It reflects the types of troops that were available to defend France at the time. Therefore there is a wide difference in quality.

General of the Division	Able
1st Brigade commander	Able
1st Line Infantry Regiment	Experienced Steady
2nd Line Infantry Regiment	Experienced Steady
3rd Line Infantry Regiment	Experienced Steady
4th Line Infantry Regiment	Green Cautious
5th Line Infantry Regiment	Green Cautious
6th Line Infantry Regiment	Raw Cautious
2nd Infantry Brigade Commander	Able
1st National Guard Regiment	Green Cautious
2nd National Guard Regiment	Green Cautious
3rd National Guard Regiment	Green Cautious

WARGAME SCENARIOS

4th National Guard Regiment — Green Cautious
5th National Guard Regiment — Raw Cautious
6th National Guard Regiment — Raw Cautious

3rd Infantry Brigade Commander — Able
1st Naval Infantry Regiment — Green Cautious
2nd Naval Infantry Regiment — Green Cautious
3rd Naval Infantry Regiment — Raw Cautious
1st Provisional Regiment — Green Cautious
2nd Provisional Regiment — Green Cautious

Cavalry Brigade Commander — Able
1st Chasseur a Cheval Regiment — Green Cautious
2nd Chasseur a Cheval Regiment — Green Cautious
Notes: These cavalry regiments are light cavalry
Foot Artillery Battery – 3 medium guns, 1 medium Howitzer — Experienced Steady

Italy and Naples in Spain 1812

This is a force that was deployed in the Peninsula in 1812. They were involved in a number of anti-guerrilla operations.

General of the Division — Able
1st Brigade commander — Able
1st Léger Regiment — Experienced Steady
2nd Léger Regiment — Experienced Steady
1st Line Regiment — Experienced Steady
2nd Line Regiment — Experienced Steady
Notes: The two Léger regiments are light infantry units

2nd Brigade Commander — Able
3rd Line Regiment — Green Cautious
4th Line Regiment — Green Cautious
5th Line Regiment — Green Cautious
6th Line Regiment — Green Cautious

Neapolitan Brigade Commander — Able
1st Léger Regiment — Raw Cautious
Du Roi Regiment — Experienced Confident
De la Reine Regiment — Experienced Confident

ARMIES OF THE PENINSULAR WAR

Chasseur a Cheval Regiment   Raw Cautious
Notes: The Léger Regiment and the Chasseurs are light troops.

French Cavalry Brigade Commander   Able
4th Hussar Regiment   Experienced Steady
13th Cuirassier Regiment   Veteran Confident
Notes: The Hussars are light troops and the Cuirassiers are heavy cavalry

Foot Artillery Battery – 3 medium guns,   Experienced Steady
   1 medium Howitzer

Spain 1811

This is essentially an irregular force that fought against the French during the Peninsular War. It contains some decent units, but the rest are rather unreliable.

General of the Division   Cautious
Vanguard Brigade commander   Cautious
Murcian Light Infantry   Green Cautious
Canarias Regiment   Green Cautious
Leon Regiment   Green Cautious

2nd Brigade Commander   Able
Rea Regiment   Green Cautious
Zamora Regiment   Green Cautious
Voluntarios de Navarra Regiment   Green Cautious

3rd Brigade Commander   Cautious
2nd Guards Regiment   Veteran Confident
Walloon Guards Regiment   Veteran Confident
Irlanda Regiment   Veteran Confident
Patria Regiment   Veteran Confident
Toledo Regiment   Green Steady
Legionestranjera Regiment   Green Steady

Cavalry Brigade Commander   Able
Santiago Regiment   Green Steady
Castilla Hussar Regiment   Experienced Steady
Granderos Regiment   Veteran Confident
De Instrucion Regiment   Veteran Confident

WARGAME SCENARIOS

Notes: All regiments are heavy cavalry except the Hussars, which are light

Foot Artillery Battery – 3 medium guns   Green Cautious

Historical Orders of Battle

Wellington's Army in Portugal: September 1810

1st Division – Gen Spencer	
Stopford's Brigade	1st Coldstreams, 1st Scots Guards
Blantyre's Brigade	24th, 42nd (Highland), 61st Foot
Loewe's Brigade	1st, 2nd, 5th, 7th KGL
Pakenham's Brigade	7th Foot, 79th (Highland)
2nd Division – Gen Hill	
Stewart's Brigade	3rd, 31st, 48th, 66th Foot
Inglis' Brigade	29th, 48th, 57th Foot
Crawford's Brigade	28th, 34th, 39th Foot
Hamilton's Portuguese Division	Fonseca's Brigade & Campbell's Brigade
3rd Division – Gen Picton	
Mackinnon's Brigade	45th, 74th, 88th Foot
Lightburne's Brigade	5th, 83rd, 90th Foot
Champlemond's Portuguese Brigade	9th, 21st Line
4th Division – Gen Cole	
Campbell's Brigade	7th, 11th, 53rd Foot
Kemmis' Brigade	27th, 40th, 97th Foot
Collins' Portuguese Brigade	11th, 23rd Portuguese Line Regiments
5th Division – Gen Leith	
Barnes' Brigade	1st, 9th, 38th Foot
Spry's Portuguese Brigade	Lusitanian Legion, 8th Portuguese Line
Light Division – Craufurd	
Beckwith's Brigade	43rd, 95th, 3rd Caçadores
Barclay's Brigade	52nd, 95th, 1st Caçadores

ARMIES OF THE PENINSULAR WAR

Independent Portuguese Infantry

1st Brigade (Pack)	1st, 16th Portuguese Regiments and 4th Caçadores
5th Brigade (Campbell)	6th, 18th Portuguese Line Regiments and 6th Caçadores
6th Brigade (Coleman)	7th Portuguese Line Regiment
Bradford's Brigade	12th and 13th Portuguese Line, and 5th Caçadores
Lisbon Garrison	88th, 58th Foot, Lisbon Militia Fixed Artillery – Lines of Torres Vedras
Cavalry Division: Major General Cotton	Able
De Grey's Brigade	3rd Dragoon Guards, 4th Dragoons
Slade's Brigade	1st Dragoons, 14th Light Dragoons
Anson's Brigade	16th Light Dragoons, 1st Hussars (KGL)
Fane's Brigade	13th Light Dragoons, Portuguese Cavalry
Attached Artillery to field army	3 horse batteries, 6 foot batteries, 2 KGL and 8 Portuguese medium batteries

In addition to this force, there were garrison troops at:

- Elvas – one regiment of regulars and one militia
- Peniche – two militia
- Abrantes – two militia
- Almeida – 2 regular and five militia

It is important to remember that there were also Portuguese militia units:

- Lecor's Militia at Castello Branco
- Miller's Militia at Oporto
- Silveira's Militia at Tras-os-Montes
- Trant's Militia between the Douro and Mondego
- Miranda's Militia at Thomar

At the time, the Spanish could muster the following:

WARGAME SCENARIOS

- In Estremadura – **Vanguard Division (La Carrera);** Principe, 1st and 2nd of Catalonia, Vitoria: **1st Division (Garcia);** Leon, Regt del General, La Union, 1st Barcelona, Catalan volunteers, Osuna, Zafra, Valladolid, La Serena, 2nd Seville: **2nd Division (O'Donnell);** Zamora, Rey, Toledo, Hibernia, Princesa, 1st Seville, Castilla Tiradores, Navarre Volunteers: **3rd Division (Ballasteros);** Barbastro, Pravia, Lena, Castropol, Cangas de Tineo, Infiesto; **4th Division (Zayas);** 2nd and 4th Spanish Guards, Irlanda, Patria, Toledo, Legion Estranjera, 4th Walloon Guards, Ciudad Real. There were also the following cavalry units: Carabineros Reales, Reina, Infanta, Borbon, Algarve, Sagunto, Lusitania, Hussares de Estremadura, Perseguidores de Andalusia, Imperiales de Toledo, Granaderos de Llerena, Cruzada de Albuquerque, Santiago, Hussaras de Castilla, Granederos, Escuadron de Instrucion and a single horse artillery unit, and three foot batteries.
- There was a reasonably-sized garrison in Badajoz and Ciudad Rodrigo with artillery

Massena's Army of Portugal: 15 September 1810
2nd Corps – General Reynier

1st Division – Gen Merle	Sarrut's Brigade – 2nd Léger & 36th Line
Graindorge's Brigade – 4th Léger	
2nd Division – Gen Heudelet	Foy's Brigade – 17th Léger & 70th Line
	Arnaud's Brigade – 31st Léger & 47th Line
Cavalry Brigade – Gen Soult	1st Hussars, 22nd Chasseurs, Hanoverian Chasseurs & 8th Dragoons, plus artillery

6th Corps – Marshal Ney

1st Division – Gen Marchand	Maucune's Brigade – 6th Léger & 69th Line
	Marcognet's Brigade – 39th Line & 76th Line

ARMIES OF THE PENINSULAR WAR

2nd Division – Gen Mermet	Bardet's Brigade – 25th Léger & 27th Line
	Labassee's Brigade – 50th Line & 59th Line
3rd Division – Gen Loison	Simon's Brigade – 26th Line, Legion du Midi & Legion Hanovrienne
	Ferey's Brigade – 32nd Léger, 66th Line & 82nd Line
Cavalry Brigade – Gen Lamotte	3rd Hussars, 15th Chasseurs & artillery
8th Corps – General Junot	
1st Division – Gen Clausel	Menard's Brigade – 19th, 25th, 28th & 34th Line
	Taupin's Brigade – 15th Léger, 46th Line & 75th Line
	Godard's Brigade – 22nd Line
2nd Division – Gen Solignac	Gratien's Brigade – 15th Line & 86th Line
	Thomiere's Brigade – 65th Line, Regiment Irlandais and Regiment de Prusse
Cavalry Division – Gen Ste Croix	1st, 2nd, 4th, 9th, 14th and 26th Dragoons & artillery
Reserve Cavalry – General Montbrun	Lorcet's Brigade – 3rd & 6th Dragoons
	Cavrois' Brigade – 11th Dragoons
	Ornano's Brigade – 15th & 25th Dragoons
	Plus horse and reserve artillery

British Regiments in the Peninsula

It can be very confusing to follow the progress and the distribution of British troops in the Peninsula over the period involved. The following listing, which aims to be as comprehensive as possible, notes the appearance and departure of the various British regiments. It is derived primarily from French sources.

WARGAME SCENARIOS

Cavalry

Unit	Date Arrived	Date Left	Battles or Campaigns
Household			
1 Life Guard (2 sqdns)	January 1813	end of the war	VIT, TOU
2 Life Guard (2 sqdns)	January 1813	end of the war	VIT, TOU
Royal Horse Guard (2 sqdns)	January 1813	end of the war	VIT, TOU
Line			
3 Dragoon Guard	May 1809	end of the war	TAL, ALB, USA, VIT
4 Dragoon Guard	April 1811	April 1813	
5 Dragoon Guard	September 1811	end of the war	SAL, VIT, TOU
1 Dragoon	October 1809	end of the war	FDO, ELB, MAG, VIT
3 Dragoon	August 1811	end of the war	MAG, SAL, VIT, TOU
4 Dragoon	May 1809	end of the war	TAL, ALB, USA, SAL, VIT
7 Light Dragoon	November 1808	January 1809	SAH, BEN
	September 1813	end of the war	ORT
9 Light Dragoon	July 1811	May 1813	ADM
10 Light Dragoon	November 1808	January 1809	SAH, BEN
	April 1813	end of the war	VIT, ORT, TOU
11 Light Dragoon	June 1811	May 1813	ELB
12 Light Dragoon	June 1811	end of the war	SAL, VIT, NLE, NVE
13 Light Dragoon	April 1810	end of the war	ALB, USA, NLE, ORT
14 Light Dragoon	November 1808	end of the war	DOU, TAL, FDO, ELB, SAL, PYR, NVE, ORT
15 Light Dragoon	November 1808	January 1809	SAH
	April 1813	end of the war	VIT, ORT, TOU
16 Light Dragoon	April 1809	end of the war	DOU, TAL, FDO, ELB, VIT
18 Light Dragoon	September 1808	January 1809	SAH, BEN
	April 1813	end of the war	VIT, TOU
20 Light Dragoon	August 1808	July 1809	VIM, DOU
	August 1812	end of the war	(E), CAS, ORD
23 Light Dragoon	June 1809	November 1809	TAL
German			
1 Dragoons KGL	January 1812	end of the war	GCH
2 Dragoons KGL	January 1812	end of the war	GCH
1 Hussars KGL	May 1809	end of the war	TAL, FDO, ELB, SAL, TOU
2 Hussars KGL	April 1811	end of the war	(C), BAR, ADM
3 Hussars KGL	September 1808	January 1809	SAH, BEN
Brunswick Hussars	August 1812	end of the war	(E), ORD

ARMIES OF THE PENINSULAR WAR

Infantry

Unit	Bn	Date Arrived	Date Left	Battles or Campaigns
Guard				
1 Foot Guards	1	October 1808	January 1809	COR
	2	October 1812	end of the war	NLE, NVE, BAY
		October 1808	January 1809	COR
	3	April 1810	November 1811	(C), BAR
		November 1811	end of the war	(C) 10/1812 then NLE, NVE, BAY
Coldstream Guards	1	March 1809	end of the war	DOU, TAL, FDO, SAL, BUR, BID, NLE, NVE, BAY
	2 (2 Companies)	April 1810	November 1811	(C), BAR
3 Foot Guard	1	March 1809	end of the war	DOU, TAL, FDO, SAL, BUR, BID, NLE, NVE, BAY
	2 (2 companies)	April 1810	November 1811	(C), BAR
Line				
1 Foot	3	October 1808	January 1809	COR
		April 1810	end of the war	FDO, SAL, VIT, SAN, BID, NLE, NVE, BAY
2 Foot		August 1808	January 1809	VIM, COR
		March 1811	end of the war	SAL
With the 2nd battalion 53 Foot they formed the 2nd provisional battalion				VIT, RON, SOR, NLE, TOU
3 Foot	1	August 1808	end of the war	DOU, TAL, ALB, VIT, RON, SOR, NLE, STP, ORT
4 Foot	1	August 1808	January 1809	COR
		November 1810	end of the war	BAD2, SAL, VIT, SAN, BID, NLE, NVE
5 Foot	1	August 1808	January 1812	ROL, VIM, COR
	2	May 1812	end of the war	SAL, VIT, NLE, ORT, TOU
		December 1809	October 1812	BUS, FDO, ELB, CIU, BAD2, SAL
6 Foot	1	August 1808	January 1809	ROL, VIM, COR
		November 1812	end of the war	NLE, MAY, SOR, ORT
7 Foot	1	July 1810	end of the war	BUS, ALB, BAD2, SAL, VIT, NLE, ORT, TOU
	2	April 1809	June 1811	DOU, TAL, ALB
9 Foot	1	August 1808	January 1809	ROL, VIM, COR
	2	March 1810	end of the war	BUS, FDO, BAD2, SAL, VIT, SAN, BID, NLE, NVE, BAY
		August 1808	June 1809	
		February 1812	May 1811	VIM, COR, DOU (G), BAR (2 companies)
10 Foot	1	August 1812	end of the war	(E), CAS, TAR, ORD
	2	December 1812	April 1813	(E), CAS (1 co)
11 Foot	1	August 1808	end of the war	SAL, SOR, NLE, TOU
	2	October 1811	September 1812	TFA (2 companies)
14 Foot	1	October 1808	January 1809	COR
20 Foot		August 1808	January 1809	VIM, COR
		December 1812	end of the war	VIT, RON, SOR, NLE, ORT, TOU

WARGAME SCENARIOS

Regiment	Battalion	From	To	Battles
21 Foot	1	December 1812	April 1813	(E) (1 co), CAS
23 Foot	1 2	November 1810 October 1808	end of the war January 1809	ALB, BAD2, SAL, VIT, RON, SOR, NLE, ORT, TOU COR
24 Foot	2	April 1809	end of the war	TAL, BUS, FDO, SAL, BUR
With the 2nd battalion 58 Foot they formed the 3rd provisional battalion				SOR, PYR, NLE, ORT
26 Foot	1	October 1808	January 1809	COR
27 Foot	1	November	end of the war	(E), CAS, TAR, ORD
28 Foot	1 2	August 1808 February 1809 July 1811 September 1809	January 1809 March 1811 end of the war August 1811	COR (G) BAR ADM, VIT, MAY, NLE, STP, TOU ALB
29 Foot		August 1808	October 1811	ROL, VIM, DOU, TAL, ALB
30 Foot	2	October 1810	May 1813	FDO, BAD2, SAL
31 Foot	1 2	December 1812 November 1808	April 1813 end of the war	(E) (1 co), CAS TAL, ALB
With the 2 bat 66 Foot they formed the 1 provisional battalion				VIT, RON, SOR, NLE, STP
32 Foot	1	August 1808 July 1811	January 1809 end of the war	ROL, VIM, COR SAL, SOR, NLE, TOU
34 Foot	2	July 1809	end of the war	ALB, ADM, ALM, VIT, MAY, NLE, STP, TOU
36 Foot	1	August 1808 March 1811	January 1809 end of the war	ROL, VIM, COR SAL, SOR, NLE, TOU
38 Foot	1 2	August 1808 June 1812 April 1810	January 1809 end of the war December 1812	ROL, VIM, COR SAL, VIT, SAN, NLE, BID, NVE BUS, BAD2, SAL
39 Foot	2	July 1809	end of the war	ALB, ADM, ALM, VIT, MAY, NLE, STP, TOU
40 Foot	1	August 1808	end of the war	ROL, VIM, TAL, BUS, ALB (1 co), BAD2, SAL, VIT, RON, SOR, NLE, ORT, TOU
42 Foot	1 2	September 1808 March 1812 July 1809	January 1809 end of the war May 1812	COR SAL, BUR, SOR, NLE, ORT, TOU BUS, FDO
43 Foot	1 2	October 1808 June 1809 August 1808	January 1809 end of the war January 1809	 BUS, SAB, FDO, CIU, BAD2, SAL, PYR, BID, NLE, NVE VIM, COR
44 Foot	1 2	July 1813 October 1810	end of the war May 1813	(E) FDO, BAD2, SAL
45 Foot	1	August 1808	end of the war	ROL, VIM, TAL, BUS, SAB, CIU, BAD2, SAL, VIT, SOR, NLE, ORT, TOU
47 Foot	2	May 1810	end of the war	(C) September 1812, BAR, TFA, VIT, SAN, BID, NLE, NVE, BAY
48 Foot	1 2	June 1809 April 1809	end of the war June 1811	TAL, ALB, BAD2, SAL, VIT, RON, SOR, NLE, ORT, TOU DOU, TAL, ALB

ARMIES OF THE PENINSULAR WAR

50 Foot	1	August 1808 September 1810	January 1809 end of the war	ROL, VIM, COR FDO, ADM, ALM, VIT, MAY, STP, ORT, TOU
51 Foot		October 1808 February 1811	January 1809 end of the war	COR FDO, BAD1, SAL, VIT, SOR, NLE
52 Foot	1 2	August 1808 June 1809 August 1808 March 1811	January 1809 fin de la guere January 1809 February 1812	COR BUS, SAB, FDO, CIU, BAD2, SAL, VIT, BID, NVE, ORT, TOU VIM FDO, CIU
53 Foot	2	April 1809	end of the war	DOU, TAL, SAL, VIT, RON, SOR, NLE, TOU
With the 2 Foot they formed the 2 provisional battalion				
57 Foot	1	October 1809	end of the war	ALB, VIT, RON, NLE, STP
58 Foot	1 2	August 1812 June 1809	end of the war end of the war	(E), CAS, TAR SAL, BUR
With the 2 bat du 24 Foot formed the 3 provisional battalion				
59 Foot	2	October 1808 September 1809 April 1813	January 1809 March 1813 end of the war	COR (C) VIT, SAN, BID, NLE, NVE
60 Foot	5 8 *	August 1808 November 1813	end of the war end of the war	ROL, VIM, DOU, TAL, BUS, SAB, FDO, ELB, CIU, BAD2, ALM, SAL, BUR, VIT, MAY, ROL, SOR, BID, NLE, NVE, STP, ORT, TOU, BAY (C)
61 Foot	1	June 1809	end of the war	TAL, SAL, SOR, NLE, ORT, TOU
62 Foot	1 2	December 1812 October 1813	April 1813 end of the war	(E) 1co CAS NVE
66 Foot	2	April 1809	end of the war	DOU, TAL, ALB, VIT, RON, SOR, NLE, STP
With the 2 battalion 31 Foot they formed the 1 provisional battalion				
67 Foot	1 2	December 1812 December 1810 January 1812 May 1813	March 1813 January 1812 May 1813 end of the war	(E) 1 co (C) BAR (CT) (E) TAR
68 Foot		July 1811	end of the war	SAL, VIT, SOR, NLE
71 Foot	1	August 1808 September 1810	January 1809 end of the war	ROL, VIM, COR FDO, ADM, ALM, VIT, MAY, STP, ORT, TOU
74 Foot		February 1810	end of the war	BUS, FDO, CIU, BAD2, SAL, VIT, SOR, NLE, ORT, TOU
75 Foot		December 1812	April 1813	(E) 1 co, CAS
76 Foot		October 1808 July 1813	January 1809 end of the war	COR NLE, NVE
77 Foot		July 1811	end of the war	ELB, CIU, BAD2
79 Foot		August 1808 February 1810 September 1810	January 1809 September 1810 end of the war	COR (C) FDO, SAL, BUR, SOR, NLE, TOU

WARGAME SCENARIOS

81 Foot	1	August 1812	end of the war	(E), CAS, TAR, ORD
	2	October 1808	January 1809	COR
82 Foot	1	August 1808	January 1809	ROL, VIM, COR
		October 1810	October 1810	(G) FUE
		December 1811	June 1812	(G) TFA 2 companies
	2	June 1812	end of the war	VIT, MAY, SOR, NLE
		February 1811	March 1811	(G) BAR 2 companies
83 Foot	2	April 1809	end of the war	DOU, TAL, BUS, SAB, FDO, ELB, CIU, BAD2, SAL, VIT, NLE, ORT, TOU
84 Foot	2	July 1813	end of the war	NLE, NVE
85 Foot		March 1811	October 1811	FDO, BAD1
		July 1813	end of the war	NLE, NVE
87 Foot	2	April 1809	end of the war	TAL, (C), BAR, TFA, VIT, NLE, ORT, TOU
88 Foot	1	February 1809	end of the war	TAL, BUS, SAB, FDO, ELB, CIU, BAD1, SAL, VIT, SOR, NLE, ORT, TOU FDO
	2	September 1810	July 1811	
89 Foot	2	October 1810	October 1810	(G) FUE 4 companies
91 Foot	1	August 1808	January 1809	ROL, VIM, COR
		October 1812	end of the war	SOR, NLE, ORT, TOU
92 Foot	1	August 1808	January 1809	COR
		October 1810	end of the war	FDO, ADM, ALM, VIT, MAY, STP, ORT
94 Foot		February 1810	end of the war	(C) February - September 1810, SAB, FDO, ELB, CIU, BAD2, SAL, VIT, NLE, ORT, TOU
95 Foot	1	August 1808	January 1809	VIM 2 companies, COR 5 companies BUS, SAB, FDO, CIU, BAD2, SAL, VIT, PYR, NLE, NVE, TOU 4 companies ROL, VIM (C) BAR 2 companies, TFA 1 co, CIU, BAD2 2 companies, FDO 1 co, SAL 4 companies, 6 companies VIT, BID, NLE, NVE (C) BAR 2 companies, FDO 1 co, CIU 5 companies BAD2, VIT, PYR, BID, NLE, NVE, TOU:
	2	June 1809	end of the war	
		August 1808	January 1809	
		March 1811	end of the war	
	3	June 1810	end of the war	
97 Foot		August 1808	October 1811	VIM, DOU, TAL, ALB 1 co
Germans and others				
KGL Bat. Léger	1	August 1808	January 1809	
		March 1811	end of the war	ALB, SAL, VDP, VIT, BID, NLE, NVE, BAY
KGL Bat. Léger	2	August 1808	January 1809	
		March 1811	end of the war	ALB, SAL, VDP, VIT, BID, NLE, NVE, BAY

KGL Bat. Line	1	August 1808	end of the war	DOU, TAL, BUS, FDO, SAL, BUR, BID, NLE, NVE, BAY
KGL Bat. Line	2	August 1808	end of the war	DOU, TAL, BUS, FDO, SAL, BUR, BID, NLE, NVE, BAY
KGL Bat. Line	3	December 1812	April 1813	(E) 2 companies CAS
KGL Bat. Line	4	August 1812	end of the war	(E) CAS, TAR, ORD
KGL Bat. Line	5	August 1808	end of the war	DOU, TAL, BUS, FDO, SAL, BUR, BID, NLE, NVE, BAY
KGL Bat. Line	6	August 1812	April 1813	(E) CAS
KGL Bat. Line	7	August 1808	July 1811	DOU, TAL, BUS, FDO
KGL Bat. Line	8	December 1812	April 1813	(E) CAS 1 co
Oels light infantry		November 1810	end of the war	FDO, BAD2, SAL, VIT, RON, MAY, SOR, SAN, BID, NLE, NVE, ORT
Rgt Suisse de Roll		August 1812	end of the war	(E) 3 companies, CAS, TAR, ORD
Rgt Suisse de Dillon		August 1812	end of the war	(E) 5 companies, CAS, TAR
Rgt Suisse de Watteville		October 1811	April 1813	(C), (CT)
Chasseurs Britanniques		January 1811	end of the war	FDO, BAD1, SAL, VIT, SOR

WARGAME SCENARIOS

Table Key:
(C): Cadix
(CT): Cartagène
(E): côte Orientale
(G): Gibraltar
ADM: Arroyo dos Molinos (28/10/1811)
ALB: Albuera (16/05/1811)
ALM : pont d'Almaraz (18/05/1812)
BAD1 : Badajoz (mai-juin 1811)
BAD2 : Badajoz (06/04/1812)
BAR : Barossa (05/03/1811)
BAY : sortie de Bayonne (15/04/1811)
BEN : Benevente (01/01/1809)
BID : Bidassoa (07/10/1813)
BUR : Burgos (September-October 1812)
BUS : Busaco (27/09/1810)
CAS : Castalla (13/04/1813)
CUI : Cuidad-Rodrigo (19/01/1812)
COR : Retreat from Corogne (01/1809)
DOU : passage de Douro (Oporto) (12/05/1809)
ELB : El Bodon et Carpio (25/09/1811)
FDO : Fuentes De Onoro (3 and 5/05/1811)
FUE : Fuengirola (13/10/1810)
GCH : Garcia Hernandez (23/07/1812)
MAG : Maguilla (11/06/1812)
MAY : Maya (25/07/1813)
NLE : Nivelle (10/11/1813)
NVE : Nive (9 et 12/12/1813)
ORD : Ordal and Villafranca (12 and 13/09/1813)
ORT : Orthez (27/02/1814)
PYR : Pyrénées (25/07 et 02/08/1813)
ROL : Rolica (17/08/1808)
RON : Roncevaux (25/07/1813)
SAB : Sabugal (03/04/1811)
SAH : Sahagun (21/12/1808)
SAL : Salamanca (22/07/1812)
SAN : San Sebastien (27/07 et 31/07/1813)
SOR : Sorauren (28-30//1813)
STP : Saint-Pierre (13/12/1813)
TAL : Talavera (27-28/07/1809)
TAR : Tarragonne (06/1813)
TFA : Defence of Tarifa (12/1811 et 01/1812)
TOU : Toulouse (10/04/1814)
USA : Usagre (25/05/1811)
VDP : Venta del Poza (23/10/1812)
VIM : Vimeiro (21/08/1808)
VIT : Vitoria (21/06/1813)

Chapter 7

The War in the Peninsula

This chapter aims to provide practical solutions to the wargamer to organise and run wargame campaigns in the theatre. This chapter begins by providing a basic campaign system and also covers weather and other considerations.

Campaign Rules

One of the most challenging and exciting aspects of wargaming is to run or take part in a campaign. With one-off battles, your army is at full strength and maximum fitness, with bellies full and with pockets and pouches stuffed with ammunition. In a campaign game, you have a chance to see exactly what it could have been like for a general trying to cope with an army lacking supplies; a force dispirited after a recent defeat and depleted regiments wracked with disease and desertion.

Normally you will also need an umpire, but if you trust your opponent (and many don't), you can work out the map moves and possible encounters yourselves. The major advantage of having an umpire is that the players can tell the umpire where their troops and supply depots are based, where they want to move and when the troops are expected to arrive. This means that the umpire carries out all of the map moves and he is the only person who actually knows with any certainty where both sides' units and supplies are at a given time.

Categorizing forces for movement

As far as movement is concerned, it is essential to attempt to categorize the different types of forces on the march. The following table explains the different types of force you are likely to create:

WARGAME SCENARIOS

Type of Force	Description of force
Scouts and couriers	Single figures or less than a regiment representing a scouting force or an individual figure with despatches
Light mounted force	Cavalry only consisting of one or more regiments
Mounted force	Cavalry accompanied by horse artillery
Light infantry force	Infantry only consisting of one or more regiments
Mixed force	Any mixture of infantry, cavalry and artillery and all forces accompanied by baggage or supplies

Movement

Normally troops would only move on roads. Obviously they do go cross-country, but for ease of understanding and to highlight the importance of the road network, you will see in the movement table that the cross-country moves are seriously reduced.

In effect there are three different types of road; these are shown in the following table:

Type of Road	Description and implications
Main road	A major road or a metalled road, actually far more numerous than you would expect. These are the ideal roads for maximum movement
Dirt road	A basic road either dirt or in some cases reinforced with planks. A standard local road, inferior to a road, but better than a track for movement
Track	Essentially a country lane which may or may not be marked on the map. As it is only really used by local farm traffic, it will be rutted and uneven. Despite this, it is still marginally better than marching cross-country

THE WAR IN THE PENINSULA

Campaign movement

Troops would normally undertake one or two marches per day. The first march would begin just after dawn and end for a rest and food at around noon. After two hours or more, the troops would get underway again and undertake their second march of the day. The following table shows the map distances in miles that can be covered by the different types of force in each march:

Type of Force	Main Road	Dirt Road	Track	Open Ground	Rough Ground
Scouts and couriers	40	25	20	12	8
Light mounted force	25	20	12	10	5
Mounted force	20	15	10	6	3
Light infantry force	15	12	10	8	5
Mixed force	12	10	8	5	2

Additional marching considerations

The force will be preparing for a morning march from first light and will commence the march at dawn. If the force has marched at dawn, they are to be assumed to have not had breakfast. Therefore the following applies:

Troop Type	Impact of marching at dawn if engaged in a battle before having food
Green	Count as disordered
Trained	Count as Green
Experienced	Count as Green
Veteran	Count as experienced
Elite	Count as experienced

Troops cannot march for more than three periods (a day and half): they must rest for a half day after three marches. If the troops have marched for three periods and then are expected to fight a battle then they are affected as shown in the above table.

For the purposes of movement open terrain is essentially farmland and rough terrain includes marches and forests. If so agreed or decreed by the umpire, the defending forces, knowing the region, can count open and rough ground as track. The invading force, unless the route has been fully scouted, counts the region as shown on the map.

WARGAME SCENARIOS

As far as rivers are concerned, a force crossing a bridge or using a ford loses a quarter of that marching period distance to simulate the delay in crossing. Optionally, this can also be applied to built-up areas if the force is passing through a village or town.

Transforming from map movement to table
The purpose of map movement is to manoeuvre elements of your command into position to launch attacks on the enemy. Ideally, the positions should be advantageous to you in terms of the terrain (better suiting your troops), or to threaten and capture key enemy positions such as supply dumps, river crossings and centres of population. It is also the purpose of the map movement to work around the enemy and hit his forces unprepared or to force weaker columns of his troops into action against your own superior forces.

At some point in the map movement, your troops will make contact with the enemy. You should always state the order in which your troops are marching, as this will determine the first troops that enter the table. Remember that men, horses and equipment take up considerable amounts of space on the roads and that your forces will be marching in column one unit behind another. Choose your lead units well as these will have to deal with the enemy on the wargame table until the rest of the troops can arrive and deploy.

In effect, when the first of your units enter the table itself, the battle begins. You will have to start issuing orders to your brigades and regiments as they appear. In the first turn, you may deploy only the leading infantry brigade, cavalry regiment or artillery unit as appropriate. It is also advisable to have your force commander as near the front of the column as possible.

After the arrival of the first element of your force, you may deploy up to three other elements each successive turn until all of your troops have been deployed on the table.

You may not, necessarily, wish to deploy all of your troops onto your baseline. You may wish to send troops around the flanks so that they arrive on the table edges or even to the rear of the enemy forces. Normally an umpire will decide how long these flanks marches will take to complete. The enemy will be unaware of this movement unless they have scouts or other troops carrying out similar flanking moves.

In some cases you may encounter a prepared enemy. Obviously some of the encounters that will lead to a battle will be as a result of two opposing forces using map movement. In other cases you will come on an enemy that is dug in, defending a position or in camp resting after a march.

This is why it is important for players to state when their troops will ready themselves for the day. If the enemy is caught in camp, in the early hours of the morning, they will not be able to deploy as quickly as those who are already up, had their breakfast and are mustered for roll call.

The players will nominate a time for their troops to rise. Add two hours for breakfast and to break down the camp and then they are ready for action or movement. Once this period has passed, the player may deploy a brigade each turn in order to move them into the battle line.

Scouting advantages on the map and on the table

Scouts and pickets were the eyes and ears of the armies. As far as map movement and scouting are concerned, players should detach a stand of cavalry to cover a mile of front. As an alternative, a player may choose to detach a stand of infantry and post them as either pickets or signallers. These too can cover a mile of frontage. Assessing the value of what pickets or scouts see is a problem, but if you are using an umpire, it is a relatively straightforward procedure. In either case, you should use the following table:

D10 roll	Direction of march	Location	Other Activity	Enemy Strength
0,1,2	Not given	To within 10 mls	None	Only that the enemy is present
3,4	Wrong	Correct	Vague	Huge over-estimate
5,6	Correct	To within 10 mls	Vague	Under-estimate by half
7	Correct	To within 5 mls	Report if obvious	About right
8	Correct	Correct	Report if obvious	Approximate number of brigades regiments and batteries
9	Correct	Correct	Highly detailed	As above, but detailed information on name and strength of units

WARGAME SCENARIOS

Table modifiers

- Add one if the scouts manage to take prisoners or if the scouts are led by a named and graded officer
- Deduct one if the scouts or pickets have been on duty for more than 8 hours
- Deduct two if enemy scouts screen the enemy force

Dealing with patrols, scouts and pickets in contact

When positioning or sending out a patrol or similar, the player must state whether the patrol has one of the following orders:

Patrol orders	Implications
Lie low and watch	Patrol acts as if it has hold orders and is cautious. In combat add 1 against 'Aggressively Patrol'
Watch and actively scout	Patrol acts as if it has engage orders and is steady. In combat add 1 against 'Investigate'
Investigate	Patrol acts as if it has advance orders and is confident. In combat add 1 against 'Aggressively patrol'
Aggressively patrol	Patrol acts as if it has assault orders and is impetuous. In combat add 1 against 'Watch and Actively scout'

Total the number of figures and then add any bonuses from the table above. Adjust the score by the following:

- If Green troops, minus 2
- If Green, minus 1
- If Experienced, add 1
- If Steady, add 2
- If Confident, add 3
- If Arrogant, minus 2
- If cavalry, add 2

Each player now throws a D10, with (1)0 being zero. Add the modifiers to the score and compare the totals. The highest score effectively screens the enemy force and if the difference is 5 or more then the enemy patrol is captured.

Fatigue

At the beginning of a campaign, each regiment or artillery unit is assigned an initial level of fitness. Experienced, Veteran or Elite troops begin with a value of 100, Trained troops 90 and Green troops 80. You should modify each unit's fitness on a daily basis using the following list of factors:

- -20 if they have taken part in a battle that has been lost
- -10 if they have taken part in a battle that they have won
- -5 for each of three successive marches without a break
- -5 if they have fought during the night or have marched at night
- -5 if it has been raining
- -5 for each day they have been under bombardment
- -5 if they have taken part in or have been the victims of a raid
- -10 for each day they have been unsupplied
- -20 for each day they have not had fresh water
- +10 if they have rested for a full day
- +5 if they have been fully supplied that day

Use the following table to assess their battlefield effectiveness:

Modified fitness value	Effects
60	The troops are tired. They count as disordered on the battlefield and may only march once per day.
40	Exhausted. Troops may not be given assault or advance orders on the battlefield. For map movement thrown one D10 per stand in the unit. A score of 0 means that stand has been lost due to desertion.
20	The unit is broken. They may not be given assault, advance or engage orders on them battlefield. They may only carry out retreats on a map and, if called upon to rally, they will rout.
0	The unit is destroyed. The entire regiment has deserted, or if appropriate surrendered to the enemy.

WARGAME SCENARIOS

Lines of Communication and Supply

As the old saying goes, 'an army marches on its stomach'. It was vital to ensure that there was a steady trickle of supplies to the front, in order to ensure that the army remained an effective fighting force. If an enemy positions at least one stand of scouts or pickets on a supply route, it is considered to be broken until those enemy units have been dispersed.

As far as the campaign is concerned, you should think of these supply routes as being a steady movement of wagons backwards and forwards along the supply route. The supply route will lead back to a main supply area. In this supply area there will be stocks of medical supplies, food, replacement weapons and of course ammunition.

Normally there would be a commissariat positioned relatively close to the army. Gradually the army would move its supply bases forward so that the distance between it and the army was as short as possible. Obviously this made the commissariat a tempting target for the enemy and its loss would have a drastic impact on the effectiveness of the troops in the field.

As far as the campaign rules are concerned, once a force has been deprived of its supplies from the commissariat for two days it should be classified as being unsupplied. Supplies are also important as far as garrisons or defence forces are concerned. Troops in a defensive position should be allocated a number of days of supply. After this they will be classed as being out of supply, thus forcing the commander owning the garrison units to attempt to relieve them, or they will surrender.

If an army has fought an engagement and is out of supply then it is considered to have run out of ammunition. In extreme circumstances a player can state that his troops will be placed on half rations and told to conserve ammunition. In these cases an army can operate on short supplies for 5 days, after which it becomes unsupplied. Equally, if the army is told to conserve ammunition then it may fight two engagements before being unsupplied.

Optionally, you may choose to consider that if a unit has not suffered any casualties during a battle it has not been sufficiently engaged in the fight to have expended any ammunition.

In the movement section of these rules we designated certain units as being 'light', in the sense that they do not have their own commissariat. These troops are deemed to be able to last self-sufficiently on their rations for 5 days and to be able to fight 2 battles. If they visit one of their own depots they can immediately be re-supplied. Alternatively they could raid an enemy town or depot and similarly be re-supplied.

THE WAR IN THE PENINSULA

After the battle

Although the rules designate full stand losses in battle, these losses are meant to simulate the fact that some of the men have been killed, wounded or have simply deserted. During the Peninsular War, both sides suffered greatly by men disappearing in action.

If the battle was won or was a stalemate you have the opportunity to try to retrieve some of your lost stands. Use the following table to work out how many stands will return to action for the next engagement:

Number of stands lost	D10 roll
1	5 – 9, stand returns
2	5 – 7, one stand returns 8 – 9, two stands return
3	5 – 6, one stand returns 7 – 8, two stands return 9, three stands return
4	5 – 6, one stand returns 7, two stands return 8, three stands return 9, four stands return
5	5, one stand returns 6, two stands return 7, three stands return 8, four stands return 9, five stands return
6+	5, one stand returns 6, two stands return 7, three stands return 8, four stands return 9, all stands return

Routed regiments

It is highly likely that some of your units did not rally on the battlefield and ran off into the countryside. If a unit has fled the battlefield, after the battle roll a D10 to see if you can recover the unit. The target score on a

WARGAME SCENARIOS

D10 is 7, modified by the following factors (a 0 will count as zero in the throw):

- +2 if elite
- +1 if veteran or experienced
- +2 if the battle was won
- -1 if Green
- -2 if battle was lost

Chasing the enemy and capturing equipment

If an army has won a battle it can opt to retreat without any danger of being attacked. Even a defeated army would often wait for a day after having been beaten in order to deal with its wounded and try to gather up any routed troops.

If the victorious army chooses to pursue, the defeated army does not have any option but to retreat. It will lose all of its routed units and may only roll to see if it can regain them when it reaches a safe haven and is unmolested by the pursuing force. A victorious army can begin a new march in the next map movement period after the battle.

If an army is in possession of the battlefield at the end of an engagement, it may opt to re-equip troops with better firearms, stand for stand, for every enemy stand lost or enemy stand taken prisoner. If cavalry has been destroyed or captured, the force in possession of the battlefield may re-equip a unit to make them mounted infantry or replace losses it may have suffered during the battle. If artillery has not been destroyed or spiked by the enemy then the player can opt to reassign infantry to become Green artillery crew. A stand of infantry is required to man each new gun.

Benefits of experience

After a battle that has seen a unit actively engaged, there is an opportunity for it to improve its status. Either the umpire or the other player should agree that a unit is worthy of attempting to improve its status. Use the following table for each relevant unit:

Transition	Roll required on D10
Veteran to Elite	9, 0
Experienced to Veteran	9, 0
Trained to Experienced	8, 9, 0
Green to Trained	7, 8, 9, 0

THE WAR IN THE PENINSULA

Replacements

If a regiment has suffered casualties during a campaign then replacements can be assigned to it. Use a D10 to determine whether the regiment's overall status has been affected by the arrival of the replacements. Throw a D10 with 0 requiring a second throw. Compare your die roll to the number of stands you have needed to replace. If it is less than or equal to those number of stands then reduce the status of the regiment by one level.

Scenario builder, Terrain generator and Weather

Scenario Builder

You can design your own wargame scenarios with the minimum of complications by simply deciding to agree the overall strength of the two armies. Begin by designing scenarios for a brigade or two per side and then work up to divisions and eventually corps as you build up your forces.

In effect, a scenario should take into account the year and the theatre in which the battle is being fought. Beyond that, you need to nominally decide which of the two sides is the aggressor and which is the defender. This means that unbalanced sides can fight one another whilst the defender, being weaker in terms of number of regiments, guns, training, supplies and cavalry, will not be disadvantaged if they have possession of the better terrain.

The following tables are examples or themes of different battles: many of them you will recognise as being somewhat like the real-life encounters from the Peninsular War:

Encounter Battle

Situation	Both sides are fighting in terrain unknown to them, the armies blunder into one another
Balance of forces	Roughly equal in terms of infantry, cavalry and artillery
Terrain placement	Players take it in turns to place terrain from an agreed range of terrain features
Set up	Players throw a D10 and the highest scoring player chooses the side of the table they prefer

WARGAME SCENARIOS

Tactical Defence of Position

Situation	The defender chooses the battlefield
Balance of forces	Roughly equal, perhaps a slight advantage to the aggressor
Terrain placement	Defender sets up the terrain
Set up	Defender can choose which side of the table to deploy

Organised Defence

Situation	The aggressor has a numerical superiority, but faces a prepared defensive line
Balance of forces	The aggressor should have a numerical advantage of at least 25%
Terrain placement	The defender lays out the terrain including field defence works
Set up	The defender sets up along their line of field works

Delaying Action

Situation	The defender must hold and deny specified positions (such as a town or road junction) from the aggressor for a specified number of turns
Balance of forces	The defender's available regiments and other elements should be no more than 50% of that of the aggressor
Terrain placement	Defender lays out the terrain including some hastily dug defence works
Set up	Defender sets up along the table edge with the defence works or around the terrain objective

THE WAR IN THE PENINSULA

Unpleasant Surprise

Situation	The aggressor, a smaller force, attacks an unprepared larger army
Balance of forces	The defender should have a numerical superiority of 100%, but will be scattered around the table
Terrain placement	The aggressor lays out the terrain
Set up	The aggressor chooses one or two separate entry points on to the table (usually roads), the defender then deploys either as a long line across the table in column of march or scattered around the table with each separate command at least 15cm from each other. If the latter, the defender counts as disordered for the first three turns after having seen the enemy

Lured

Situation	The defender is in unknown territory and has been lured into a poor position by the aggressor
Balance of forces	Roughly equal
Terrain placement	The aggressor places the terrain
Set up	The defender must place all of their troops on the table. The aggressor can then choose to deploy on any other table edge

Under Siege

Situation	A numerically inferior defender is under siege by a larger aggressor
Balance of forces	The defender's forces should be roughly half that of the aggressor
Terrain placement	The defender places the terrain. If a fortification this should cover one table corner and at least half a table length. A

WARGAME SCENARIOS

Set up	town should occupy at least a quarter of a table length from the centre If defending a town, this can be surrounded be defensive positions. In each case, after the placement of the defenders fortifications, the aggressor may place an earthwork position for artillery facing each of the defenders artillery emplacements

Prime Objective

Situation	The aggressor's goal is to capture a specified static position or baggage belonging to the defender
Balance of forces	The aggressor should have a numerical advantage of at least 25%
Terrain placement	The aggressor lays out the terrain, then the defender nominates a building or bridge as the prime objective. Alternatively, the defender's baggage can be nominated as the target
Set up	The defender may deploy on the table edge closest to the prime objective if it is a static position. If the prime objective is mobile – a commander, wounded men, ammunition baggage or a train – then it cannot move for the first three turns of the game. The winner is the possessor of the prime objective after 12-15 turns

Hold Until Relieved

Situation	The defender must hold their positions for a specified number of turns until the remainder of the force arrives
Balance of forces	Initially, the aggressor outnumbers the defender by at least 50%. After eight turns, this should be reduced to 25%, after 10

THE WAR IN THE PENINSULA

Terrain placement Set up	turns, the forces should be equal and then after 12 turns the defender should have a 50% advantage The defender lays out the terrain The defender chooses the table edge and must have at least one intact unit to trigger off the arrival of the reinforcements, these may either appear on his baseline (with a D10 throw of 0,1,2,3,4 or 5), the left edge (6 or 7), or the right edge (8 or 9)

Fall Back in Good Order

Situation	The aggressor is chasing a retreating defender and has caught up with the rearguard units
Balance of forces	The aggressor should outnumbered the defender by 25% at the beginning of the battle
Terrain placement	Both players take it in turn to lay out a piece of terrain
Set up	The defender chooses the table edge. He must place his forces no less than a quarter of the width of the table from the table edge or 2 feet, whichever is the least. The defender must secretly nominate a regiment, brigade or division as his rearguard. The purpose of the exercise is to extricate his whole force from the table. He may do this one formation at a time: once one has exited, the next can begin, finally leaving with the nominated rearguard unit or units

WARGAME SCENARIOS

Encircled

Situation	The aggressor has advanced too quickly and is now surrounded by a better placed, if inferior enemy force
Balance of forces	The aggressor begins with a 50% advantage in terms of numbers. After five turns, the advantage is reduced to 25%, after eight the sides are equal, and after ten the aggressor is outnumbered by 50%
Terrain placement	The defender lays out the terrain
Set up	The aggressor deploys first along one table length and one table width. The defender deploys on the opposite table length. The defender may bring on his reinforcements either on his baseline or on either table edge. The aggressor wins if he still has at least 10% of his force intact on the table on turn 15 and has managed to withdraw at least 50% of his army in good order with the minimum of losses

Last Round

Situation	The aggressor, larger in number, is on the verge of annihilating the defender
Balance of forces	The aggressor should have a 100% superiority in numbers
Terrain placement	The defender lays out the terrain
Set up	The defender must position his forces in the centre of the table with no more than 25% of his force on his baseline as a reserve. The attacker can opt to set upon his baseline and/or either of the table widths. The defender may attempt to retreat off the table exiting no earlier than turn 15. If at that stage he has any intact units, he has won the game. The aggressor wins by either destroying or routing (they must exit the table) all of the defenders units

THE WAR IN THE PENINSULA

Meeting Engagement

Situation	The two opposing forces are sucked into an escalating battle as they collide with one another
Balance of forces	The forces should be equal but split into at least five separate commands
Terrain placement	Players take it in turns to lay out the terrain. Ideally, there should be 2 roads leaving each base line and one on each table width
Set up	Players use a D10 to decide which table edge they deploy; the winner has the choice of table edge. Each commander chooses a line of march from one of the roads on their table edge to one of the roads exiting from the opponent's table edge. The commander and 20% of the army arrive on the table edge; they should begin moving towards the nominated road exit. On turns 3, 5, 7 and 9 another 20% of the army arrives following the same route. Obviously, by then the two armies will be engaged. The winner is the army which has either decisively beaten the opponent or exited 40% of their army via the nominated road

Scorched Earth

Situation	The aggressor is deep in enemy territory and is intent on destroying valuable food stocks and munitions
Balance of forces	The aggressor should have a 50% numerical superiority
Terrain placement	The defender lays out the terrain. He should add up the number of separate formations in his army (brigades or similar) and halve this total, then nominate that number of strategic objectives on the table. If the defender wishes these may be baggage, mobile munitions, a train or a herd of cattle or horses
Set up	The aggressor must destroy all of the strategic objectives nominated by the defender

WARGAME SCENARIOS

Terrain Generator

If you have chosen a contemporary map or drawn your own campaign map then you will already have some idea as to the terrain of the area. Some of the contemporary maps, however, aside from noting roads, forests, towns and rivers, fail to indicate the actual local geography of the particular area. As we have also seen, a battle begins when two armies collide with one another following movement on the map. It may be readily apparent which of the armies can be considered to be the aggressor and which one is the defender. As a general rule of thumb, the aggressor is the force that is operating in what is or was enemy-held territory. However, a defence force can become an aggressor if it chooses to launch a counteroffensive against the aggressor, thereby taking the initiative away from the invading force.

We have already detailed rules that determine who lays out the terrain on a wargames table, dependent upon the different scenarios you will be fighting. You can find all of these instructions in the section *Scenario Builder*. The two players can agree as to which type of engagement is being fought, or if you have an umpire then s/he will make the ultimate decision. The first necessary step is to determine where the engagement is being fought. The following table outlines the possibilities:

Region	0-1	2-3	4-5	6-7	8	9
France	F	F	F	F	R	H
Belgium/Holland	F	F	F	R	R	C
Germany	F	F	F	R	M	H
Northern Italy	F	F	R	H	M	M
Northern Spain	F	F	W	R	P	H
Central Spain	F	F	W	R	M	H
Southern Spain/ Portugal	F	F	W	H	P	P
Central Russia	F	F	F	P	P	H
Southern Russia	F	F	W	H	S	D
Austria	F	W	R	M	H	H
Ireland	F	F	W	R	C	S

Key to table:

- F = Farmland
- W = Wilderness
- R = Riverbank
- M = Mountains
- S = Swampland
- H = Hilly region
- P = Plain
- D = Desert
- C = Coastal

THE WAR IN THE PENINSULA

Once you have determined the dominant type of terrain that will be on the wargames table you now need to determine the terrain in each area of the table itself. For example, a wargames table 8' x 6' would be four areas long and three areas deep: in other words a total of 12 areas. You will use the random terrain table appropriate to the dominant type of terrain identified on the first chart we have given you.

Farmland

Defender's Dice	Aggressor's Dice			
	0-2	3-5	6-7	8-9
0-1	Steep hill	Field/Crops	Settlement	Farm
2-3	Hill	Field, Fenced	Fenced road	Farm
4-5	Rise	Field, Walled	Sunken lane	Farm
6-7	Wood	Wood	Road	Building
8	Stream	Wall	Fence line	Field/Crops
9	Field, Fenced	Stream	Field/Crops	Choice

Wilderness

Defender's Dice	Aggressor's Dice			
	0-2	3-5	6-7	8-9
0-1	Scrub	Steep Hill	Stream	Farm
2-3	Stream	Marsh	Pool	Building
4-5	Track	Road	Farm	Hill, Rocky
6-7	Field, Fenced	Woodland	Field	Clearing
8	Hill, Bare	Clearing	Woodland	Hill
9	Clearing	Scrub	Field, Crops	Rise

WARGAME SCENARIOS

Riverside

Defender's Dice	Aggressor's Dice			
	0-2	3-5	6-7	8-9
0-1	Steep Hill	Marsh	Railroad	Settlement
2-3	Hill	Marsh	Fenced Road	Farm
4-5	Rise	Stream	Ditch	Pool
6-7	Wood	Wood	Road	Building
8	Stream	Hill+Cliff	Fence Line	Steep banks
9	Field	Rocks	Forest edge	Choice

Mountains

Defender's Dice	Aggressor's Dice				
	0-2	3-4	5-6	7-8	9
0-1	Steep Hill	Stream	Road	Farm	Mtn Spur
2-3	Long Hill	Pool	Farm	Building	Wood
4-5	Stream	Scrub	Track	Forest	Cliff
6-7	Wood	Ravine	Forest	Clearing	Stream
8	Mtn Spur	Scree	Steep Hill	Hill+Cliff	Scrub
9	Rocks	Hill+Scree	Hill+Wood	Rise	Forest

Swamplands

Defender's Dice	Aggressor's Dice			
	0-2	3-5	6-7	8-9
0-1	Hill	Marsh	Road	Settlement
2-3	Rise+ Field	Marsh	Fenced Road	Farm
4-5	Rise	Lake	Ditch	Clearing
6-7	Wood	Wood	Road	Building
8	Stream	Pool	Fence Line	Embankment
9	Field	Scrub	Forest edge	Dry

Hill Country

Defender's Dice	Aggressor's Dice			
	0-2	3-5	6-7	8-9
0-1	Hill	Rise	Rocks	Settlement
2-3	Hill	Scrub	Hill	Farm
4-5	Ravine	Steep Hill	Road	Building
6-7	Steep Hill	S. Hill+ Scree	Pool	Field
8	Scrub	S. Hill + Cliff	Stream	Wood
9	Wood	Farm	Field	Choice

Plains

Defender's Dice	Aggressor's Dice		
	0-3	4-6	7-9
0-1	Hill	Rocks	Settlement
2-3	Marsh	Pool	Farm
4-5	Rise	Stream	Building
6-7	Wood	Scrub	Scrub
8	Forest	Rise	Field
9	Ravine	Road	Choice

Desert

Defender's Dice	Aggressor's Dice		
	0-3	4-6	7-9
0-1	Steep hill	Rocks	Settlement
2-3	Hill	Dunes	Farm
4-5	Rise	Dry river bed	Building
6-7	Ravine	Scrub	Ruin
8	Scree	Enclosure	Cliff
9	Dunes	Soft sand	Soft sand

WARGAME SCENARIOS

Coastal

| | Aggressor's Dice | | |
Defender's Dice	0-3	4-6	7-9
0-1	Creek	Ditch	Embankment
2-3	Field	Rise	Settlement
4-5	Marsh	Wood	Farm
6-7	Marsh	Scrub	Field
8	Pool	Field	Building
9	Stream	Banked Road	Orchard

Being sensible about terrain placement

Any settlement should have a road running into and out of it, exiting on both a table length and width. Any two settlements should be linked together with roads. Any wood next to a settlement could be an orchard.

Roads or tracks crossing streams or creeks will either have a bridge or a ford. Individual stream pieces should be converted into dry watercourses.

Optional Weather Rules

Before the battle, roll on this table.

Roll on 1D10	Apr	May	Jun	Jul	Aug	Sept	Oct
0	Snow	Cold	Heavy Rain	Heavy Rain	Heavy Rain	Cold	Snow
1	Cold	Heavy Rain	Heavy Rain	Heavy Rain	Heavy Rain	Heavy Rain	Cold
2	Heavy Rain	Light Rain	Light Rain	Light Rain	Light Rain	Light Rain	Heavy Rain
3	Heavy Rain	Light Rain	Light Rain	Light Rain	Light Rain	Light Rain	Heavy Rain
4	Light Rain	Fair	Fair	Fair	Fair	Fair	Light Rain
5	Light Rain	Fair	Fair	Fair	Fair	Fair	Light Rain
6	Fair	Fair	Fair	Showers	Showers	Fair	Fair
7	Fair	Fair	Showers	Showers	Showers	Fair	Fair
8	Fair	Showers	Showers	Hot	Hot	Showers	Fair
9	Showers	Showers	Hot	Hot	Hot	Hot	Showers

On successive days, roll a D10, if the result is 0-5, then the weather remains the same as the day before. If 6-9 is thrown, then consult the weather table again for a change in conditions.

Effects of weather

Light Rain — reduce movement by a quarter, on the second day treat as heavy rain

Heavy Rain — reduce movement by a half. Fords impassable

Showers — Roll a D10: if 0-3 is scored then there is no effect; 4-7, treat as light rain; 8-9 treat as heavy rain

Hot — Roll a D10; if 0-2 is rolled then stands are removed from the regiment as stragglers; if 3-4 is rolled, then one stand is lost as stragglers; if 5-6 is thrown then the regiment will not respond to anything other than a HOLD order for the first two turns after arrival on the battlefield; if 7-9 is thrown then there is no effect on the regiment

Cold — Treat as with the hot conditions

Snow — As cold conditions, but all difficult terrain is classed as impassable. Streams and minor rivers can be forded at any point

If there is rain for four or more days, then reduce all movement to a quarter of the normal movement rates. All fords become impassable; they become passable after three days of dry weather. After four days of rain, there is no bonus for moving on roads, they recover after two days of dry weather.

Chronology

Date	Event
1808	
2 May	Dos de Mayo Rising in Madrid
25 May	The Austrias declare war on France
8 June	French win the battle at the Alcolea Bridge, Andalusia French win the battle at Tudela, Navarre
10 June	French win the battle at Llobregat, Catalonia
12 June	French win the battle at Cabezon Bridge, Leon French win the battle at Mallen, Aragon
15 June	Siege of Saragossa begins in Aragon
18 June	French defeated when they attack Gerona, Catalonia
21 June	French win the battle at the River Cabriel, Valencia
23 June	General Merle seizes Santander, Old Castile.
24 June	French win battle at the Cabrillas, Valencia
26 June	French attack Valencia and withdraw on June 28
14 July	French win battle of Medina de Rio Seco, Leon Castaños launches his Baylen offensive in Andalucia
19 July	Allies win battle of Baylen, Andalucia
24 July	French attack Gerona, Catalonia
29 July	French win battle at Evora, Portugal
1 August	British land in Portugal
13 August	French forced to abandon their siege of Saragossa, Aragon
15 August	Allies win battle at Obidos, Portugal
16 August	French abandon their siege of Gerona, Catalonia
17 August	Allies win battle of Roliça, Portugal
20 August	General Duhesme besieged in Barcelona, Catalonia
21 August	Allies win battle of Vimiero, Portugal
13 September	French initiate their evacuation of Portugal
25 October	French win battles at Logrono and Lodosa, Navarre
30 October	French complete their evacuation of Portugal
31 October	French win battle at Zornoza, Biscay
7 November	General St-Cyr surrounds Rosas, Catalonia
10 November	French win battle of Gamonal, Old Castile
11 November	French win battle of Espinosa, Old Castile
23 November	French win battle of Tudela, Navarre
28 November	French take Rosas, Catalonia

CHRONOLOGY

30 November	French win battle at Somossierra, Old Castile
4 December	Napoleon seizes Madrid, New Castile
16 December	French win battle of Cardadeu, Catalonia
17 December	French relieve Barcelona, Catalonia
20 December	The second siege of Sarogssa, Aragon begins
21 December	French win battle of Molins de Rey, Catalonia. French win battle at Sahagun, Leon
26 December	Allies win battle at Benavente, Leon
30 December	French win battle at Mansilla, Leon

1809

3 January	Allies win battle at Cacabellos, near Villafranca, Galicia
13 January	French win battle of Uclés, New Castile
16 January	Allies win battle of Corunna, Galicia
21 January	French General Soult takes Ferrol, Galicia
20 February	The second siege of Saragossa finishes, Aragon
25 February	French win battle of Valls, Catalonia
5 March	French win battle at Moterey, Galicia
12 March	French General Soult takes Chaves, Portugal
20 March	French win battle at Braga, Portugal
26 March	French win battle of Ciudad Real, New Castile
28 March	French win battle of Medellin, Estremadura
29 March	French win battle for Oporto, Portugal
2 May	French win battle at Amarante, Portugal
10 May	Allies win battle at Grijon, Portugal
12 May	Allies win second battle for Oporto, Portugal
14 May	French win battle at Alcantara, Estremadura
19 May	French take Oviedo, Austurias
23 May	Allies win battle of Alcaniz, Aragon
24 May	Beginning of the third siege of Gerona, Catalonia
15 June	French win battle of Maria, Aragon
18 June	French win battle at Belchite, Aragon
28 July	Allies win battle of Talavera, New Castile
8 August	French win battle at Arzobispo, Estremadura
11 August	French win battle of Almonacid, New Castile
12 August	French win battle of Baños, Estremadura
18 October	Allies win battle of Tamames, Leon
11 November	French win battle at Ocaña, New Castile
19 November	French win battle of Ocaña, New Castile
28 November	French win battle of Alba de Tormes, Leon
11 December	End of the third siege of Gerona, Catalonia

WARGAME SCENARIOS

1810

12 January	French under Victor take Almaden, New Castile
19 January	French win battle at La Carolina, Andalucía
23 January	French win battle at Jaen, Andalucía
24 January	French under General Augereau relieve Barcelona, Catalonia
31 January	French under Bonnet take Oviedo, Austurias
1 February	French under King Joseph take Seville, Andalucía
5 February	French under Victor begin their siege of Cadiz, Andalucía
20 February	French win battle at Vich, Catalonia
6 March	French under Suchet begin their blockade of Valencia, Valencia
10 March	French withdraw from Valencia, Valencia
21 March	Allies win battle at Villafranca, Catalonia
15 April	French under Suchet begin their siege of Lerida, Catalonia
21 April	French under Junot take Astorga, Galicia
23 April	French win battle of Lerida-Margaleff, Catalonia
12 May	French take Hostalrich, Catalonia
14 May	French take Lerida, Catalonia
15 May	French under Suchet begin their siege of Mequinenza, Catalonia
30 May	French under Ney begin their siege of Ciudad Rodrigo, Leon
18 June	French under Suchet take Mequinenza, Catalonia
9 July	French take Ciudad Rodrigo, Leon
24 July	French win battle at the River Coa, Portugal. French under Ney begin their siege of Almeida, Portugal
28 July	French take Almeida, Portugal
14 September	O'Donnell raids Gerona, Catalona
27 September	Allies win battle of Bussaco, Portugal
11 October	French under Massena move up to the Lines of Torres Vedras, Portugal
4 November	French win battle near Baza, Granada
19 December	French under Suchet begin their siege of Tortosa, Catalonia

1811

2 January	French under Suchet take Tortosa, Catalonia
21 January	French under Soult take Olivenza, Estremadura
27 January	French under Soult begin their siege of Badajoz, Estremadura
4 March	French under Massena retreat from Santarem, Portugal
5 March	Allies win battle of Barrosa, Andalucía
10 March	French under Soult take Badajoz, Estremadura

CHRONOLOGY

12 March	Allies win battle at Redinha, Portugal
14 March	Allies win battle at Cassal Nova, Portugal
15 March	Allies win battle at Fozd'aronce, Portugal. French under Latour-Maubourg take Albuquerque, Estremadura
25 March	French win battle at Campo Mayor, Portugal
3 April	French under Macdonald begin their siege of Figueras, Catalonia
	Allies win the battle of Sabugal, Portugal
11 April	French under Massena retreat from Salamanca, Leon
3 May	Allies win first battle of Fuentes de Oñoro on the Leon and Portuguese border
5 May	Allies win second battle of Fuentes de Oñoro on the Leon and Portuguese border
6 May	Allies under Beresford begin their siege of Badajoz, Estremadura
8 May	French under Suchet begin their siege of Tarragona, Catalonia
10 May	French pull out of Almeida, Portugal
16 May	Allies win battle of Albuera, Estremadura
10 June	Allies abandon their siege of Badajoz, Estremadura
28 June	French under Suchet take Tarragona, Catalonia
2 July	French under Soult relieve Niebla, Andalucía
9 August	Allied offensive under Freire fails in Granada
19 August	French under Macdonald take Figueras, Catalonia
23 September	French under Suchet begin their siege of Saguntum, Valencia
25 September	French win battle at El Boden, Leon
25 October	French win battle of Saguntum, Valencia
28 October	Allies win battle at Arrayo dos Molinos, Estremadura
20 December	French under Leval begin their siege of Tarifa, Andalucía
25 December	French under Suchet begin their siege of Valencia, Valencia
29 December	French win battle at Merida, Estremadura

1812

8 January	Allies under Wellington begin their siege of Ciudad Rodrigo, Leon
	French take Valencia, Valencia
19 January	Allies under Wellington take Ciudad Rodrigo, Leon
16 March	Allies under Wellington begin their siege of Badajoz, Estremadura
7 April	Allies under Wellington take Badajoz, Estremadura
19 May	Allies win battle at Almaraz, Estremadura

WARGAME SCENARIOS

14 June	Allies under Wellington begin their siege of the Salamanca Forts, Leon
22 June	Allies under Popham take Lequeitio, Biscay
27 June	Allies under Wellington take the Salamanca Forts, Leon
8 July	Allies under Popham take Castro Urdiales, Biscay
19 July	Allies under Popham fail to take Guetaria, Biscay
21 July	French win battle at Castalla, Valencia
22 July	Allies win battle of Salamanca, Leon
3 August	Allies under Popham take Santander, Old Castile
11 August	French win battle at Majalahonda, New Castile
12 August	Allies take Madrid, New Castile
19 September	Allies under Wellington begin their siege of Burgos, Old Castile
21 October	Allies under Wellington raise their siege of Burgos, Old Castile
23 October	French win battle at Venta Del Pozo, Old Castile
25 October	Allies win battle at Villa Muriel, Old Castile
2 November	French retake Madrid, New Castile
13 November	Allies under Wellington take the Huerba, Leon

1813

12 April	Allies win battle at the Pass of Biar, Valencia
13 April	Allies win battle of Castalla, Valencia
3 June	Allies under Murray begin their siege of Tarragona, Catalonia
12 June	Allies under Murray abandon their siege of Tarragona, Catalonia
21 June	Allies win the battle of Vitoria, Navarre
27 June	Allies win the battle at Tolosa, Navarre
28 June	Allies besiege San Sebastian, Biscay
10 July	French under Paris abandon Saragossa, Aragon
25 July	Allies win battles at Maya and Roncesvalles on the French and Spanish border
28 July	Allies win first battle of Sorauren, Navarre
30 July	Allies win second battle of Sorauren, Navarre
	French win battle at Lizaso, Navarre
31 August	Allies storm San Sebastian, Biscay
	Allies win battle of San Marcial, Biscay
8 September	The citadel at San Sebastian finally surrenders to the Allies
13 September	French win battle at Ordal, Catalonia
7 October	Allied forces cross the Spanish French border at Bidassoa

CHRONOLOGY

31 October	The French at Pamplona surrender, Navarre
10 November	Allies win battle of the River Nivelle on the Spanish French border
9-10 December	Allies win battle of the Nive, Gascony
13 December	Allies win battle of Saint Pierre, Gascony

1814

27 February	Allies begin their siege of Bayonne in southern France
	Allies win battle of Orthez, southern France
20 March	Allies win battle at Tarbes, southern France
6 April	Napoleon Bonaparte abdicates
10 April	French win battle of Toulouse, southern France
14 April	French fail in their attempt to break out at Bayonne, southern France
27 April	French surrender at Bayonne, southern France

Further Reading

(Non-Fiction)

Esdaile, Charles J, *The Peninsular War: A New History*, (Penguin Books, 2003)
Fitchett, W H, *Battles & Sieges of the Peninsular War: Corunna, Busaco, Albuera, Ciudad Rodrigo, Badajos, Salamanca, San Sebastian & Others*, (Leonaur Ltd, 2007)
Gates, David, *Spanish Ulcer: A History of the Peninsular War*, (Da Capo Press, 2001)
Glover, Michael, *The Peninsular War, 1807-1814: A Concise Military History*, (Penguin Classic Military History, 2001)
Grehan, John, *The Lines of Torres Vedras: The Cornerstone of Wellington's Strategy in the Peninsular War 1809-1812*, (Spellmount Publishers, 2000)
Haythornthwaite, Philip J, *The Peninsular War: The Complete Companion to the Iberian Campaigns 1807-14*, (Brassey's, 2004)
Paget, Julian, *Wellington's Peninsular War*, (Leo Cooper Ltd, 2005)
Robertson, Ian, *Wellington Invades France: The Final Phase of the Peninsular War, 1813-1814*, (Greenhill Books, 2003)

(Fiction)

The Sharpe novels by Bernard Cornwell:

Sharpe's Rifles: Richard Sharpe and the Invasion of Galicia, January 1809
Sharpe's Havoc: Richard Sharpe is back in the Peninsula in 1809 in Oporto, Portugal
Sharpe's Eagle: Richard Sharpe and the Talavera Campaign, July 1809
Sharpe's Gold: Richard Sharpe and the Destruction of Almeida, August 1810
Sharpe's Escape: Richard Sharpe and the Battle of Busaco, 1810
Sharpe's Fury: Richard Sharpe and the Battle of Barossa, March 1811
Sharpe's Battle: Richard Sharpe and the Battle of Fuentes de Oñoro, May 1811
Sharpe's Company: Richard Sharpe and the Siege of Badajoz, January to April 1812
Sharpe's Sword: Richard Sharpe and the Salamanca Campaign, June and July 1812
Sharpe's Skirmish: Richard Sharpe and the defence of the Tormes, August 1812
Sharpe's Enemy: Richard Sharpe and the Defence of Portugal, Christmas 1812
Sharpe's Honour: Richard Sharpe and the Vitoria Campaign, February to June 1813
Sharpe's Regiment: Richard Sharpe and the Invasion of France, June to November, 1813
Sharpe's Christmas: Sharpe's Christmas is set in 1813, towards the end of the Peninsular War
Sharpe's Siege: Richard Sharpe and the Winter Campaign, 1814